Voices
of the
HOLOCAUST

Voices of the HOLOCAUST

VOLUME 2

Resisters
Liberation
Understanding

LORIE JENKINS McELROY

AN IMPRINT OF GALE

DETROIT • NEW YORK • LONDON

Voices of the
HOLOCAUST

Lorie Jenkins McElroy, Editor

Staff

Elizabeth Des Chenes, *U·X·L Senior Developmental Editor*
Carol DeKane Nagel, *U·X·L Managing Editor*
Thomas L. Romig, *U·X·L Publisher*

Margaret Chamberlain, *Permissions Specialist*
Shalice Shah, *Permissions Associate*

Shanna P. Heilveil, *Production Assistant*
Evi Seoud, *Production Manager*
Mary Beth Trimper, *Production Director*

Tracey Rowens, *Art Director*
Cynthia Baldwin, *Product Design Manager*
Linda Mahoney, *Typesetting*

Library of Congress Cataloging-in-Publication Data

Voices of the Holocaust/Lorie Jenkins McElroy, editor
      p. cm.
    Includes bibliographical references and index.
    Contents: v. 1. Antisemitism, escalation, holocaust—2. Resisters, liberation, understanding.
    Summary: Presents six theme-based original documents, such as speeches, letters, and book excerpts, from 1020 to approx. 1950, which examine the Holocaust.
    ISBN 0-7876-1746-6 (set: alk. paper). — ISBN 0-7876-1747-4 (v. 1: alk. paper).— ISBN 0-7876-1748-2 (v. 2: alk. paper)
    1. Holocaust, Jewish (1939-1945)—Juvenile literature. 2. Righteous Gentiles in the Holocaust—Juvenile literature. 3. Anti-Nazi movement—Juvenile literature. 4. World War, 1939-1945—Jews—Rescue
    Juvenile literature. [1. Holocaust, Jewish (1939-1945). 2. Righteous Gentiles in the Holocaust. 3. Anti-Nazi movement. 4. World War, 1939-1945—Jews—Rescue.]
    I. McElroy, Lorie Jenkins.
    D804.34.V66. 1998
    940. 53' 18—dc21.

                                         97-33195
                                       CIP AC

Printed in the United States of America
10 9 8 7 6 5 4 3 2 1

contents

Bold type indicates volume numbers
Regular type indicates page numbers

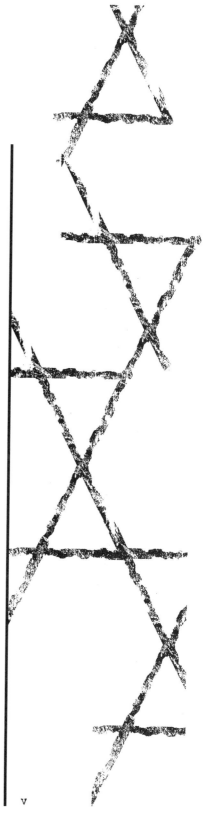

volume 1

antisemitism

volume 2

resisters 2: 253

liberation 2: 348

reader's guide

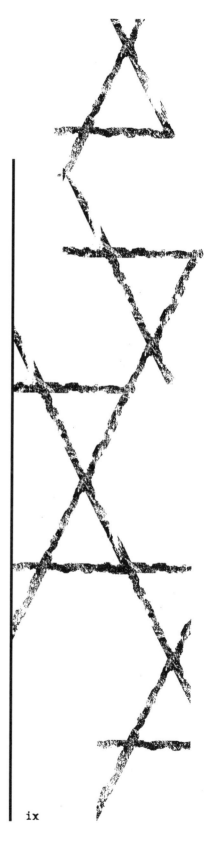

Voices of the Holocaust presents 34 excerpted documents written by people whose lives were forever changed by the events of the Holocaust. The autobiographical essays, diary entries, newspaper articles, court transcripts, letters, and reminiscences in these two volumes reflect the experiences of oppressors, resisters, liberators, witnesseses, and survivors. Some entries, such as the selections from Adolf Hitler's memoir *Mein Kampf* or Albert Speer's *Inside the Third Reich,* explore the development and inner workings of the Nazi regime. Other excerpts, including Janina David's *A Square of Sky,* Gonda Redlich's *Terezin Diary,* and Kim Malthe-Bruun's *Heroic Heart,* reflect the horrors faced by ordinary citizens during the Holocaust years. The search for justice and understanding is the focus of documents such as *Eichmann in Jerusalem* by Hannah Arendt, *Maus* by Art Spiegelman, and "Why I Write" by Elie Wiesel.

Format

Both *Voices of the Holocaust* volumes are divided into three chapters. Each of the six chapters focus on a specific theme: Antisemitism, Escalation, Holocaust, Resisters, Liberation, and Understanding. Every chapter opens with an historical overview, followed by four to seven document excerpts.

Each excerpt is divided into six sections:

- **Introductory material** places the document and its author in an historical context

- **Things to Remember** offers readers important background information about the featured text

- **Excerpt** presents the document in its original spelling and format

- **What happened next...** discusses the impact of the document on both the speaker and his or her audience

- **Did you know...** provides interesting facts about each document and its author

- **For Further Reading** presents sources for more information on documents and speakers

Additional Features

Many of the *Voices of the Holocaust* entries contain a short boxed biography on the speaker. In addition, call-out boxes within entries examine related events and issues, while black-and-white illustrations help illuminate the text. Each excerpt is accompanied by a glossary running alongside the primary document that defines terms, people, and ideas. Both volumes contain a timeline of important events and cumulative index.

Comments and Suggestions

We welcome your comments and suggestions for documents to feature in future editions of *Voices of the Holocaust.* Please write: Editor, *Voices of the Holocaust,* U·X·L, 835 Penobscot Bldg., Detroit, Michigan, 48226-4094; call toll free: 1-800-347-4253; or fax: 313-961-6347.

acknowledgments

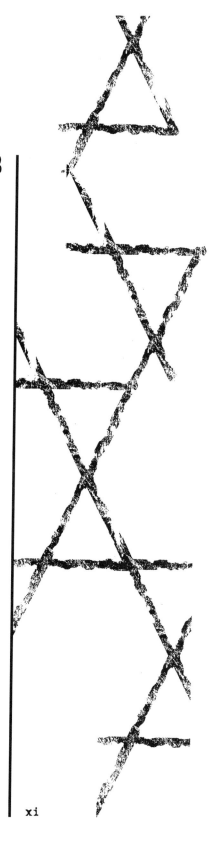

Special thanks are due for the invaluable comments and suggestions provided by the Holocaust Reference Library advisors:

Dr. William J. Shulman, President, Association of Holocaust Organizations, and Director, Holocaust Resource Center & Archives in New York; Linda Hurwitz, Director, The Holocaust Center in Pittsburgh, Pennsylvania; Max Weitz, Director, Holocaust Resource Center of Minneapolis, Minnesota; Jonathan Betz-Zall, Children's Librarian, Sno-Isle Regional Library System, Edmonds, Washington; and Debra Lyman Gniewek, Library Services Coordinator, Office of Information Technology, School District of Philadelphia, Pennsylvania.

The editor extends added thanks to Ina Gallon for her careful and thoughtful research and material selection, and to Don Sauvigne for his assistance throughout the project. Acknowledgment also goes to the staff of the United States Holocaust Memorial Museum in Washington, D.C., for its help with photographs and research material.

HOLOCAUST timeline

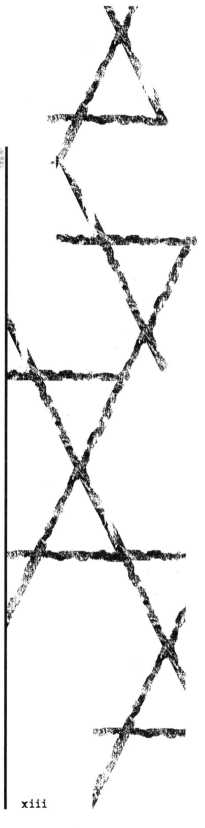

1899 Houston Stewart Chamberlain publishes *The Foundations of the Nineteenth Century,* a book that uses racialism to explain European history.

1903 Russian antisemites circulate *The Protocols of the Elders of Zion,* a forgery that describes the master plan of an alleged Jewish conspiracy to dominate the world.

1923 Alfred Rosenberg reissues an official Nazi party version of *The Protocols.*

1925 Adolf Hitler describes his racial beliefs concerning the superiority of German people and the inferiority of Jews in his memoir *Mein Kampf* ("My Struggle").

1933 Adolf Hitler becomes Chancellor of Germany and appoints Joseph Goebbels as Reich Minister of Public Enlightenment and Propaganda.

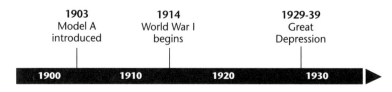

1903
Model A
introduced

1914
World War I
begins

1929-39
Great
Depression

| 1900 | 1910 | 1920 | 1930 |

1933 Inge Deutshkron, a young Jewish girl living in Berlin, witnesses a nation-wide boycott against Jewish-owned businesses.

1933 The Nazis conduct book burnings and impose censorship throughout Germany.

1935 The Nazi government orders Franziska Schwartz, a deaf German teenager, to appear at a health center for sterilization.

1935 Wilhelm Frick drafts the Nuremberg Laws, which deny German citizenship rights to Jews and prohibit marriage and sexual relationships between Jews and non-Jews.

1936 Participation in Hitler Youth becomes mandatory. All ten-year-old boys are required to register at government offices for group membership.

1938 *New York Times* reporter Otto D. Toliscus gives an account of the two-day campaign of violence against Jews known as "Kristallnacht."

1939 Several hundred Jews attempt to emigrate from Germany on board the steamship *St. Louis,* but are forced to return to Europe.

1939 Wilhelmine Haferkamp and other fertile German women receive the Mother's Cross, a medal honoring their child-bearing accomplishments.

1939 In accordance with the principles of the Jehovah Witness faith, young Elisabeth Kusserow refuses to salute the Nazi flag and is sent to reform school for six years.

1939 Adolf Hitler appoints Hans Frank Governor-General of certain sections of Poland that later become the "resettlement" areas for Jews and others deemed unfit for Reich citizenship.

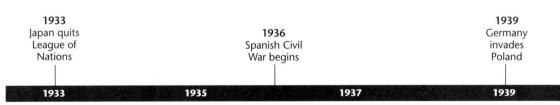

1933 Japan quits League of Nations		1936 Spanish Civil War begins		1939 Germany invades Poland
1933	**1935**	**1937**		**1939**

1939 Reinhardt Heydrich issues a directive to Nazi task forces ordering the "resettlement" of Jewish Poles to urban centers near railroad lines.

1940 Writing in his diary, Chaim A. Kaplan records his observations about the formation of a Jewish ghetto in the Polish city of Warsaw.

1940 The Warsaw ghetto becomes "closed," sealing Janina David and her parents off from surrounding neighborhoods.

1940 The Nazis imprison Christian Reger for defying the state-sponsored religion known as the German Faith Movement.

1941 Rudolph Höss, Commandant of the Auschwitz concentration camp, oversees the first experiments using poisonous gas for the extermination of large masses of human beings.

1941 Avraham Tory, a Lithuanian Jew, survives a Nazi-ordered "action" that removes nearly 10,000 people from the Kovno ghetto, about half of whom are children.

1941 Gonda Redlich arrives at the ghetto in Theresienstadt, Czechoslovakia, which the Nazis portray as a "model Jewish settlement."

1942 A small group of high-ranking Nazi party and government officials meet to discuss the "Final Solution," a code name for their plan to eliminate all European Jews.

1942 Anne Frank and her family move into a secret annex built on the top stories of a house in Amsterdam.

1942 Etty Hillesum assists new arrivals at the Westerbork transit camp where Dutch Jews are held before deportation to death camps in Poland.

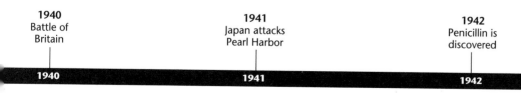

1940
Battle of
Britain

1941
Japan attacks
Pearl Harbor

1942
Penicillin is
discovered

1940   1941   1942

1942 Hirsch Grunstein and his brother go into hiding in Belgium to escape the Nazis. The boys stay with a couple who volunteers to give them shelter.

1942 Wladyslaw Bartoszewski, a Catholic Polish resister, helps form a Jewish relief committee called Zegota.

1943 Hans and Sophie Scholl are arrested on a Munich university campus for distributing pamphlets for the White Rose resistance group.

1943 After abandoning his university studies to fight fascism, a young Jewish Italian man named Primo Levi is captured by the Nazis and sent to Auschwitz.

1944 Corrie Ten Boom and her family are imprisoned by the Gestapo for their involvement in an underground operation to aid Jews in Holland.

1944 Hannah Senesh, a Jew living in Palestine, parachutes behind enemy lines as part of a British-sponsored rescue mission to reach Jews and other resisters.

1944 A young Swedish businessman named Raoul Wallenberg arrives in Hungary to help save the surviving Jews trapped in Budapest.

1944 Oskar Schindler seeks permission from the Nazis to spare Jewish prisoners from death by employing them at a munitions factory in Czechoslovakia.

1944 Kim Malthe-Bruun joins the Danish resistance movement and is arrested by the Gestapo.

1945 American reporter Edward R. Murrow broadcasts his impressions of the Buchenwald concentration camp shortly after its liberation.

1945 British forces liberate French prisoner Fania Fénelon from the Bergen-Belson concentration camp in northern Germany.

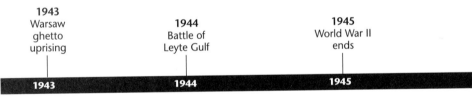

1943
Warsaw
ghetto
uprising

1944
Battle of
Leyte Gulf

1945
World War II
ends

1943   1944   1945   1946

1945 Heinrich Himmler, the senior Nazi official responsible for overseeing the mass murder of six million European Jews, is captured by the Allies and commits suicide.

1945 Robert H. Jackson gives the opening address for America before the International Military Tribunal at Nuremberg.

1947 Survivor Simon Wiesenthal forms the Jewish Historical Documentation Center in Austria to track down Nazi war criminals.

1957 After emigrating to the United States, Gerda Weissmann Klein writes a memoir called *All But My Life.*

1960 Elie Wiesel publishes *Night,* an autobiographical account of his experiences during the Holocaust.

1961 Hannah Arendt attends the trial of Adolf Eichmann, a notorious Nazi criminal who fled to Argentina after the war.

1970 After serving 20 years in prison, former Nazi Albert Speer publishes his autobiography *Inside the Third Reich.*

1992 Art Spiegelman wins a Pulizer Prize for *Maus,* a cartoon-style novel about the author's experiences as a child of Holocaust survivors.

1993 The United States Holocaust Memorial Museum opens in Washington, D.C.

1997 Riva Shefer, a 75-year-old Latvian Jew who survived a Nazi labor camp, becomes the first recipient of money from a $200 million Swiss fund established to aid Holocaust survivors.

1953
Soviets
launch
Sputnik

1961
Berlin wall is
constructed

1973
Vietnam
War ends

1998
Vatican
issues
Holocaust
declaration

1950   1960   1970   1990

credits

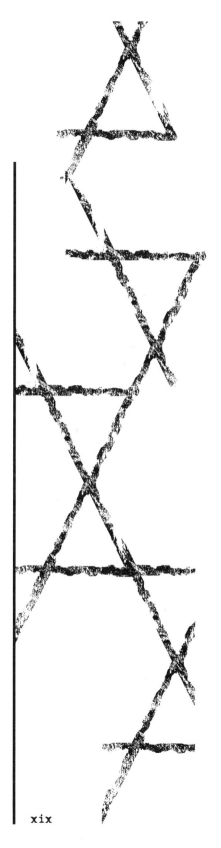

The editors wish to thank the copyright holders of the excerpted documents included in this volume and the permissions managers of many book and magazine publishing companies for assisting us in securing reproduction rights. What follows is a list of the copyright holders who have granted us permission to reproduce material for *Voices of the Holocaust*. Every effort has been made to trace copyright, but if omissions have been made, please contact the publisher.

Deutschkren, Inge. From *Outcast: A Jewish Girl in Wartime Berlin*. Translated by Jean Steinberg. Fromm International Publishing Corporation, 1989. Translation copyright © 1989 Fromm International Publishing Corporation. Reproduced by permission.

Fénelon, Fania with Marcelle Routier. From *Playing for Time*. Atheneum, 1977. English translation copyright © 1977 by Michael Joseph Ltd and Atheneum Publishers. All rights reserved. Reproduced by permission of Michael Joseph, Ltd. In the U.S. by Atheneum, a division of Simon & Schuster, Inc.

Frank, Anne. From *The Diary of A Young Girl: The Definitive Edition*. Edited by Otto H. Frank & Mirjam Pressler, translated by Susan Massotty. Bantam Books, 1995. English translation copyright © 1995 by Doubleday, a division of Bantam Doubleday Dell Publishing Group, Inc. Reproduced by permission of Bantam Books, a division of Bantam Doubleday Dell Publishing Group, Inc.

Friedman, Ina R. From *The Other Victims: FirstPerson Stories of Non-Jews Persecuted by the Nazis*. Houghton Mifflin Company, 1990. Copyright © 1990 by Ina R. Friedman. All rights reserved. Reproduced by permission.

Friedman, Saul S. From *The Terezin Diary of Gonda Redlich*. Translated by Laurence Kutler. The University Press of Kentucky, 1992. Copyright © 1992 by The University Press of Kentucky. Reproduced by permission of The University Press of Kentucky.

Greene, Bette. From *Summer of My German Soldier*. The Dial Press, 1973. Copyright © 1973 by Bette Greene. All rights reserved. Reproduced by permission.

Haferkamp, Wilhelmine. From "Motherhood Times Ten, and Food to Spare," in *Frauen: German Women Recall the Third Reich,* by Alison Owings. Rutgers University Press, 1993. Copyright © 1993 by Alison Owings. All rights reserved. Reproduced by permission.

Hillesum, Etty. From *An Interrupted Life—The Diaries, 1941-1943 and Letters from Westerbork*. Translated by Arnold J. Pomerans. Pantheon Books, 1986. Copyright © 1986 by Random House, Inc. Reproduced by permission.

Höss, Rudolph. From *Death Dealer: The Memoirs of the SS Kommandant at Auschwitz*. Edited by Steven Paskuly, translated by Andrew Pollinger. Prometheus Books, 1992. Copyright © 1992 by Steven Paskuly. All rights reserved. Reproduced by permission.

Jens, Inge. From *At the Heart of the White Rose: Letters and Diaries of Hans and Sophie Scholl*. Edited by Inge Jens, translated by J. Maxwell Brownjohn. Harper & Row, Publishers, 1987. © 1987 HarperCollins Publishers, Inc. Reproduced by permission of Harpercollins Publishers, Inc.

Kaplan, Chaim A. From *Scroll of Agony: The Warsaw Diary of Chaim A. Kaplan*. Translated and edited by Abraham I. Katsh. Collier Books, 1973. Copyright © 1963, 1973 by Abraham I. Katsh. All rights reserved. Reproduced by Hamish Hamilton Ltd. In the U.S. reproduced by permission of Macmillan Publishing Company, a division of Simon & Schuster, Inc.

Keneally, Thomas. From *Schindler's List*. Touchstone Book, 1982. Copyright © 1982 by Serpentine Publishing Co. Pty, Ltd. Reproduced by permission.

Klein, Gerda Weissmann. *From All But My Life*. Hill and Wang, 1995. Copyright © 1957, 1995 by Gerda Weissmann Klein. Reproduced by permission of Hill and Wang, a division of Farrar, Straus and Giroux, Inc.

Levi, Primo. From *Survival in Auschwitz: The Nazi Assault on Humanity*. Translated by Stuart Woolf. Collier Books, 1993. Reproduced by permission.

Malthe-Bruun, Kim. From *Heroic Heart*. Edited by Vibeke Malthe-Bruun, translated by Gerry Bothmer. Random House, 1955. Copyright, 1955, renewed 1983 by Random House, Inc. All rights reserved. Reproduced by permission.

Murrow, Edward R. From *In Search of Light: The Broadcasts of Edward R Murrow, 1938-1961*. Alfred A. Knopf, 1967. © Copyright 1967 by the Estate of Edward R. Murrow. Reproduced by permission.

New York Times, November 11, 1938. Copyright © 1938, renewed 1966 by The New York Times Company. Reproduced by permission.

Rosenberg, Maxine B. From *Hiding to Survive: Stories of Jewish Children Rescued from the Holocaust*. Clarion Books,

Voices of the HOLOCAUST

HOLOCAUST resisters

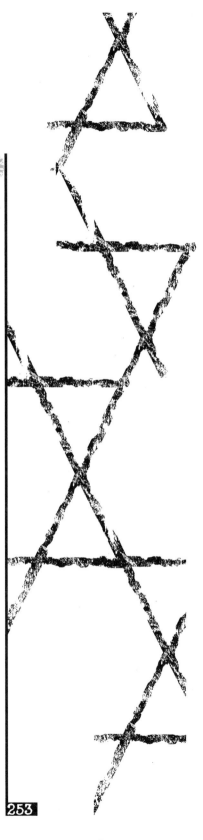

When Adolf Hitler came to power in 1933, he represented renewed hope and national pride for many people humiliated by Germany's defeat in World War I. While Hitler denounced many political parties, influences, and even countries, he primarily held Jewish people accountable for all the ills that befell Germanic, or "Aryan," people. Despite his messages of hate, many Germans truly believed he was the only person capable of saving their country from ruin. While promising a glorious future to millions of disenchanted and unemployed citizens of Germany, Hitler did not give specific details of the way he planned to solve the "Jewish problem." But after the Nazis seized control of the German government and outlawed all political opposition, few people in Germany could safely disagree with Nazi policies.

As Germany invaded one European country after another, the Nazis instituted a similar pattern of suppression and domination. The party restricted civil rights, demanded loyalty

to their regime, and brutally punished those who resisted. Anti-Jewish measures stripped Jews of their citizenship rights, jobs, and assets (land, homes, businesses, and other valuables) and segregated all people of Jewish ancestry into restricted areas known as ghettos. Although they first imposed a strict program of forced emigration and imprisonment on the Jewish people, by 1941 the Nazis had turned to mass murder as a way of solving the "Jewish problem." The following year, Hitler and other top-level Nazi leaders formally approved a plan—code-named the "Final Solution"—for the annihilation of all European Jews. By the summer of

1942, reports of the systematic extermination of Jews began to leak to the free world.

When the shocking news of Nazi atrocities reached Jewish settlers living in British-occupied Palestine, many decided to attempt rescue missions. One young woman, a volunteer parachutist agent named **Hannah Senesh**, offered to be dropped behind enemy lines. Senesh was one of 32 parachutists who participated in British-sponsored missions between 1943 and 1945. Her writings, published as *Hannah Senesh: Her Life & Diary,* describe her ideals and dreams during this tumultuous period in world history.

Like Senesh, many other courageous people attempted to overthrow Nazi rule. Such resisters operating in occupied territories were called "partisans." These individuals evaded German orders, committed sabotage (destructive acts that hinder a nation's war effort), refused to fulfill production quotas, and disobeyed forced labor assignments. While some partisan groups acted mainly by opposing Nazi occupation through demonstrations and the like, others actually attempted to save Jews; all risked their lives. One Nazi leader made sure Jews and resisters met with ruthless brutality. His name was **Heinrich Himmler**. Himmler was the senior official responsible for carrying out the "final solution" to the "Jewish problem" and oversaw the administration of all occupied countries.

One of the most inspiring examples of resistance took place in Denmark. The behavior of the Danish people and government was unique among Nazi-controlled countries— nearly all 8,000 Jews living in Denmark survived the war. **Kim Malthe-Bruun**, a young seaman who joined the underground resistance movement in 1944, exemplifies the exceptional bravery and character of the Danes. His humanitarian spirit is reflected in his writings, which were published in 1955 as *Heroic Heart: The Diary and Letters of Kim Malthe-Bruun, 1941-1945.*

In the early 1940s, Poland contained the largest Jewish population of any country in Europe. Many factors made it difficult for Poles to help their 3.3 million fellow Jewish countrymen. Antisemitism was widespread, and all Poles were potential targets for Nazi persecution. As a further deterrent, the Germans imposed the death penalty on all people

Jews from the Lodz (Poland) ghetto being deported to Auschwitz.

who helped hide Jews. But, despite these grave risks, many Poles such as **Wladyslaw Bartoszewski** assisted the Jews during the Holocaust. In his book *The Warsaw Ghetto: A Christian's Testimony,* Bartoszewski chronicles his experiences working for the relief committee called Zegota, which attempted to help the 20,000 to 30,000 Jews hiding in Warsaw, Poland.

Corrie Ten Boom was a Christian resister who lived in Holland. Ten Boom, her sister, and her father willingly placed themselves in danger by hiding Jews in their ancient little house on a main street in Haarlem. Ten Boom gives an account of her experiences as a leader of the underground movement in her book *The Hiding Place.*

Unlike the people living in occupied countries, German citizens who resisted the Nazis faced an additional danger—the charge of treason, or betrayal of their own country, which was punishable by death. Only one group dared to oppose Hitler's dictatorship and voice dissent against its

murderous policies. Members of the White Rose movement, which was founded at the University of Munich, distributed leaflets critical of the Nazi government. Founder **Hans Scholl** and his sister, **Sophie Scholl**, believed it was worth risking their lives to try to persuade other Germans to turn against the Nazis. A small glimpse of their hopes was captured in the book *At the Heart of the White Rose: Letters and Diaries of Hans and Sophie Scholl.*

During World War II, **Raoul Wallenberg** left the security of Sweden, his neutral homeland, to aid the Jewish population living in Hungary. The grandson of a diplomat, Wallenberg was ideally suited for the unusual role of providing false documents to nearly 100,000 Hungarian Jews. These documents guaranteed their holders safety from Nazi deportation to death camps. The book *Letters and Dispatches, 1924-1944: Raoul Wallenberg* contains the thoughts of this courageous businessman who was captured by the Soviets and

A group of Jewish parachutists waits to leave Palestine for Cairo in May 1944.

disappeared behind the Iron Curtain—Soviet-dominated territory in Eastern Europe—after World War II.

When the Nazi government began to prepare for the Soviet invasion in 1941, they called on businesses in occupied Poland to produce war supplies for the German troops. **Oskar Schindler** responded to this request by opening a cookware factory in the Polish city of Cracow. To operate the plant, he relied on the Jewish population interned (or held) in the local ghetto and labor camp. At some point, Schindler ceased being an ordinary employer and began functioning more as a savior to his Jewish workers. As described in the book *Schindler's List,* he concocted a plan to relocate his Jewish workforce to a safer location—for the supposed purpose of producing armaments for the war efforts. His heroic actions saved over 1,200 Jews.

Hannah Senesh

Excerpt from *Hannah Senesh:
Her Life & Diary*, written
between 1934 and 1944

This edition published in 1986

Resisters, or government opponents, operating in Nazi-occupied territories were called "partisans." These individual citizens of occupied countries evaded German orders, committed sabotage (destructive acts that hinder a nation's war effort), refused to fulfill production quotas, and disobeyed forced labor assignments. When the Nazis outlawed organized resistance to their party's goals, these groups began operating secretly and came to be known as segments of the "underground" movement.

The Allied powers (those countries fighting against Germany in World War II) had various expectations of resistance members. The Soviet Union expected partisans to fight the Nazis during military attacks and destroy communication lines and industrial plants. On the other hand, the United States and Great Britain asked partisans to provide intelligence (information to help win the war), aid in the escape of prisoners of war, and carry out specific military missions.

In the summer of 1942, reports of the systematic extermination of Jews in Nazi-occupied countries began to travel to the free world. When this shocking news reached Jewish settlers living in British-occupied Palestine, many decided to attempt rescue missions. After considerable debate, the British agreed to train volunteers as parachutist agents; these agents would then be dropped behind enemy lines in order to carry out specific missions. Because many of the volunteers were natives of the target countries, they had the necessary linguistic (language) skills and familiarity with the terrain to blend in with the citizenry and perform the desired duties. Some 250 men and women volunteered; 110 received train-

Heinrich Himmler (1900-1945)

Heinrich Himmler was the senior Nazi official responsible for carrying out the "Final Solution," the code name for the mass extermination of European Jews. Himmler—the second most powerful man in wartime Germany—was born near Munich, Germany, to devout Catholic parents. He received a *gymnasium* (high school) education before joining the Bavarian army as a cadet-clerk in World War I. After the war, Himmler earned a diploma in agriculture from a technical college and worked as a sales consultant for a fertilizer manufacturer.

In 1923, Himmler joined the National Socialists (NASDP or Nazi party) and participated in an attempted overthrow of the German government, an action now known as the Beer Hall Putsch. From 1925 to 1930, he served as the acting propaganda leader of the party. After marrying Magarete Boden, Himmler tried his hand at poultry farming, but was unsuccessful. Then, in January 1929, Hitler selected Himmler to head his personal bodyguard detail, known as the *Schutzstaffel,* or SS. This appointment became the foundation of Himmler's rise to power within the Reich (pronounced RIKE; German word for "empire"). Himmler expanded the SS, also known as the Black Guard, from 300 to 50,000 men in four years.

Himmler was appointed chief of police in Munich in 1933 and was later made head of the Gestapo organization (the Nazi political police). Acting in his role as police chief, he set up the first concentration camp at Dachau to house "enemies" of the Nazi party. By 1936,

ing. However, due to operational and technical difficulties, only 32 of the volunteers actually parachuted in missions between 1943 and 1945.

Hannah Senesh was one of the Palestinian-Jews who parachuted into occupied Europe as an emissary, or agent, to aid Jews living under Nazi oppression. Originally from Budapest, Hungary, Senesh had immigrated to Palestine in 1939 when she was 19 years old. A talented writer and poet, she lived on the Kibbutz Sedot Yam near Caesarea. (A kibbutz

(Continued from previous page)

Himmler had gained control over the entire political and criminal police system of the Third Reich, becoming *Reichsführer* of the SS and head of the German police.

When war broke out in 1939, Himmler mobilized his SS forces to follow the regular army into occupied territories. Under his command, SS forces captured civilians and brutally killed them. Millions of so-called "racial degenerates" were either displaced from their homes or murdered. While witnessing a mass execution staged especially for him, Himmler reportedly grew faint from the bloodbath and hastened the construction of death camps with gas chambers to allow for "a more humane means" of execution.

In late 1944, when the tides of the war turned against Germany, Himmler tried to cover traces of his mass murder apparatus by ordering the death camps closed and crematoriums and gas chambers destroyed. Himmler proposed that Germany should surrender to then-U.S. general Dwight D. Eisenhower and the western Allies (the non-Asian forces fighting against Germany during World War II), while continuing to fight the Soviets in the East. Hitler regarded Himmler's suggestion as treasonous, became enraged, and stripped him of all his offices and responsibilities. When Germany finally surrendered, Himmler assumed a false identity and attempted to escape Germany. He was arrested by British troops and committed suicide by swallowing cyanide (a fast-acting poison) on May 23, 1945.

is a communal farm or settlement.) After learning of the fate of fellow Jews trapped in Europe, she became determined to attempt the rescue of Jews stranded in Hungary and neighboring countries.

Senesh volunteered in 1943 and received training in Egypt. Like the other men and women who offered their services to the resistance effort, Senesh was willing to place herself in tremendous danger by parachuting behind Nazi lines. She believed that even if she and her comrades did not succeed in rescuing their Jewish brothers and sisters, their courage and sacrifice would inspire Jews throughout Europe. Of the 32 parachutists, Senesh was one of five who was able to penetrate into her target country. She parachuted into Yugoslavia on March 13, 1944, determined to cross into Hungary.

Things to Remember While Reading the Diary Entries and Letters of Hannah Senesh:

- In the first diary entry excerpted below, Senesh mentions that she had become a Zionist. As a teenager growing up in Budapest, Hungary, she was exposed to many different factions within the Zionist movement. Members of this worldwide initiative were committed to the creation of a Jewish homeland in Palestine.

- Due to the nature of her mission, Senesh wrote a letter to her brother George in case she did not return alive. However, when George arrived in Palestine before she left for Cairo, Egypt, she allowed him to see the letter. Written on December 25, 1943, it contains an apology for undertaking a deed that would perhaps cost Senesh her life.

- Senesh wrote the last two letters cited below on the day she parachuted into Yugoslavia. Also included below is the last poem written by Senesh, which she composed while in prison in Budapest. Notice she was not yet 23 years old.

Hannah Senesh: Her Life & Diary

Zionist: Person who supports the creation of a Jewish nation in Palestine. (Mount Zion is the site of Jerusalem, the capital of Israel.)

October 27, 1938

I don't know whether I've already mentioned that I've become a **Zionist**. *This word stands for a tremendous number of things. To me it means, in short, that I now consciously and strongly feel I am a Jew, and am proud of it. My primary aim is to go to* **Palestine**, *to work for it. Of course this did not develop from one day to the next; it was a somewhat gradual development. There was first talk*

Palestine: A region in the
Middle East bordered on
the west by the Mediter-
ranean Sea and to the east
by the Dead Sea. It has
long been the scene of
fighting between the Arab
and Israeli peoples—
especially along the West
Bank area near the River
Jordan. Palestine is considered the historic homeland
of the Jews.

Vehemently: Passionately
or strongly.

Knuckle down: Get busy;
make a serious attempt at
doing something.

*of it about three years ago, and at that time I **vehemently** attacked
the Zionist Movement. Since then people, events, times, have all
brought me closer to the idea, and I am immeasurably happy that
I've found this ideal, that I now feel firm ground under my feet,
and can see a definite goal towards which it is really worth striv-
ing. I am going to start learning Hebrew, and I'll attend one of the
youth groups. In short, I'm really going to **knuckle down** properly.
I've become a different person, and it's a very good feeling.*

One needs something to believe in, something for which one can have whole-hearted enthusiasm. One needs to feel that one's life has meaning, that one is needed in this world. Zionism fulfills all this for me. One hears a good many arguments against the Movement, but this doesn't matter. I believe in it, and that's the important thing.

*I'm convinced Zionism is Jewry's solution to its problems, and that the outstanding work being done in Palestine is not **in vain**.*

Caesarea
February 22, 1943

*How strangely things work out. On January 8 I wrote a few words about the sudden idea that struck me. A few days ago a man from **Kibbutz** Ma'agan, a member of the **Palmach**, visited the kibbutz and we chatted awhile. In the course of the conversation he told me that a Palmach unit was being organized to do—exactly what I felt then I wanted to do. I was truly astounded. The identical idea!*

My answer, of course, was that I'm absolutely ready. It's still only in the planning stage, but he promised to bring the matter up before the enlistment committee since he considers me admirably suited for the mission.

*I see the hand of destiny in this just as I did at the time of my **Aliyah**. I wasn't master of my fate then either. I was **enthralled** by one idea, and it gave me no rest. I knew I would emigrate, despite the many obstacles in my path. Now I again sense the excitement of something important and vital ahead, and the feeling of inevitability connected with a decisive and urgent step. The entire plan may **miscarry**, and I may receive a brief notification informing me the matter will be postponed, or that I don't qualify. But I think I have the capabilities necessary for just this assignment, and I'll fight for it with all my might.*

In vain: Without success.

Kibbutz: Hebrew for communal settlement or farm.

Palmach: Elite unit of the underground military force in British-occupied Palestine.

Aliyah: Hebrew for the immigration of Jews to Israel.

Enthralled: Charmed; held spellbound.

Miscarry: Failure to achieve what was intended.

*I can't sleep at night because of the scenes I **envisage**: how I'll conduct myself in this or that situation ... how I'll notify Mother of my arrival ... how I'll organize the Jewish Youth. Everything is still indefinite. We'll see what the future brings....*

January 11, 1944

This week I leave for Egypt. I'm a soldier. Concerning the circumstances of my enlistment, and my feelings in connection with it, and with all that led up to it, I don't want to write.

I want to believe that what I've done, and will do, are right. Time will tell the rest.

Haifa
December 25, 1943

Darling George!

Sometimes one writes letters one does not intend sending. Letters one must write without asking oneself, 'I wonder whether this will ever reach its destination.'

Day after tomorrow I am starting something new. Perhaps it's madness. Perhaps it's fantastic. Perhaps it is dangerous. Perhaps one in a hundred—or one in a thousand—pays with his life. Perhaps with less than his life, perhaps with more. Don't ask questions. You'll eventually know what it's about.

*George, I must explain something to you. I must **exonerate** myself. I must prepare myself for that moment when you arrive inside the frontiers of the Land, waiting for that moment when, after six years, we will meet again, and you will ask, 'Where is she?' and they'll abruptly answer, 'She's not here.'*

I wonder, will you understand? I wonder, will you believe that it is more than a childish wish for adventure, more than

Envisage: To have a mental picture of something before it becomes real.

Exonerate: To relieve of a responsibility or clear from blame.

youthful romanticism that attracted me? I wonder, will you feel that I could not do otherwise, that this was something I had to do?

There are events without which one's life becomes unimportant, a worthless toy; and there are times when one is commanded to do something, even at the price of one's life.

I'm afraid, George, that feelings turn into empty phrases even though they are so impassioned before they turn into words. I don't know whether you'll sense the doubts, the conflicts, and after every struggle the renewed decision.

It is difficult because I am alone. If I had someone with whom I could talk freely, uninhibitedly—if only the entire burden were not mine, if only I could talk to you. If there is anyone who would understand me, I think you would be that one. But who knows ... six years is a long time.

But enough about myself. Perhaps I have already said too much. I would like to tell you a few things about the new life, the new home, as I see them. I don't want to influence you. You'll see for yourself what the country is. But I want to tell you how I see it.

*First of all—I love it. I love its hundred faces, its hundred climates, its **many-faceted** life. I love the old and the new in it; I love it because it is ours. No, not ours, but because we can make ourselves believe it is ours.*

And I respect it. Not everything. I respect the people who believe in something, respect their idealistic struggle with the daily realities. I respect those who don't live just for the moment, or for money. And I think there are more such people here than anywhere else on earth. And finally, I think that this is the only solution for us, and for this reason I don't doubt its future, though I think it will be very difficult and combative.

As far as the kibbutz is concerned, I don't think it is perfect, and it will probably pass through many phases. But in today's cir-

Many-faceted: Many sided.

A group of Jewish parachutists with members of the Yugoslovian underground.

cumstances it best suits our aims, and is the closest to our concept of a way of life—about this I have absolutely no doubt.

We have need of one thing: people who are brave and without prejudices, who are not robots, who want to think for themselves and not accept **outmoded** ideas. It is easy to place laws in the hands of man, to tell him to live by them. It is more difficult to follow those laws. But most difficult of all is to impose laws upon oneself, while being constantly *self-analytical* and *self-vigilant*. I think this is the highest form of law enforcement, and at the same time the only just form. And this form of law can only build a new, **contented** life.

I often ask myself what the fate of the kibbutz will be when the magic and novelty of construction and creation wear off, when

Outmoded: No longer acceptable or stylish.

Self-analytical: An individual's attempt to understand himself or herself.

Self-vigilant: Watching out for oneself.

Contented: Satisfied.

Senesh **267**

*the struggle for existence assumes reality and—according to plan— becomes an organized, abundant **communal** life. What will the **incentive** of the people be, what will fill their lives? I don't know the answer. But that day is so far in the future that it is best to think of existing matters.*

Don't think I see everything through rose-coloured glasses. My faith is a subjective matter, and not the result of outer conditions. I see the difficulties clearly, both inside and out. But I see the good side, and above all, as I said before, I think this is the only way.

I did not write about something that constantly preoccupies my thoughts: Mother. I can't.

Enough of this letter. I hope you will never receive it. But if you do, only after we have met.

And if it should be otherwise, George dear, I embrace you with everlasting love.

Your sister.

P.S. I wrote the letter at the beginning of the parachute training course.

March 13, 1944

*Dearest **Comrades:***

On sea, land, in the air, in war and in peace, we are all advancing towards the same goal. Each of us will stand at his post. There is no difference between my task and that of another. I will be thinking of all of you a great deal. That's what gives me strength.

Warmest comradely greetings.

Communal: Group.

Incentive: Motivation.

Comrades: Fellow soldiers; intimate or close friends.

Hannah Senesh (1921-1944)

Hannah Senesh (pronounced "SZENES") was born in Budapest, Hungary. She came from a distinguished family of poets, writers, and musicians. At the age of 13, she began keeping a diary, displaying remarkable talent as a writer and poet. Senesh became a Zionist at the age of 17, immigrated to Palestine two years later, and joined the Kibbutz Sedot Yam near Caesarea.

In 1943, Senesh volunteered to participate in a secret parachute mission organized by the British military and intelligence service. She parachuted into Yugoslavia in March of 1944 and was captured three months later in Nazi-occupied Hungary. After five months of imprisonment and torture in a prison in Budapest, she was brought to trial and convicted of treason against Hungary. Senesh was executed shortly before the city of Budapest fell to the advancing Russian army.

March 13, 1944

Mother Darling,

In a few days I'll be so close to you—and yet so far. Forgive me, and try to understand. With a million hugs.

One—Two—Three*

One—two—three ...
*   eight feet long,*
Two strides across, the rest is dark ...
Life hangs over me like a question mark.
One—two—three ...
*   maybe another week,*
Or next month may still find me here,
But death, I feel, is very near.
I could have been
*   twenty-three next July;*

I gambled on what mattered most,
The dice were cast. I lost.

Budapest 1944

[*Her last poem, written in prison;
translated from the Hungarian by Peter Hay.]
(Senesh, pp. 63, 127, 131-34, 167, 257)

What happened next...

After parachuting into Yugoslavia in March of 1944, Senesh and her team spent several months traveling throughout the countryside working with numerous resistance groups. They witnessed firsthand the destruction caused by German forces; entire villages and towns were burnt and pillaged. Dressed as British officers, the four parachutists received the cooperation of numerous partisans engaged in guerrilla tactics (aggressive acts of warfare carried out by independent fighting units) against the Nazis.

Because of her gender and charisma, Senesh impressed civilians and partisans everywhere she went. She was fearless, perceptive, inspirational, and completely devoted to the cause of saving Jews and fighting the Nazis. When Senesh and her comrades met one particular group of Jewish partisans, they revealed their true identities and connections to Palestine. This chance meeting inspired Senesh to write the poem "Blessed Is the Match," which she gave to her fellow parachutist Reuven Dafni just before her departure into Hungary. This poem later became famous throughout Israel.

In June of 1944, Senesh crossed into Nazi-occupied Hungary and was immediately captured. She spent five months in a prison in Budapest, where she was tortured by the Gestapo (the Nazis' secret police force). The Nazis attempted to force Senesh to reveal the secret codes for her transmitter radio. Even when Gestapo officers threatened to kill her mother, Senesh maintained her resolve. On October 28, 1944, she appeared before a military tribunal (or court) and was convicted of treason against Hungary. Senesh's eloquent and forceful defense affected the judges, who decided to postpone her sentencing for over a week. Amidst heavy bombing by Allied air forces and the approach of the Russian army, the judges who had tried Senesh fled Budapest. She was executed by firing squad on November 7, a month before the Soviets completely encircled Budapest.

Today, Hannah Senesh is considered a national heroine in Israel, where her legacy symbolizes courage and moral strength. Her story is the subject of numerous plays, books, and a motion picture. In 1950, her remains were brought to Israel and buried in the national military cemetery at Mount Herzl in Jerusalem.

Did you know...

- Thirty-two Palestinian-Jews under British sponsorship parachuted behind enemy lines in Europe. Twelve were captured; seven were executed. Senesh is buried along with six other parachutists in the national cemetery in Jerusalem. An outline of a parachute is carved on each headstone, and their graves form the shape of V.

- Most modern Israelis can recite from memory Senesh's poem "Blessed Is the Match," which in Hebrew is "Ashrei ha-Gafrur." She wrote the poem in May 1944, a month before her capture by the Nazis. Like a match that is consumed by its use, Senesh believed her life was worth sacrificing for a higher cause.

- In Israel, over 30 streets bear Senesh's name, as do two farming settlements, a forest, and a ship.

For Further Reading

Atkinson, Linda. *In Kindling Flame: The Story of Hannah Senesh.* Lee & Shepard, 1985.

Kertyesz, Imre. *Fateless.* Evanston, IL: Northwestern University Press, 1992.

Senesh, Hannah. *Hannah Senesh: Her Life & Diary.* First English edition, Nigel Marsh, 1971. New York: Schocken Books, 1972. Reprinted, Hakibbutz Hameuchad Publishing House Ltd., 1986.

Kim Malthe-Bruun

Excerpt from Heroic Heart:
The Diary and Letters of Kim
Malthe-Bruun, 1941-1945

Edited by Vibeke Malthe-Bruun
Published in 1955

When the forces of Nazi Germany invaded Denmark in 1940, about 8,000 Jews lived in the country—that number represented less than 1 percent of the total population of Denmark. The actions taken by the Danish people and government were unique among all European countries under Nazi rule; nearly all Jews in Denmark survived the war. Although greatly outmatched and overpowered by German military forces, Denmark responded in a way that demonstrates the potential power of nonviolent action and resistance. Unlike the experience in other countries, antisemitism, or anti-Jewish sentiment, never received much support in Denmark. Despite efforts by Nazi occupiers to convey their prejudices, the country remained steadfast in its support of Jewish citizens and refugees (those who flee to a foreign country to escape danger and persecution).

After invading Denmark, Germany officially declared that it had no intention of seizing any of the country's territory or suppressing its political independence. The country's democratic administration continued, with King Christian X retaining his sovereignty, Danish parliament carrying out its functions, and the Danish army, navy, and police remaining intact. The German accord with Denmark also contained a provision that prohibited Germany from harming the Jews living in Denmark. For the first few years of occupation, this clause remained in effect despite German pressure and the efforts of the small Danish Nazi party that tried to stir up antisemitism.

Unlike the experience of Jews in other countries, the situation for Jews in Denmark remained unchanged under German occupation—at first. No anti-Jewish measures were introduced, not even the typical provision requiring Jews to wear yellow badges in the shape of the Star of David. No Jewish property was confiscated, and no Jews were forced from government posts. In fact, the Germans did not even succeed in creating a legal distinction between native Danes of Jewish origin and Jewish refugees. By preventing preparatory measures designed to strip Jews of their rights, Danish leaders delayed the implementation of more drastic measures such as the creation of ghettos (restricted areas of cities where Jews were forced to live) and deportations (forced exits) to extermination camps.

In the spring of 1943, tensions began to increase between the two governments as Danish resistance operations gathered momentum. The growing strength of the Allied forces (those countries fighting against Germany during World War II) encouraged Danish citizens to organize strikes and acts of sabotage (destructive acts that hinder a nation's war effort) against the Germans.

In August, a crisis erupted when government officials, including German-appointed Nazi leaders stationed in Denmark, objected to Germany's attempt to tighten its control over Denmark. German military forces entered the capital city of Copenhagen, disarmed the Danish army, imprisoned the king, and dissolved the government. The newly appointed German military leader, General von Hannecken, declared a state of emergency (a need for immediate action) and imposed martial law (military law applied in occupied territory).

No longer content with postponing the "final solution" to the "Jewish problem," the Nazis sent one of their ruthless antisemites, Rolf Gunther, to Copenhagen to organize the deportation of all Jews. Rather than send the Jews to concentration and extermination camps, the Germans consented to deport them to the Theresienstadt ghetto in Czechoslovakia.

To assist with the deportation operation, Nazi officials arranged for the transfer to Copenhagen of German transport vessels and Gestapo police units. They scheduled the mass arrest and deportation of Jews to begin the night of October 1, 1943, which was Rosh Hashanah, or the Jewish New Year. A few days before the planned seizure, news of the maneuver reached Georg Ferdinand Duckwitz, a German embassy official who was responsible for all shipping affairs in Copenhagen. Duckwitz decided to reveal his knowledge of the planned attack to local Danish Social Democrats who, in turn, told members of the Jewish clergy. Jewish rabbis warned their congregations and many people worked intently to spread the word throughout Copenhagen, where most Danish Jews resided. When the Nazi Gestapo raided Jewish residences over the course of several days, they found less than 500 people; the rest were safely hidden. Many of those arrested were elderly and apparently did not comprehend the significance of the warning.

At first the Danes acted spontaneously to alert Jews and help them move into hiding. With the assistance of Danish fisherman, many Jews were smuggled across the narrow strait of water to Sweden, which remained neutral during the war. Soon, Danish partisans, or resisters, stepped in and helped organize the massive flight that occurred when the Swedish government publicly declared that it was willing to take in all refugees from Denmark. A large-scale rescue operation began, involving many groups of Danish society. King Christian X formally objected to the German actions, church leaders published a strong protest and urged their followers to help the Jews, and universities closed for a week so students and professors could help with the rescue efforts. Over the course of three weeks, some 7,200 Jews were ferried to Sweden, where they remained in safety until the end of the war. (Even though the Nazi-planned roundup was considered a failure, the Germans did manage to ship 472 captured Jews to Theresienstadt at the end of October 1943.)

As a result of the successful rescue operation, the Danish resistance movement grew in size and strength. For the next two years (until the war ended), partisans helped maintain a reliable escape route to Sweden. Although the Germans lifted the state of emergency in October 1943, Danish sabotage and resistance efforts intensified. General strikes (military attacks) swept across the country in response to the news of an assassination attempt on Adolf Hitler in July 1944.

Kim Malthe-Bruun was just 21 years old when he joined the Danish partisan underground in September 1944. He had spent the previous three years as a merchant seaman travel-

Jewish refugees being ferried out of Denmark by Danish fisherman in October 1943.

ing throughout Europe. When he docked in various ports, he became a firsthand witness to Nazi oppression and the atrocities committed against the Jews. Like his fellow citizens, Malthe-Bruun was deeply upset by what was going on around him and decided to try to help stop the persecution.

In December 1944, Malthe-Bruun and several other partisans were arrested by the Gestapo. During his four months in prison, he was harassed and tortured by guards who tried to force him to confess. During his career as a seaman and throughout his captivity, Malthe-Bruun kept a diary and wrote letters to his mother; his girlfriend, Hanne; and his older cousin, Nitte. The portions of his writings excerpted below reflect the various stages of his life—from his observations while traveling through Germany to his impressions of his first resistance activities in the fall of 1944.

As he awaited his trial, Malthe-Bruun reviewed his life and the world events that so greatly affected him. With remarkable eloquence, he explains in his writings his simple beliefs about life—beliefs that remained unshaken in the face of death and continue to inspire readers today.

Things to Remember While Reading *Heroic Heart: The Diary and Letters of Kim Malthe-Bruun, 1941-1945*:

- Malthe-Bruun, like many other Danes, possessed remarkable moral and political virtues. Unlike people in other Nazi-occupied countries who feared involvement in the resistance effort, large numbers of ordinary citizens in Denmark united in opposition to the Nazis for the protection of the Jews.

- The Nazis attempted to turn the tide of public opinion in Denmark against the Jews. The propaganda campaigns (ideas and information spread to further the Nazi cause) that had worked well in other occupied countries failed in Denmark, due to the long history of tolerance among the Danes.

- Resistance in Denmark depended on the participation of the fishermen and sailors who worked along the coastlines. Some ferried Jewish refugees to Sweden, while others—like Malthe-Bruun and his comrades—transported armaments for resistance efforts.

Heroic Heart: The Diary and Letters of Kim Malthe-Bruun, 1941-1945

LUBECK

7 March 1944

Gave vent to: Let out.

Indignation: Frustrations or anger aroused by injustice.

*... Tonight I've been talking to an Austrian Saloon-keeper. He was burning up with hatred for the Germans. He put his face close to mine and the whites of his eyes showed as he **gave vent to** all his **indignation**. He trembled with rage and seemed for once to be*

able to let himself go. But it was quite a shock to see how humble he became when another guard passed by.

*The town is covered with posters—all telling the same story. One **depicts** a railway station crowded with happy Germans, taken from above. Over the picture lies the heavy shadow of a man in a big coat, and underneath is printed in large letters: "The enemy is listening." Two of the posters preach economy, and I'll never be able to forget the last one. It shows an ugly face reflected in a hand mirror, looking very much like a rat and with a **loathsome** expression over his features. Almost **in relief** is an angular, **semitic** nose and the caption under the poster reads: "Look at yourself in the mirror. Are you a Jew or aren't you?" How rotten all of these people must be in order not to react violently to this. The Germans are like a ripe fruit that has been damaged and now the rottenness has come to the surface.*

17 October 1944

How I long for a dash of cold salt water in my face and the sound of sails flapping in the wind, a bicycle ride on a black night, and to arrive at my destination and see a light shining from the top-floor window at Loendal! Now it's always: "Come over right away." "Can't you do this?" "That has to be done right away," etc. It's an exhausting and difficult job, but I wouldn't change it for anything.

HELLERUP
28 November 1944

Dear Nitte,

*You must forgive me for having neglected you for so long, but I know you understand that my present life takes all of my time and that my thoughts are filled with everything that comes my way in these **crucial** days.*

Depicts: To represent by or as if by a picture.

Loathsome: Disgusting.

In relief: Depicting sharpness of outline or projection of detail.

Semitic: Characteristic of the Semites; Jewish.

Crucial: Extremely important; necessary.

This is an extraordinary time we're living in, and it has brought forth many extraordinary people. It's almost beyond my grasp. But I do know that there is no other time in which I would prefer to have lived than the one we are now going through. Everything is trembling and the agony which is part of every birth is everywhere. Never has the world been exposed to such suffering, but never has the feeling of life been as strong or as intense as now. I'm living a fantastic life among fantastic people, and it is through this that I have come close to them. And because true feelings are always exposed when nerves are on edge, I'm getting to know people in a different way than I ever did before.

I used to look at the world through the eyes of a dreamer, and to me it's always had a special glow. Every night I went to sleep with a smile on my lips and a smile in my heart, and every morning I woke up rested and filled with wonder at the life to which I was born.

Now at night I fall into a heavy sleep, taking with me all that is on my mind. But when I wake up, it isn't because I can't sleep any longer, but because something tells me that I have work to do. It is only the present that counts. I feel that I must always follow my inner convictions, always be prepared for the unexpected, always be ready to spring into action. You know what this is like, living for the moment only and with our lives at stake. The group with which I'm working has completely accepted this.

VESTRE PRISON
13 January 1945

Dear ____

As I have the feeling that we will probably be sent south very soon, I'm sending you this message. A hundred and sixty-five left last night.

To begin with, I want as many of you as possible to profit from the experiences I've had since my arrest. I wish that all the clandestine newspapers would publish an urgent appeal to everyone who is working for our country. We don't want to hear anything more about the gruesome methods of the **Gestapo** and about the unfortunate people who fall into their hands. All this should be kept off the front pages even if the victims happen to be ministers of the gospel. We should print instead all that will serve our best interests, and only this should be put before us in print during the long job that lies ahead.

Many of us do a fine job as long as we ourselves can set the pace, but we fail when we are under **duress**. Let me give an example. When I was in the toilet the other day a young kid came running in like a scared rabbit, because he was about to undergo questioning. "Will they torture me in there?" He was white as a sheet. "Take it easy and don't betray your friends; nothing is going to happen to you," I said, trying to calm him down. During the questioning he immediately admitted everything and not until later did I realize that I, as well as many others who have been doing a lot of careless thinking and writing, were at fault. I should have talked to him as a man and told him that he would most likely get all hell beaten out of him, but that it wouldn't be too bad if he didn't let himself go to pieces over something so unimportant.

Everyone goes around picturing these horrors, but no one thinks that it might happen to him, just as no one thinking of death believes that he can also be touched by it himself....

No one should feel that the fight is over the minute he has fallen into the hands of the enemy. That is only the beginning of the struggle to safeguard everything that others as well as you have won by fighting hard. This is the time to show whether you're a man or a coward....

Please remember this. If one day you find yourself in the hands of the **traitors** or the Germans, brace yourself and look them straight in the eyes. The only difference is that they are now the masters over you physically. Otherwise they are the same low

Clandestine: Secret.

Gestapo: Secret police force of the Nazi party.

Duress: Forced or compelled by threat.

Traitors: People who betray their country.

breed of life they were before your arrest. Take a good look at them, and you will see that the only harm they can do you is to give you some blue spots and sore muscles....

*You enter a room or a corridor and are told to stand with your face against a wall. Don't stand there in a panic thinking about death. If you're afraid to die, it means that you aren't old enough to take part in the struggle for freedom, or at least not mature enough. If the thought of brute force is enough to frighten you, you are the ideal victim for questioning. Suddenly and without reason they slap you. If you're weak, the physical blow, plus the humiliation of it, will give you such a shock that the Gestapo will immediately gain the upper hand and **inoculate** you with so much fear that everything will move according to their wishes.*

*Be calm and show neither hatred nor **contempt**, since both of these strike out at their easily wounded **vanity**. Regard them as human beings and make use of this vanity to strike back at them— but very cautiously. It's amazing how easily they fall into the trap....*

*Still one more thing: The Danes must change their attitude toward the Gestapo. Remember that you belong to a select group while they for the most part are a mob gone wild and therefore without **scruples**. Remember that this isn't a game and that you can't wave a white flag in the middle of it. This is important for the sake of our country as well as for us personally....*

VESTRE PRISON
January 1945
[smuggled out]

Dearest Mother,

You ask if I want anything. There is only one thing: to get out of here. Otherwise I don't need anything. You know that I've always been able to get along on very little.

Inoculate: In this case, to introduce into the mind of.

Contempt: Lack of respect.

Vanity: Overinflated pride.

Scruples: An ethical principle that inhibits action.

Thank you for what you said in your letter. It's meant a great deal to me. Your calmness and your wisdom make me very happy. You say that I've fulfilled all your expectations. I'm afraid that all of you see me in some sort of rosy light and forget to look at the facts. You forget that my daily life has prepared me for hardships much worse than the ones I've been exposed to here. Therefore you must realize that none of all the things that are so tough on the others—the food, the bed, the confinement, the questioning, have affected me in the least. I wouldn't have missed this experience for anything. Don't forget either that adventure is in my blood, and at the time of my arrest I was more excited at the thought of the experiences that were ahead of me than anything else. Neither the Gestapo nor anyone else has frightened me in the least. It's the primitive ones who are the most interesting. When they took me ... for questioning I thought that I felt the way an animal trainer must

The Danish public and government administration refused to abandon the several hundred Jews who had been sent to the Czechoslovakian ghetto of Theresienstadt (pictured above).

*feel when he enters a cage of wild animals. The trainer probably has a sort of affection for the animals, even if he knows that some of them are **mangy** and have to be destroyed. I've never been afraid of dogs, although I know that you have to proceed with caution when dealing with wild ones.*

*Until now I haven't been harmed. I had to take my clothes off, but that was all. The man standing beside me looked as if he were about to spring on me, but each time I ignored him without being directly impolite and started to talk to his colleague. Only once did we confront each other, and I realized what would happen if he lost control of himself. I calmly asked him, "Are you afraid?" Never have I seen a more astonished look on anyone's face. Then he flew into a rage but had to check himself because I had turned toward the other fellow, who was apparently his superior. After that he didn't flare up quite so much and did his job with a little less **zest**....*

*I learned fast never to say no or answer a question in the negative because it gives them the chance to fly at you and scream that you're a liar, etc. But if you answer their questions in the **affirmative**, even with the most ridiculous nonsense, they often think that you've misunderstood the question, that you really don't know anything about it and let it drop....*

VESTRE PRISON
21 January 1945
[smuggled out]

Mangy: Infected with mange, a contagious skin/hair condition caused by mites that affects mainly animals; shabby.

Zest: Keen enjoyment.

Affirmative: An expression of confirmation; a positive answer; agreement.

Dearest Hanne,

I've just been lying here and thinking about what a marvelous girl you really are. There are so many things in you that I appreciate and love....

A lot of things have happened to me while I've been here which don't happen to everybody. Don't be angry with me, but if I *don't manage to get out of here I would like to be sent to Germany, first to **Froeslev** to get to know the life there, and then to Germany to see the collapse of the **Reich** inside its borders. It's going to be enormously interesting. Have faith in me. I don't think that there are many as well-equipped to get through it as I am.*

I've always felt that there is a reason for everything and that this chain of events is leading me some place. I feel this more strongly now than ever before. I'd feel cheated if I didn't get out of here either to see the end of the occupation and the people wild with joy here at home or else see the tragedy and breakdown in Germany.

I'm not quite sure how you stand on this, but I think you feel as I do that our lives follow lines which are not accidental and that what happens to us is always for our greatest good....

*I must say that up to the present time I've been very lucky to have the chance to live a life so full of change and movement with so many new impressions. It's really wonderful to be alive. I still don't know what death is like, but it would seem to me that it's the high point of our lives. I can't help thinking of this when I see how nervous the Gestapo and the **collaborators** are when they go into town. But I'm a bit different from them just the same.*

VESTRE PRISON
GERMAN SECTION, CELL 411
4 April 1945

Dearest Mother,

*Today I went before the military **tribunal** together with Joergen, Niels and Ludwig. We were condemned to die. I know that you're strong and that you will be able to take this. But listen to me, Mother. It isn't enough that you are able to take it. You must also understand it. I'm not of importance and will soon be forgotten, but the ideas, the life, the inspiration which filled me will live on.*

Froeslev: Concentration camp in Denmark.

Reich: Pronounced RIKE; the German word for "empire."

Collaborators: In this case, the people who were cooperating with or assisting the Nazis.

Tribunal: A court of justice.

*You will find them everywhere—in the new green of spring, in people you will meet on your way, in a loving smile. Perhaps you will also find what was of value to me, you will love it and you won't forget me. I would have liked to grow and mature, but I will still live in your hearts and you will live on because you know that I am in front of you on the road and not behind, as you had perhaps thought at first. You know what has always been my greatest wish and what I thought I would become. Mother dear, come with me on my journey. Don't stop at the last stage of my life, but instead stop at some of the **preceding** ones and you may find something which will be of value to the girl I love and to you, Mother.*

*I have followed a certain path and I don't regret it. I've never betrayed what is in my heart, and now I seem to see the unbroken line which has run through my life. I'm not old, I ought not to die, and still, it seems so simple and natural to me. It's only the brutal way which at first terrifies us. I have so little time left; I don't quite know how to explain it, but my mind is completely at peace. I have always wanted to be like **Socrates**, but although I have no one to talk to as he had, I feel the same **tranquility** of spirit and very much want you, Hanne and Nitte to understand this....*

*How strange it seems to be writing this **testament**! Each word will stand; it can never be **amended**, never **revoked**, never changed. I'm thinking of so many things. Joergen is sitting here in front of me writing a letter to his daughter for her **Confirmation**—a document for life. We have lived together as friends and now we're going to die together....*

Finally there are the children who have recently come to mean so much to me. I had so been looking forward to seeing them and being with them again. Just to think of them makes me happy and I hope they will grow up to be men who will be able to get more out of life than what lies on the surface. I hope that their character will develop freely and never be subjected to prejudice.

Give them my love, my godson and his brother.

Preceding: Immediately before.

Socrates: An ancient Greek philosopher.

Tranquility: Calmness.

Testament: An expression of an intense belief or conviction.

Amended: Changed for the better.

Revoked: Recalled or taken back.

Confirmation: Christian rite conferring—usually on a young person—the gift of the Holy Spirit and full church membership.

I see what the situation in our country is leading up to and I know that Grandfather is right. But remember all of you that the aim shouldn't be to return to the period before the war, but that it is up to you, young and old, to create a broad, human ideal which everyone can recognize. This is the thing that our country needs; something that even a simple peasant boy can look up to and be happy in the thought that he is working and fighting for.

*Then, finally, there is my Hanne. Make her see that the pilot stars are still shining and that I was only a **beacon** on her route. Help her to keep going. She can now become very happy.*

In haste—your oldest and only son. (Malthe-Bruun, pp. 107-69)

Beacon: A source of light, inspiration, or guidance.

What happened next...

The Danish public and government administration refused to abandon the several hundred Jews who had been sent to the Czechoslovakian ghetto of Theresienstadt in October 1943. They sent a steady flow of food parcels to the ghetto and warnings to the German government. The Danish ministry also demanded that a delegation (a group of representatives) be allowed to inspect the ghetto. In June 1944, the Germans finally granted permission for representatives of the Danish and International Red Cross to gain entry into Theresienstadt. Unfortunately, delegates were shown a fake "model ghetto," complete with cafes and stores, which had been built expressly for their visit. But, due to the persistent Danish interest in the fate of their deported countrymen, no Danish Jews were sent to Auschwitz for extermination. Some 50 Danish Jews died in Theresienstadt out of the original group of 477, a death rate that reflects the higher standard of care they received compared to other prisoners.

In April 1945, the Danish prisoners were transferred by bus from Theresienstadt to Swedish custody. During their travels to Sweden, the buses passed through Denmark, where hundreds of thousands of Danes filled the streets to greet the return of their fellow citizens. A month later, the British Army entered Copenhagen and accepted the German surrender. Shortly thereafter, the Jewish refugees began returning from Sweden.

After liberation, one of the partisans clearing out the Vestre Prison found a letter Malthe-Bruun had received from his cousin Nitte. The back of the sheet of paper was covered with tiny writing by Malthe-Bruun. Written after he had been tortured, the letter had been hidden within the walls of his cell. His mother, Vibeke Malthe-Bruun, collected and edited his diaries and letters, publishing them in 1955—a decade after his death.

Did you know...

- After the war, Danish Jews returned from hiding to find that their homes, belongings—and even their pets and plants—had been cared for by neighbors. Some returning refugees came home to newly-painted houses and rooms full of fresh flowers.

- While Sweden remained neutral throughout the war, its allegiances changed depending on the circumstances. The Swedish government kept a restrictive immigration policy regarding Jews fleeing Nazi terror, yet citizens harbored some 20,000 Norwegian and Finnish children of Jewish descent. Also, the government formally offered to accept Danish Jews in September 1943.

- Under the direction of the Danish government, relief organizations packed and shipped food and clothing to the Danes imprisoned at Theresienstadt. By using a shipping service that required a signed receipt, the Danes ensured that most parcels reached the deportees.

For Further Reading

Flender, Harold. *Rescue in Denmark.* New York: Simon & Schuster, 1963.

Holliday, Laurel. *Children in the Holocaust and World War II: Their Secret Diaries.* New York: Simon & Schuster, 1995.

Malthe-Bruun, Kim. *Heroic Heart: The Diary and Letters of Kim Malthe-Bruun, 1941-1945.* Edited by Vibeke Malthe-Bruun. Translated by Gerry Bothmer. New York: Random House, 1955.

Wladyslaw Bartoszewski

Excerpt from
The Warsaw Ghetto:
A Christian's Testimony

Translated by Stephen G. Cappellari
Published in 1987

Some 3.3 million Jews lived in Poland at the outbreak of World War II, representing about 10 percent of the total population. After the German invasion and occupation in 1939, Polish Jews became isolated from non-Jewish Poles through a series of measures imposed by the Nazis. Jews were expelled from the area of Poland incorporated into Germany, known as Warthegau. In the remaining portion, called the Generalgouvernement, the German Nazis drove the Jews into large cities, concentrating them within designated areas, or ghettos.

By the end of 1941, the Nazis began constructing a series of extermination camps in Poland built specifically for systematic mass murder. As these camps became operational, Jewish prisoners were deported by train from the ghettos as part of "resettlement" programs. In reality, the Nazis were transporting Jewish Poles—and eventually Jews from other countries—to specially designed gas chambers.

Many factors made it difficult for non-Jewish Poles to help Jews. Separated by walls and Nazi guards, inhabitants of the Jewish ghettos could not easily interact with those Poles living in the "Aryan" sections. Since antisemitism, or anti-Jewish sentiment, was widespread within Polish society, Jews could not automatically trust their fellow compatriots. In addition, the Nazis imposed the death penalty upon those people who hid Jews—in fact, all persons found in the house, including children, were executed. Finally, Nazi terror brutally victimized all Poles since the Germans viewed them as a subhuman group.

Corrie Ten Boom: A Christian Resister in Holland

Corrie Ten Boom was living a peaceful and satisfying life in the small city of Haarlem in the Netherlands when the Nazis invaded and conquered Poland in 1940. Middle-aged and unmarried, Ten Boom and her sister Betsie kept house for their elderly father and helped with the family's watch business. The family lived together in a tiny centuries-old house called the Beje (pronounced BAY-yay), typical of old Haarlem buildings.

Two years after occupation started, the Ten Boom family began to receive a special type of visitor at their home. Jewish neighbors, fearful for their lives, sought shelter at the Beje. When the first person appeared at their doorstop asking for help, the Ten Booms did not hesitate to take him in. Corrie became the leader of an underground—or secret—operation based in her tiny home. The family sheltered victims at the Beje either permanently or until they could be safely transported to the countryside. Corrie arranged to obtain valuable ration

Despite the riskiness of their actions, many Poles did help Jews by offering refuge in private homes. Historians estimate that as much as 2.5 percent of the Aryan population (or 160,000 to 360,000 people) gave help to the Jews in the eastern portion of Poland. Relief efforts took place in two main areas: Krakow and Warsaw, where 20,000 to 30,000 Jews were in hiding. As German occupation persisted and violence toward the Jews escalated, underground (secret) organizations formed to provide aid throughout Poland. These organizations, which included trade unions, religious groups, and political parties, began to coordinate their aid through a central group called Zegota, which was code name for the Council for Aid to Jews.

In operation from December 1942 to January 1945, Zegota was the only relief organization that was run jointly by Jews and non-Jews. Its board of representatives included

(Continued from previous page)

cards so that farmers in the rural areas could afford to feed and house Jewish victims. Despite her age, the 50-year-old resistance leader ventured out on her bike at night after curfew, meeting with other people who worked in the underground. She even had a secret hiding place built in one of the small attic bedrooms so that her Jewish house guests could remain safely concealed during any Gestapo raid.

On February 28, 1944, the Ten Booms were arrested by the Gestapo and taken to prison. Betsie and her father died during their imprisonment, but Corrie survived and was released from Ravensbruck on New Year's Day 1945. After the war, Corrie helped open a relief home for survivors of the war years. She also traveled extensively, giving talks about her resistance experiences, which she credited to divine guidance (direction from God). Today, the Ten Boom home still stands on Barteljorisstraat in the center of Haarlem. The Ten Booms' story is chronicled in *The Hiding Place,* written by Corrie Ten Boom with John and Elizabeth Sherrill.

members of five Polish and two Jewish political movements—all from a wildly varied political spectrum. Zegota provided an important necessity to the Jews living in Poland—false Aryan documents. Members of Zegota used various methods to obtain or manufacture tens of thousands of forged documents, including birth and marriage certificates and employment papers, which they gave free of charge to Jews.

In addition, Zegota placed some 2,500 Jewish children in specially arranged public orphanages, which were frequently run by convents, and helped connect Jews who needed medical care with a secret network of trusted doctors. After repeated attempts, Zegota also successfully convinced the Polish government-in-exile to issue formal appeals to the Polish population at large, urging them to give aid to the Jews.

Opposite page: *A view of the*
Warsaw ghetto in the
summer of 1941.

Wladyslaw Bartoszewski was one of the many Catholic Poles who assisted the Jews in Poland during the Holocaust. Along with several hundred other Poles, Bartoszewski had been arrested by the Nazis in 1940 during a large-scale operation directed against members of Polish intellectual circles. After spending nearly a year in Auschwitz as a political prisoner, he returned to the city of Warsaw to find a newly created Jewish ghetto enclosed by a 3-meter-high wall. His time at Auschwitz convinced him of the importance of aiding victims of Nazi terror. In December 1942, he helped form a relief committee that later became Zegota. As a member of Zegota's board, Bartoszewski represented an underground group of young Catholics called "Front Odrodzenia Polski," or Front for Poland's Renewal.

Bartoszewski wrote about his experiences as a Christian Pole who dared to help the Jews in his book *The Warsaw Ghetto: A Christian's Testimony.* The excerpt below begins with a description of his early attempts to provide aid and ends with a mention of the Warsaw Ghetto Uprising, which began in April 1943.

Things to Remember While Reading the Excerpt from *A Christian's Testimony*:

- Bartoszewski first began helping Jews living in hiding, or "underground," in the winter of 1941-1942. He obtained false documents for the Jews living in the Warsaw area, which provided them with "Aryan" identities.

- He worked closely with many people in the resistance movement including Zofia Kossak-Szatkowska and Wanda Krahelska-Filipowicz—two women who helped create the Provisional Committee for Aid to Jews in September 1942. This organization later became the Council for Aid to Jews in December, and used the code name of "Zegota."

- The Warsaw ghetto uprising began on April 19, 1943, the eve of Passover. This month-long siege was the first urban uprising in German-occupied Europe.

- Bartoszewski worked hard to keep the Polish government-in-exile informed of events as they unfolded in Warsaw and throughout Poland. For several years he served as a "Delegatura," or underground representative for the Polish government-in-exile.

Early in the summer of 1941 I returned to Warsaw with several hundred other men who had been released from Auschwitz. I had been arrested in 1940 during the course of a large-scale operation directed against the **intelligentsia** of Warsaw and taken to the camp where I was **detained** as a political prisoner, with the "protective custody inmate" number 4427. At the time I was just nineteen years old. But I was soon to gather experiences bitter beyond any that I had known, even though this was a time when there were as yet no gas chambers and mass executions—only "normal" deaths from exhaustion brought about by excessive work, unimaginable hunger, and brutal beatings. Before my arrest I was an employee of the Polish Red Cross in occupied Warsaw. The problems of charity work and of aiding people who had suffered the **ravages** of war were thus not unknown to me. In the camp, where I saw and experienced the deepest human misery, I developed the conviction that helping the victims of Nazi terror was of the utmost importance.

Prior to my **internment** in Auschwitz there was no ghetto in my home town. The encirclement of a section of Warsaw with a wall three meters high and the forced resettlement of a half a million people behind it were the most significant changes I encountered there upon my return. In the Christian Polish community, on the "**Aryan**" side of the wall, several thousand Jews, perhaps more than ten thousand, lived illegally. They needed birth certificates and certificates of baptism issued in "Aryan" names, forged work permits and identification papers, a roof over their heads, and often financial support as well. My first attempt to help those living **underground** (this was during the winter months of 1941/42) involved obtaining documents for people I did not know personally, but only from a photograph attached to the documents. At the time, my most important source of free documents was my friend Zbigniew Karni-

Intelligentsia: Intellectuals who form an artistic, social, or political vanguard or elite.

Detained: Held.

Ravages: Violently destructive effects.

Internment: Confinement.

Aryan: According to the Nazis, Germans were descendants of this supposedly superior race.

Underground: Organization conducted in secret.

bad, a medical student my own age, who worked in an illegal **cell** involved in manufacturing forged documents for a section of the **Home Army.** At the time many members of the various underground organizations as well as Catholic priests were involved in aiding Jews hidden in and around Warsaw and in forging documents. In mid 1942 I established contact with two people, both respected in prewar Poland, who were active in completely different ideological-political areas. One of them, Zofia Kossak-Szatkowska, a Catholic author well known throughout Europe, had been living in Warsaw illegally since the beginning of the Nazi occupation and was wanted by the **Gestapo** for her anti-Nazi views, which she held before the war; the other, Wanda Krahelska-Filipowicz, was close to **socialist** circles during her student years and, as a young student before World War I, was responsible for the famous bomb attack on the Russian governor of Warsaw, General Skallon. For many months the two had been heading a secret rescue operation of refugees from the ghetto, mainly for women and children, in which they provided material goods, documents, and shelter. Their large circle of friends and their social standing helped them greatly in this endeavor. They devoted themselves to the underground whole-heartedly and gladly welcomed anyone who was willing to risk participation in their undertaking. I began working with Zofia Kossak immediately, and from that point on I frequently played the role of intermediary between her and various persons, Polish Christians as well as Jews, with whom she cooperated. It was my responsibility to deliver documents and money and, if necessary, warnings.

At the beginning of 1943 those of us in Warsaw did not have the slightest idea that we would soon be witnesses to the **hitherto** most heroic and stunning event in the history of the resistance to the occupying forces in Poland: the armed April revolt of the Warsaw ghetto.

On 13 March shots were once again fired in the streets of the Warsaw ghetto: a Jewish combat group was offering armed resistance to the police and to members of the German Industrial Pro-

Cell: Small unit of a larger organization.

Home Army: Polish secret military resistance organization.

Gestapo: Secret police of the Nazi Party.

Socialist: Advocates of a political and economic system based on government control of the production and distribution of goods. Socialists champion the removal of private property in a quest to attain a classless society.

Hitherto: Up to that time.

*tection Unit engaged in **looting**. In **retribution**, the **SS** mowed down several dozen people on the street. The command of the Jewish Combat Organization in the ghetto posted flyers during the night of 14/15 March informing the population of a new "action" being planned.*

*We soon found out that the tragic fate of the Jewish community in Krakow had been sealed on 13 March. There were still about 10,000 people living in the ghetto there who had survived the June and October 1942 "resettlements" to the extermination camps. Now some of them—those who had been declared able-bodied—were killed on the spot or sent to their deaths in Auschwitz; some where taken to the camp in Plaszow near Krakow, where they were forced into slave labor that ultimately proved fatal. Only a few individuals were saved. These survivors had been sheltered by Christian Poles in Krakow and its surroundings with the help of Christian friends or by establishing contacts with the Council of Aid to Jews in Krakow. Dr. Julian Aleksandrowicz, an outstanding **hematologist**, was one of those who managed to escape from the Krakow ghetto during those critical days in March. He later participated in the fight against the Germans as a member of the Home Army. He is now an academic known throughout Europe and **professor emeritus** at the hospital for Internal Medicine at the Krakow Medical Academy.*

*The alarming news from Krakow increased the anxiety of those of us in Warsaw. In view of our experiences during the past few years we were well aware of the fact that Berlin's centrally coordinated extermination campaigns were guided by an **ulterior** criminal purpose and that the Warsaw ghetto, which still had 70,000 inhabitants, would soon be a target. But the members of the two Jewish combat groups, the Jewish Combat Organization and the Jewish Military Association, were not wasting any time: the network of **bunkers** and fortifications was expanded systematically; considerable numbers of **Molotov cocktails** and hand*

Looting: Robbing; Seizing and carrying away by force.

Retribution: Receiving of reward or punishment.

SS: Political police of the Nazi Party.

Hematologist: Doctor specializing in disorders of the blood.

Professor emeritus: Retired college educator who retains an honorary title.

Ulterior: Hidden agenda.

Bunkers: Fortified chambers.

Molotov cocktails: Crude, homemade firebombs.

grenades were manufactured according to the guidelines supplied by the Polish Home Army.

The spring of 1943 came early. April was mild and generally warm, and there was relatively heavy traffic on the streets of Warsaw. The Easter holidays were imminent, as was Passover. On Palm Sunday, 18 April 1943, rumors spread through Warsaw that a large police action was to take place in the ghetto during the next few hours. The rumors were underscored by, among other things, a considerable concentration of the **collaborating** Ukrainian-Latvian support units in the city. In the evening, shortly before the curfew for Christian Poles, I went to the vicinity of the ghetto wall and noted an increased number of police patrols, which were also immediately noticed by the **vigilant reconnaissance** troops of the Jewish Combat Organization in the ghetto. They alarmed the com-

Jews captured during the Warsaw ghetto uprising are led away for deportation.

Collaborating: Cooperating; working together.

Vigilant: Watchful, especially looking out for danger.

Reconnaissance: Troops that conduct exploratory surveys of enemy territory.

bat groups, who took up their positions during the same night; the majority of the civilian population hid in their cellars.

"No one got any sleep during the night from Sunday to Monday," a participant in the events, an official of the Jewish National Committee, recalls in a report published in June of 1943 in the underground Catholic monthly <u>Prawda</u>:

*"The combat groups posted **sentries**. The civilian population retreated into shelters, cellars, or upper floors. The apartments were empty. The first reports of the observers came in: the walls of the ghetto were surrounded by German troops. So it <u>was</u> an action."*

*Several hours later, at daybreak of 19 April ... 850 SS troops and sixteen officers of the **Waffen-SS** marched into the ghetto protected by tanks and two armored cars. They moved along Nalewki Street—the main artery of the Jewish residential area—in the direction of the center of the ghetto. After they had gone a few hundred meters they had already encountered unexpected resistance: young members of the Jewish Combat Organization threw hand grenades and Molotov cocktails out of the windows of the adjoining houses. One of the tanks was hit and went up in flames; twelve Nazis were killed on the street, and the SS column hurriedly retreated from the ghetto. The Germans resumed the fight again after two hours, this time with greater caution and larger forces, SS brigade commander [Stroop], the major general of the police, took over the command....*

*United by a common and deeply felt sorrow, every piece of bad news from the other side of the wall touched us profoundly. Discussions of various unrealistic possibilities to save the combatants filled us with new illusions. The conditions under which we ourselves lived **precluded** any possibility of aid—to help was not in our power. Accordingly, we thought our most important task was to transmit news to the West regularly to keep it informed about the events in Warsaw. In addition, we attempted systematically to influence Christian Polish public opinion to win over as many people as possible who might assume the great risk of offering help*

Sentries: Guards who stand watch at certain points of passage.

Waffen-SS: Military unit of the Nazi political police.

Precluded: Ruled out in advance.

and shelter to refugees. We tried to exert influence through personal contacts as well as through the underground press. We stressed the important historical and moral meaning of the ghetto uprising: this was, after all, the first rebellion of a city in the history of the European resistance movement, the first **mutinous** battle in the center of a major city where there was a **contingent** of several tens of thousands of German troops. And finally, this uprising was also a turning point in the history of the Jewish people under the occupation, a phenomenon that even surpassed the goals and expectations of the organizers and leaders of the fight themselves. I can still clearly remember the impression that Anielewicz's letter made on us. It was written on 23 April 1943, the fifth day of the fighting in the ghetto, and was addressed to his representative and friend Jitzchak Cukierman, then in the "Aryan" sector. Berman translated the letter into Polish for us:

Mutinous: Disposed to rebellion.

Contingent: A representative group to be called to action if needed.

"What we are experiencing surpasses our most daring hopes. The Germans fled from the ghetto twice.... The most important thing is this: the dream of my life has been fulfilled—I am experiencing Jewish self-defense in the Warsaw ghetto in all its pride and glory."

The underground newspapers somberly directed the attention of the Christian Polish population to the heroism of the fighting Jews and appealed for its support. On 5 May 1943, while the fighting in Warsaw was still going on, the then prime minister of the Polish government in exile, General Sikorski, gave a speech on London radio and emphasized:

"We are witnesses to the greatest crime in human history. We know that you are giving all the help you can to the tortured Jews. For that, my countrymen, I thank you in my own name and in that of the government of Poland. I ask you to continue to grant them any conceivable help and at the same time to put a stop to this inhuman cruelty." (Bartoszewski, pp. 42-80)

What Happened Next...

Mass deportations of Jews from the Warsaw ghetto began on July 22, 1942. By September, 300,000 Jews had been rounded up—with 265,000 going directly to the Treblinka death camp. As many as 70,000 Jews remained in the ghetto, anxiously anticipating another transport. In January 1943, when the Germans started the next wave of deportations, they met with armed resistance for the first time. Since the Nazis captured only 5,000 to 6,000 Jews, the ghetto inmates saw their display of armed resistance as a victory that prevented the complete liquidation (or destruction) of the entire population. However, historians in the postwar era have determined that the Nazis only intended a partial deportation in the second operation. Nonetheless, the remaining Jews began to gather arms for the next and final wave of deportations—determined to fight until death.

After the success of this initial display of force, many Jews who had previously refrained from any violent action began to support resistance groups within the ghetto. On April 19, 1943, the eve of Passover, the Nazis entered the ghetto intending to round up all remaining Jews for a final deportation. This time they met with considerable resistance, which led to a month-long battle known as the Warsaw Ghetto Uprising. The total fighting force within the ghetto numbered about 750, including young men armed with pistols, home-made fire bombs, and hand grenades supplied by non-Jewish resisters from outside the ghetto.

Despite being heavily overmatched, the Jewish resistance fighters managed to push back the Nazi forces. On the first day of the uprising, German losses totaled 12 soldiers, a tank, and two armored vehicles. Following several days of street fighting, the Germans resorted to burning the ghetto one building at a time to flush out their captives. After nearly four weeks of fighting, resistance forces fell and the ghetto itself was burned. Nazi reports indicated that 56,065 Jews had been "destroyed." As the first urban uprising, the Warsaw Ghetto Uprising provided inspiration to Jews and non-Jews throughout German-occupied Europe.

Thereafter, Christian Poles and other resisters escalated their fight against the Nazis. The Zegota organization continued to operate, sheltering the Jews who managed to escape the ghetto, as well as those who had been in hiding since the German invasion. The Polish Home Army continued to resist the Nazis at every opportunity. In 1944, an armed uprising led by the Polish Home Army raged for several months in Warsaw. After the Germans overcame the resistance fighters, they burned and razed (destroyed to the ground; virtually erased) the city. Warsaw was completely destroyed. Some 170,000 Poles perished during the uprising, while 165,000 remaining occupants were sent to concentration camps or drafted for slave labor.

Bartoszewski remained active in the resistance movement throughout the war, including acting as an underground representative for the Polish government-in-exile in England. Following the war, he became a scholar and prolific author and served for many years on the faculty at the Catholic University of Lublin, a city in Eastern Poland. His studies and writings on the Nazi occupation of Poland, —particularly the Warsaw uprisings—are now considered among the most accurate accounts available. In 1963, Bartoszewski was honored by Yad Veshem in Jerusalem as "Righteous Among Nations" for his valiant efforts to save Jews in Poland during World War II.

Did You Know...

- Two different military organizations existed in the Warsaw ghetto—the ZOB, or Jewish Fighting Organization, which was the larger of the two, and the ZZB, or Jewish Military Union. Both groups developed contacts outside the ghetto to obtain arms and coordinated their efforts to fight the Nazis during the uprising.

- At the start of the Warsaw ghetto uprising, Jewish resisters marked their position by placing two flags atop a building—the flag of Poland and a Jewish national flag. When defeat seemed near after close to a month of fighting, the leaders of ZOB took their own lives rather than surrender to German forces.

- Nearly 20,000 Jews from Warsaw survived the war through hiding. In all of Poland, only 50,000 to 70,000 survived. Another 180,000 successfully fled to the Soviet Union.

- An estimated 3 million Polish Jews perished in the holocaust— that's about 90 percent of *all* Polish Jews who were alive before World War II. Some 3 million non-Jewish Poles also died in the war. Most were executed by Nazis, while others died as slave laborers.

For Further Reading

Bartoszewski, Wladyslaw. *The Warsaw Ghetto: A Christian's Testimony.* Originally published in 1983. English translation by Stephen G. Cappellari. Boston: Beacon Press, 1987.

Fluek, Toby Knobel. *Memories of My Life in a Polish Village, 1930-1949.* New York: Random House, 1990.

Gelman, Charles. *Do Not Go Gentle: A Memoir of Jewish Resistance in Poland, 1941-1945.* Hamden, CT: Archon, 1989.

Pretzel, MM. *Portrait of a Young Forger.* Knightsbridge Publishing Co., 1990.

Hans and Sophie Scholl

Excerpt from *At the Heart of the White Rose: Letters and Diaries of Hans and Sophie Scholl,* written 1937-1943

Edited by Inge Jens
Originally published in 1984

When Adolf Hitler came to power in 1933, he represented renewed hope and national pride for many people humiliated and upset by Germany's defeat in World War I. Hitler urged fierce devotion to the fatherland, fostering a type of nationalism (or loyalty) that blamed "others" for the ill-fortune crippling Germany. While Hitler condemned certain political parties, influences, and even countries, he primarily held Jewish people accountable for all that went wrong for Germanic, or "Aryan," people. According to Hitler and the Nazi party, Jews were responsible for the failing economy, defeat in the war, and the loss of national "purity." Despite his messages of hate, many Germans fully believed he was the only person capable of saving Germany from complete ruin.

While promising a glorious future to millions of disenchanted and unemployed citizens, Hitler did not give specific details of what he planned as the solution to the "Jewish problem." After the Nazis seized control of the German government and outlawed all political opposition, no one in Germany could safely disagree with Nazi policies. Unlike the people living in occupied countries, German citizens who resisted the Nazis faced an additional danger—the accusation of treason, or betrayal of their own nation.

A special law passed by the Nazi government—called the Treason Law—ordered severe punishment for offenders during wartime. This legislation made even the slightest criticism of the Nazi regime a punishable offense, which could result in imprisonment, torture, and even death. To enforce the new decree, some 40,000 Gestapo agents, or members of the secret state police, shadowed every aspect of German social life.

Members of the White Rose student resistance group in Munich. Hans Scholl is on the left; Alexander Schmorell is second from the left (hidden from view); and Sophie Scholl and Christel Probst are on the right.

Accused traitors appeared before a special court known as the *Volksgericht,* or People's Court, located in the capital city of Berlin, where the proceedings were held under bright lights and filmed by camera. Wearing a bright red robe, Roland Freisler, the presiding officer of the court, frequently shouted abuse at the defendants. Few lawyers dared to actively defend the accused, and no appeals (requests for a higher court to review a lower court's decision) were allowed. Freisler was known as the "hanging judge" for his tendency to send prisoners to the gallows. He and other powerful officials also had at their disposal 11 guillotines set up throughout Germany; the Nazis reinstituted the practice of beheading shortly after they came into power.

Only one group dared to oppose Hitler's dictatorship and voice dissent against its murderous policies. Founded at the University of Munich by Hans Scholl in 1942, the White Rose (Weisse Rose) movement distributed leaflets critical of the Nazi government. At the age of 23, Hans was nearing the completion of his medical studies when he began to organize the underground student resistance group. Six weeks before the first pamphlets appeared, Hans's sister, Sophie, arrived in Munich to start her formal college education, which had been delayed due to state-imposed labor service. When Sophie learned of her brother's anti-Nazi activities, she insisted on joining the secret group. Both knew their actions could lead to their deaths.

After serving three months on the Russian front, Hans returned to Munich in the fall of 1942 and resumed his printing activities to encourage resistance throughout Germany. The White Rose successfully spread its message to several other universities and cities, including the academic community of Hamburg. While the exact origin of the movement's name is unknown, historians believe the group chose the term "White Rose" as a symbol of purity and innocence. Determined to jolt other Germans into action, one of the White Rose pamphlets proclaimed: "We will not be silent. We are your bad conscience. The White Rose will give you no rest." In another act of defiance, Hans and a comrade painted the slogans "Freedom" and "Down with Hitler" on the campus walls.

Things to Remember While Reading the Letters and Diaries of Hans and Sophie Scholl:

- Sophie Scholl wrote many letters to her family, friends, and especially to her sweetheart, Fritz Hartnagel, an officer in the German army. Her letters contain philosophical reflections on many subjects, from the meaning of nationhood to the nature of existence. Excerpted below are some of her letters to Fritz and one to a family friend named Otl Aicher.

- Hans Scholl kept in close touch with his family and his girlfriend, Rose Nagele. Since the Nazis censored the mail, he sometimes coded his anti-Nazi comments. For example, his January 17, 1942, letter to his parents contains intentional analogies to the weather—"closer to spring" means "nearer the end of the war." Also in this letter, Hans includes a passage from German poet and dramatist Johann Wolfgang von Goethe's poem *Awakening of Epimindes,* which predicts that evil will one day vanish. Hans would include this same poem in one of the White Rose pamphlets.

- The Scholls distributed a series of anti-Nazi pamphlets during the summer of 1942. They sent the handbills to people randomly chosen from the telephone book. Notice this dangerous campaign weighs heavily on Sophie's mind in her letter to Fritz dated November 7, 1942.

- From July to October 1942, Hans—along with his younger brother, Werner, and several members of the White Rose group—served a tour of duty on the Russian front. Hans, who was part of a Student Medical Company, particularly liked Russia and wrote his observations in a little notebook, or diary.

- Hans fully understood that his treasonous actions could cost him his life. In his letter dated February 16, 1943, he attempts to explain his decisions to his girlfriend, Rose, who is upset by his choices. February 16 was the same day Hans and other members of the White Rose group printed their sixth and final handbill. Two days later Hans and Sophie were caught distributing pamphlets on the campus of the University of Munich and were arrested.

At the Heart of the White Rose: Letters and Diaries of Hans and Sophie Scholl

[In school at the Frobel Institute, where Sophie worked as a kindergarten teacher]

September 23, 1940

My dear Fritz,

I don't know for sure if my letters will be less frequent from now on, but it's in the cards. There's always so much to do when I get home from school, and I always have a lot more distractions there. (That's the wrong way of putting it, actually, because are drawing, piano playing, etc.—which I seldom get around to in spite of everything—distractions?)

Even now I'm sitting in college and should really be doing some practical work, but I'm going to put it off for half an hour. I can't answer your last letter in detail because it's at home, but many thanks indeed for your latest parcel. The stockings, which I shared with my sisters, were especially welcome.

*We're expecting Hans home any day. He was counting on some **leave** around now, but in wartime you never can tell. I'd sooner your leave didn't **coincide** with his, if you know what I mean. Then I could devote myself exclusively to each of you. But I mustn't expect too much. I'll be content if you both come at all.*

You asked me to write you my views on nationhood. I won't have the time right now, but my notion of the concept, though not clearly defined, is pretty straightforward.

*As I see it, a soldier's position **vis-à-vis** his nation is rather like that of a son who vows to stand up for his father and family come what may. If his father does another family an injustice and gets into trouble as a result, the son has to back his father regardless. Personally, I can't raise that much family feeling. To me, justice **takes precedence** over all other attachments, many of which are purely **sentimental**.*

And it would surely be better if people engaged in a conflict could take the side they consider right.

I've always thought it wrong for a father to take his child's side on principle, for instance when a teacher punishes him or her. However much he may love the child, or for that very reason. I think it's just as wrong for a German or a Frenchman, or whatever

Leave: Time off.

Coincide: Occur at the same time.

Vis-à-vis: In relation to.

Takes precedence: Is more important than; comes before.

Sentimental: Governed by feelings or emotions.

White Rose members Hans Scholl and Alexander Schmorell on the train bound for military service in Russia.

Doggedly: Stubbornly.

Subjective: Affected by personal views, experiences, or background.

Bewildered: Confused.

else a person may be, to defend his nation **doggedly** just because it's his. Emotions can often be misleading. I, too, am moved when I see soldiers on the street, possibly marching to a band, and I used to have to fight back my tears at the sound of military marches. But those are old wives' sentiments. It's absurd to let them get the better of you.

We were taught in school that a German's attitude is deliberately **subjective**. Unless it's objective as well, I can't accept it. But this subjective approach has caught on with a lot of people, and many who were looking for a pattern to fit their conflicting emotions have adopted it with a sigh of relief.

I'm sure you're **bewildered** by my often clumsy **metaphors** and wild **effusions**. I hope you can thread your way through *them. The next time I'll try to be clearer and more deliberate. It's too late today.*

Are your travels in Holland over? I hope you had a lot of good times there. Maybe I'll hear from you again now. (Not that I can complain.)

Fond love for now,
Sofie

[P.S.] I'll reply to your last letter and tell you what nationhood means to me later on.

Please forgive the exercise-book paper!

Hans also had to shoot the dog I was going to get because it got sick, so you're both in the same boat, and all my happy expectations have come to nothing.

Munich—May 2, 1941

*My dainty, **doughty** little Rose,*

*Even though May came in accompanied by rain, all the fields were bright with the loveliest green imaginable. A sunbeam pierced a little gap in the dark sea of cloud, and the world laughed and glittered in the light of heaven. I stood there **marveling** and thought, Does God take us for fools, that he should light up the world for us with such **consummate** beauty in the radiance of his glory, in his honor? And nothing, on the other hand, but **rapine** and murder? Where does the truth lie? Should one go off and build a little house with flowers outside the windows and a garden outside the door and **extol** and thank God and turn one's back on the world and its filth? Isn't **seclusion** a form of **treachery**—of desertion? Things are tolerable in succession—the youthful spirit emerges from the ruins and soars toward the light—but **simultaneities** are anti-*

Metaphors: Figures of speech that suggest the likeness of one item to another.

Effusions: Unrestrained outpourings of emotion.

Doughty: Courageous.

Marveling: Feeling a sense of wonder, surprise, or astonishment.

Consummate: Perfect in every aspect.

Rapine: Plunder; the forcible seizure of another's property.

Extol: To praise lavishly.

Seclusion: In this case, a lack of involvement in an important cause; failure to right a wrong; isolating oneself from the reality of a grave situation.

Treachery: Willful betrayal.

Simultaneities: Existing at the same time.

thetical, ruins and light at the same time. I'm weak and **puny**, but I want to do what is right.

Goethe says that if a miracle occurs in the world, it does so through the **medium** of pure, loving hearts. That **consolation** has been mine since you loved me.

Are the cherry trees in blossom with you?

I now get up almost as early as you do, but I can't see the sun yet at that time of day, the houses are too tall.

Tomorrow I'm going home for my mother's birthday. The others may also be there. Sophie, Lisl, Werner. Eve [Rose's younger sister] wrote me a nice letter. She seems to enjoy writing.

Me, I only enjoy writing to you!

Yours,
Hans

Blumberg—December 10, 1941

Dear Otl,

I just received your parcel containing the candles. I was thrilled with them and still am, not least because they got here safe and sound. I find them really lovely, especially the shape. Many thanks!

Is there no hope of your coming home for Christmas? It'll be a different skiing camp from last year....

You wrote ... that Nature is a stool mankind climbs on to reach up to God, and that it will **relapse** into nothingness once it has served its purpose. I recall that now, as I look through the window at the mountain opposite, the fields sprinkled with snow and the wintry sky beyond the leafless woods. I find it sad that all these things should someday cease to exist—sad and **inconceivable**. If they're beautiful and good, why should they someday cease to

Antithetical: Directly opposite.

Puny: Of inferior size, strength, or significance.

Goethe, Johann Wolfgang von: German poet, novelist, and playwright.

Medium: Means of conveying something.

Consolation: Comforting.

Relapse: To slip back into a former worse state.

Inconceivable: Not capable of being conceived or imagined.

exist? I delight every morning in the pure air and the sky, with the moon and stars still floating in it, and even though it's initially an unfair pleasure because I may sometimes become intoxicated with the sight, it's good in the long run because it restores things to their proper perspective (which I again find sad, but I'm nonetheless glad because otherwise I might easily overlook the essential point). —I think it's awful to create something, only to **consign** it to **limbo** afterward. Trees and flowers and animals were created too, after all, and possess a hint of spirituality.

"Nothingness was created by God." Do you find that statement ... logical? Anything that exists and was created must be something. I don't think we should try to visualize nothingness. Its name and meaning make that impossible. As someone who

Sophie Scholl bids farewell to four other members of the White Rose movement as they depart for the Russian front.

Consign: To give over to the care of another.

Limbo: A place of confinement, neglect, or uncertainty.

likes to visualize everything, I find that very hard. But that's only by the by....

*I realize that one can **wallow** in the mind (or intellect) while one's soul starves to death. That wouldn't have occurred to me once upon a time.*

Affectionate regards,
Sophie

Munich—January 17, 1942

Dear Parents,

*The severe cold, which has done you both no good, has been weighing **relentlessly** on our city, too, for the past week. It's a good thing, for all that. Even the cold is a factor that brings us closer to spring.*

I'm worried about your state of health, though, and hope you're getting over your flu. It must have come at a very inopportune time for Father.

Many thanks for the parcel, Mother. I don't own a fur coat, unfortunately, and have no idea where I could get hold of one....

I shall be paying another visit to Ulm with Hans R. in a week's time.

Much love and best wishes for body and soul,
Hans

[P.S.] A poem by Goethe from Parmenides, which the British might well bear in mind:

*That which has boldly risen from the **abyss** can,*
*by some harsh **quirk** of fate,*
conquer half the globe—
but it must then return to the abyss.

Wallow: Become abundantly supplied.

Relentlessly: Unyieldingly; without letting up or becoming less severe or intense.

Abyss: Bottomless pit; hell.

Quirk: Twist.

*Mighty dread already **looms**.*
***In vain** will he resist,*
and all who have clung to him must perish too.
[From Hans Scholl's Russian diary]

September 5, 1942

*A bizarre idea has kept me **brooding incessantly** for several days now. I'd like to create a **utopia**, but not like those we so often give vent to when we let our hair down: what the postwar world would be like if, etc. No, that would be too easy.... No, what haunts me is the strange notion that a time may come when the war is entirely forgotten, because a kindly **providence** has **effaced** its memory from every book. A truly golden age will dawn such as no one could now conceive of in his wildest dreams: peace on earth and universal **contentment** in every country under the sun. And then, while playing one day, a child unearths a fragment of some object from the sand and shows it to his **bosom** pal, and the two of them go on looking until they've assembled all the pieces. They eventually discover that it's a weapon, **scuffle** over it, one of them kills the other with the newfound weapon, etc., etc.*

*War has finally returned. The whole world goes up in flames. This war is a feeble version of the present one—everything is carried to extremes, notably human stupidity and cowardice on the one hand, **hubris** and **superbia** on the other.*

Ulm—November 7, 1942
[unintentionally dated October 7, 1942]

My dear Fritz,

Hans gets back from Russia tonight. I suppose I should be glad he's back with us, and I am. I can already picture the times we'll spend together in our modest Munich lodgings. They may well turn out to be productive times.

Looms: Takes shape.

In vain: Without success.

Brooding: Pondering anxiously; worrying.

Incessantly: Without stopping.

Utopia: An ideally perfect place.

Providence: God.

Effaced: Erased; wiped out.

Contentment: Satisfaction.

Bosom: Close or intimate.

Scuffle: Hand-to-hand struggle.

Hubris: Excessive pride or self-confidence.

Superbia: Arrogance; giving an impression of superiority; an exaggeration of worth.

But I can't feel wholeheartedly happy. I'm never free for a moment, day or night, from the depressing and **unremitting** state of uncertainty in which we live these days, which **precludes** any carefree plans for the **morrow** and casts a shadow over all the days to come. When will we finally be relieved of the **compulsion** to focus all our energy and attention on things that aren't worth lifting one's little finger for? Every word has to be examined from every angle before it's uttered, to see if it carries a hint of **ambiguity**. Faith in other people has been forcibly **ousted** by mistrust and caution. It's exhausting—disheartening too, sometimes. But, no, I won't let anything dishearten me. **Trivialities** like these can never master me while I'm in possession of other, **unassailable** joys. Strength flows into me when I think of them, and I'd like to address a word of encouragement to all who are similarly afflicted....

I'd like to go walking with you through the woods again, or anywhere at all, but that's still a remote prospect, if not an unattainable one.

A sheet of writing paper will have to **suffice** for now. It brings you many loving thoughts from

Sophie

[To Fritz Hartnagel]
Ulm—November 18, 1942

... I'm still so **remote** from God that I don't even sense his presence when I pray. Sometimes when I utter God's name, in fact, I feel like sinking into a void. It isn't [a] frightening or dizzy-making sensation, it's nothing at all—and that's far more terrible. But prayer is the only remedy for it, and however many devils scurry around inside me, I shall cling to the rope God has thrown me in Jesus Christ, even if my numb hands can no longer feel it.

Unremitting: Persistent.

Precludes: Rules out in advance.

Morrow: Future.

Compulsion: Irresistible urge.

Ambiguity: Uncertainty.

Ousted: Removed from; ejected, forced out.

Trivialities: Things of little worth or importance.

Unassailable: Not capable of being attacked or seized successfully.

Suffice: To be enough.

Remote: Distant; separated from by a great space.

Please remember me in your prayers. I won't forget you either.

Yours,
Sophie

Munich—February 16, 1943

Dear Rose,

Your last letter saddened me. I saw your tears shine through the words as I read it, and I can't dry them. Why write that way? Although I live in a permanent transition from yesterday to today and tomorrow, the beauty of the past remains intact and no less beautiful. That bygone summer still reflects its light into the present. Must its radiance be extinguished by shades of **melancholy**?

Nowadays I have to be the way I am. I'm remote from you, both outwardly and inwardly, but never **estranged**. *Never has my respect for your purity of heart been greater than it is now, when life has become an everpresent danger. But because the danger is of my own choosing, I must head for my chosen destination freely and without any ties. I've gone astray many times, I know.* **Chasms** *yawn and darkest night envelops my questing heart, but I press on regardless. As [Paul] Claudel so splendidly puts it: "Life is a great adventure towards the light."*

It might be better in the future if the sentiments conveyed in our letters owed less to emotion and more to reason. I'd welcome another letter from you soon.

Affectionate regards,
Hans (Jens, pp. 93-279)

Melancholy: Depression; sadness.

Estranged: Alienated; having broken the bonds of affection or loyalty.

Chasms: Wide differences.

Hans and Sophie Scholl

Hans Scholl (1918-1943) was born in Ingerstein, Germany, at the foots of the Alps. Sophie Scholl (1921-1943) was born in Forchtenberg, another small town in southwest Germany. Hans and Sophie were two of five Scholl children; all were close in age, with a little more than five years between the oldest, Inge, and the youngest, Werner. Their father, Robert Scholl, served as a mayor in various small towns before moving the family in 1930 to Ulm, Germany, where he opened up a business as a tax and business consultant. Magdalene Scholl, their mother, had been a deaconess in a Protestant nursing order before her marriage to Robert and remained devoutly religious throughout her life.

The Scholl family lived in a large, sunny house on Cathedral Square in Ulm, near the local cathedral, which had the highest steeple in all of Germany. At first—to the great dismay of their father—the Scholl children eagerly embraced Nazism. One by one

What happened next...

On February 18, 1943, Hans and Sophie Scholl were caught distributing pamphlets at the University of Munich. Carrying some 1,700 copies of their latest White Rose leaflet inside a suitcase, they walked through the corridors of a main building on campus depositing small piles of the pamphlet at doorways and on window sills. In the few minutes remaining before classes ended, the two dropped the last copies from the top-floor gallery, showering the empty hall with paper. A janitor, Jakob Schmid, noticed the flying leaflets and quickly locked the building doors before phoning for assistance. Gestapo agents soon arrived and arrested the Scholls.

During her interrogation, Sophie repeatedly rejected the Gestapo's offer to lighten her sentence if she repented for her treasonous actions. On February 22, Hans and Sophie Scholl, along with another White Rose member named Christel Probst, were sentenced to death and executed by guillotine.

(Continued from previous page)

the siblings participated in mandatory Hitler Youth programs, only to become disillusioned with its oppressive philosophy and regulations.

Robert and Magdalene Scholl lost three of their five children to the Nazi regime. Hans and Sophie were executed for their anti-Nazi activities in 1943. Werner died fighting with his German unit on the Russian front. After the war, Inge married Otl Aicher and began to carefully organize the writings of her heroic brother and sister. In 1952, she published *Die Weisse Rose*, which tells the story of how Hans and Sophie gave their lives in a courageous battle against tyranny and murder. An opera of the same name opened at the Dresden State Theatre to ovations and praise, and in 1961 the German Democratic Republic (the former East Germany) issued a commemorative stamp in honor of both Scholls. An honorary stamp was issued by the Federal Republic of Germany (the former West Germany) in 1964.

Roland Freisler, the notorious lead judge of the People's Court, had flown to Munich from Berlin to conduct the proceedings. In an attempt to defend herself during her trial, Sophie remarked to Freisler: "Somebody, after all, had to make a start. What we wrote and said is also believed by many others. They just don't dare to express themselves as we did."

On the evening of the executions, several thousand students assembled in Munich to voice their condemnation of the White Rose. Jakob Schmid, the janitor who turned the Scholls in, received thunderous applause as he took his bows for the capture of the two traitors. On April 19, three additional members of the group were sentenced to death. Later, eleven others were killed or forced to commit suicide, including eight members of the Hamburg branch.

The Nazis arrested members of the Scholl family for questioning in the first instance of what came to called *Sippenhaft*. To discourage resistance, the police began to arrest and punish family members of captured dissidents. The Scholls were given varying sentences, with their father, Robert, receiving the heaviest term of two years. Amidst heavy air raids and bombings, he was released from prison before his sentence was up.

Soon after the execution of the Scholls and Probst, the underground resistance began circulating a new version of the last White Rose leaflet. An added line on the front cover declared in boldfaced type: "DESPITE EVERYTHING, THEIR SPIRIT LIVES ON." Throughout the city of Munich, the same slogan appeared on walls and pavements. By the end of 1943, war planes from the British Royal Air Force were dropping millions of the White Rose pamphlets over Germany. They printed a new headline of the front page, proclaiming the leaflet to be a "Manifesto of the Munich Students." Copies of the leaflets were also circulated to Sweden, Switzerland, the United States, and the Soviet Union—news of the resisters and their handbills even reached inmates at the concentration camps in Germany and occupied countries.

Did you know...

- Today, many schools and streets throughout Germany bear the name of Hans and Sophie Scholl. The square in front of the main building at the University of Munich is called "Geschwister-Scholl Platz." *Geschwister* is a German word that means "brother and sister."

- During World War I, Robert Scholl, the father of Hans and Sophie, had been a pacifist (someone who opposes war). He refused combat duty and served instead as a medic. In August 1942, while his sons Hans and Werner were serving on the Russian front, Robert was arrested and imprisoned for having called Adolf Hitler "the scourge of God." (A scourge is a source of great torment, suffering, or anguish.)

- When exiled (exile is a period of forced absence from one's own country) German author and Nobel laureate Thomas Mann learned of the Scholls' courageous actions, he praised them publicly during a speech broadcast over the radio program *Voice of America*. Speaking in honor of the Scholls, Mann said during the radio address: "Good, splendid young people ... you shall not be forgotten."

- Some 300,000 Germans died in the unsuccessful battle at Stalingrad, Russia. Because of the large number of German casualties, local Nazi officials frequently visited neighborhoods, calling on the families of fallen soldiers. The Germans named these visitors *Totenvogel,* or "Birds of Death," after the spread-wing Nazi eagle crest that appeared on their uniforms.

- The Nazi party assigned *Blockwartes,* or block wardens, to watch German citizens for the slightest signs of party disloyalty. These snooping agents were offered awards for each captured traitor. The janitor Jakob Schmid who observed Hans and Sophie in the campus building distributing the White Rose brochures was a block warden.

- Surveillance (keeping a close eye on people and their activities) became so commonplace in Germany during World War II that the Germans coined an expression, the "German look," to refer to the sly, over-the-shoulder glance people give when they want to see if anyone is watching them.

- On February 3, 1945, while presiding over a treason trial at the People's Court in Berlin, the ruthless Nazi judge Roland Freisler was killed during an air raid by American bombers.

For Further Reading

Forman, James. *Ceremony of Innocence.* New York: Hawthorn, 1970.

Innocenti, Robert. *Rose Blanche.* Translated by Martha Coventry and Richard Graglia. Mankato, MN: Creative Education, 1985.

Scholl, Hans, and Sophie Scholl. *At the Heart of the White Rose: Letters and Diaries of Hans and Sophie Scholl.* Edited by Inge Jens. New York: Harper & Row, 1987.

Scholl, Inge. *The White Rose.* Connecticut: Wesleyan University Press, 1983.

Raoul Wallenberg

Excerpt from *Letters and Dispatches, 1924-1944*

Translated by Kjersti Board
Originally published in 1987
This version published in 1995

On March 19, 1944, Nazi Germany took control of Hungary. Immediately after seizing power, the Nazis banned all opposing political parties and trade unions and placed restrictions on the press. Anti-Jewish laws forced Jews to surrender their jobs and their assets. In preparation for deportation (forced exit) to death camps, Jews were quickly rounded up and crowded into sections of designated cities called ghettos. By July 7, some 437,000 Hungarian Jews had been transported to Auschwitz for extermination. After King Gustav V of Sweden personally appealed to the Hungarian regent, Nicholas Horthy, the Germans yielded to international protests and abruptly halted deportations.

Countries around the world, including the United States, began to reevaluate their policies regarding aid to the displaced Jews of Europe. Established in January 1944, the American War Refugee Board (WRB) sought to "rescue all victims of enemy oppression who are in imminent danger of death." While the board never received adequate funding, members decided to focus their limited energies on the plight of Hungarian Jews. The WRB, along with the World Jewish Congress, consulted with the Swedish government about possible rescue efforts. All three agencies agreed to send a young Swedish businessman, Raoul Wallenberg, to Hungary to attempt the rescue of the more than 200,000 remaining Jews in Budapest, the capital city of Hungary, located on the Danube River.

Since Wallenberg knew Budapest from his business experiences, he was ideally suited to serve as a diplomat during the Germany occupation. In addition, his connection with neutral Sweden allowed him to travel unhindered through the city. His secret funding from both the WRB and the World Jewish Council helped him to organize and manage an enormous rescue effort outside the bounds of the normal diplomatic constraints.

Immediately after his arrival in Budapest, Wallenberg concentrated on printing and distributing a new type of "protective passport" that would prevent holders from deportation. These identification papers, with the blue and yellow three-crown emblem representing Sweden, ultimately saved tens of thousands of Jews. Wallenberg gained agreement with Hungarian authorities that those with protective passports could live in certain buildings called "Swedish houses."

During the summer of 1944, a degree of stability returned to Budapest as deportations ceased and some Jews were released from internment (holding) camps. However, the calm was short-lived; Wallenberg quickly abandoned his plans of returning to Sweden. On October 15, a fanatic pro-Nazi group, the Arrow Cross party, seized control of Hungary. Armed Arrow Cross gangs roamed the streets of Budapest, robbing and killing Jewish people. The sound of submachine guns filled the night as racists thugs murdered several thousand Jews. After stealing everything from their victims, including their clothes, the Arrow Cross men shot them and threw their naked bodies into the Danube River.

Immediately after the Arrow Cross party took control of the government, Wallenberg began issuing thousands of protective passports. He successfully negotiated with both the Arrow Cross regime and the Nazi occupiers to honor not only the 5,000 Swedish passports but also similar documents arranged by other neutral parties. To help prevent Jews from being killed by the fanatical national antisemitic (anti-Jewish) forces, Wallenberg increased the number of protective "foreign houses" for Jews holding diplomatic documents issued by Sweden, the International Red Cross, and other foreign missions. This life-saving operation saw the establishment of 31 such safe houses, which were referred to collectively as the "international ghetto." Wallenberg was responsible for saving as many as 25,000 of the 50,000 Jews residing in this protective residential area.

This letter of protection, or "schutzpass," was issued to Hungarian Jew Lili Katz on August 25, 1944. The document bears Raoul Wallenberg's initials in the bottom left corner.

Things to Remember While Reading Wallenberg's Letters and Dispatches:

- Wallenberg employed 600 Jewish workers to maintain these buildings, managed food distribution, and sanitation and health services—which required large sums of money. Funding for these operations came mainly from the War Refugee Board, which received money from Jewish organizations in the United States.

- Wallenberg sent memorandums, or reports, back to the Foreign Ministry in Sweden. Excerpted below are two of these memos, which contain important information about the actions of Nazi and Hungarian officials. The reports provide readers with a glimpse into the mind and heart of Wallenberg, whose straightforward writing style nonetheless reveals a deep devotion and compassion for those he committed his life to saving.

- The Hungarian antisemitic group known as the Arrow Cross party seized control of Hungary on October 15, 1944. In his letter to his mother dated December 8, 1944, Wallenberg refers to the increased turmoil and deteriorating conditions as the Arrow Cross terrorized, plundered, and murdered the Jews of Budapest.

Letters and Dispatches, 1924–1944

Memorandum Concerning the Persecution of Jews in Hungary

Enclosed please find a summary of the current situation compiled by a well-informed source. For reasons of safety, the identity of our informant will not be revealed until later....

Conditions in Collection Centers

*The parents of one of my informants were sent away in the direction of Poland on July 1. For some reason, the train was returned to the **infamous** camp at Békásmegyer—as the result, it was thought, of Archbishop Serédi's intervention at the time. My informant received a message smuggled from his parents, which indicated that they were lacking food and water. He then went there and managed to receive permission, through bribes, to hand over a parcel with food and water. According to his statement, his parents and the other prisoners were then half-dead. They were later taken to Poland.*

Infamous: Disgraceful.

*Another informant visited the departure point at Kassa on May 25 and was shown around by the person in charge, a Baron Fiedler, to whom he had been introduced by a friend that very same day. According to Baron Fiedler, the camp, which covered an area of about 1.5 acres, had originally housed 16,000-17,000 individuals. The camp had been filled on or around May 12. On May 15, the inmates were taken to the newly created ghetto in Kassa. After three days, they were returned to the camp, and the **deportations** began sometime around May 19. When my informant visited the camp, about 8,000 persons in weakened condition remained. The temperature was about 50 degrees Fahrenheit and the weather rainy and windy. The prisoners were housed beneath narrow covers held up by wooden supports. As their names were called, they were loaded aboard the trains following an extremely **invasive body search** by the **SS**, for which both men and women were forced to disrobe. One woman tried **surreptitiously** to hide her infant under the railroad car, whereupon the child was seized by the leg and hurled headlong into the car. The car was packed so full that the passengers were forced to stand.*

According to my informant, Baron Fiedler reported that following an escape by several Jews he had ordered their relatives hung by their feet and beaten around the crotch as a warning to those following behind.

The Deportations

*A civil servant in a position to provide an overall view of the transports describes them as horrible and unspeakably brutal. Food often consists of one loaf of bread per car, sometimes of a pound of bread and 8 ounces of **marmalade**. One bucket of water is allotted to each car. The journey generally takes five days. There are many deaths.*

Treatment in Auschwitz, Birkenau, and Waldsee

The enclosed reports, which state that everybody, with the exception of able-bodied men and young women, has been put to

Deportations:
Forced exits.

Invasive body search:
Probing and humiliating search of a person's entire body, including all body cavities.

SS: Nazi political police who also ran the concentration camps.

Surreptitiously: Secretly.

Marmalade: Clear sweetened jelly containing pieces of fruit.

*death, is confirmed by the fact that postcards have been received here from these two categories of deportees, but none from older people. A journalist assigned to the Hungarian air force is **alleged** to have returned recently from the Katowice area with information confirming this. I have, however, not yet managed to speak to him.*

The Reaction of the Hungarians

*Most people you speak to are ashamed of what is happening and maintain that these brutalities are not being committed by Hungarians but only by Germans. However this is not true. Hungarian anti-Semitism is deeply rooted. Positive intervention is usually limited to helping friends by providing food and hiding places. Many **deplore** the persecution of the Jews, pointing out that it is costing the Hungarians sympathy abroad, and that they risk being treated more harshly than Romania in the event of peace, since Romania's policy toward its Jewish population is known to have become more **lenient** of late. It would appear, however, that this awareness is limited to the leaders of industry. There is a certain amount of speculation regarding the punishment awaiting those who have taken an active part in these criminal actions.*

I might mention, in this connection, that the presence of Jews is sometimes thought to constitute protection against bombing raids. Those who hold this view appear to believe that the scattering of the Jews into about 2,600 Jewish houses all over Budapest, instead of concentrating them in ghettos, is a deliberate act, and that is also the reason why the Jewish workforce has been forbidden to seek shelter during air raids.

Escape Possibilities

*The need for ration cards, baptismal certificates, identity papers; the requirement to wear the Star of David; the curfew for Jews during most of the day; the strict control of the streets at night; the lack of cash among Jews; the lukewarm sympathy of the Christian population; and the open and easily surveyable **topography** of*

Alleged: Supposed; so-called; questionably true.

Deplore: Regret strongly.

Lenient: Less strict; to go easier on.

Topography: The characteristics of the land surface.

the countryside all combine to make it difficult for the Jews to **elude** *their fate by escaping.*

Somewhere in the vicinity of 20,000 to 50,000 Jews are thought to have been hidden in Budapest by Christian friends. Of those who remain in the Jewish houses, it is likely that most are children, women, and old people. The men have been **conscripted** *for work. During the week ending on July 7, a large number of baptisms were performed by Catholic priests. Greater restrictiveness now prevails, however, and three months' instruction is now required for baptism. Many priests have been arrested. By being baptized, Jews hope to take advantage of the rumored new regulations exempting those baptized from having to wear the Star of David. The number of baptized Jews in Hungary is reported not to exceed 70,000.*

Some slight possibility evidently exists of acquiring **Aryan** *papers belonging to people who have either been bombed out or killed. These command a very high price. I do not know of any cases of false identity papers, however, and the printing establishments are under such strict control that it is, at this point, virtually impossible to escape by this method.*

The Jews of Budapest are completely **apathetic** *and do virtually nothing to save themselves.*

The Social Democratic Party is in theory pro-Jewish, but is virtually paralyzed and in all likelihood prevented from helping.

I am not familiar with the position and activities of the Communist Party.

Bribes and Corruption

A train with 1,200 Jews destined for Spain en route to Palestine departed quite some time ago, but is presently being held in Hanover. An agreement was allegedly reached between the **Jewish**

Elude: Avoid or escape.

Conscripted: Forced into service.

Aryan: Supposed master race of non-Jewish Caucasians having Nordic features.

Apathetic: Having or showing no feeling or emotion.

Council and the **Gestapo**, unbeknownst to the Hungarian government, which was told by the Gestapo that the Jews in question would be deported as usual, *i.e.*, put to death....

I am not aware of a single case in which someone has managed to escape from a detention camp, except for the one mentioned in a previous report. The embassy has also received an anonymous report of an alleged escape from the camp at Békásmegyer. Bribes are apparently much less frequent than one might assume, partly because the entire rounding-up and deportation process is so **mechanized**, swift, and impersonal that outsiders wishing to intervene have not been able to get in touch with the camp commander in question....

Budapest, July 18, 1944

[signed] Raoul Wallenberg

Memorandum Concerning the Jews in Hungary

Situation

Since my last report there has been virtually no change. Some small-scale deportations have taken place, but these are said to have comprised smaller numbers rather than whole railroad cars. This has made it difficult to verify my information.

Soldiers have continued to surround individual houses in Budapest this week, and Jews have been taken away without warning to labor service or to register for labor service. In some instances, they have then been permitted to return home.

On August 5, SS soldiers staged a **coup** against the camp at Sarvar during which the commander was forced to turn over 1,500 Jewish prisoners under threat of armored vehicles. As today is Sunday, I have been unable to verify whether they have passed Hegyeshalom. I refer to the enclosed eyewitness report, entitled "[Report of the Royal Swedish **Legation**]."

Jewish Council: Jewish leaders charged with administration within the ghetto.

Gestapo: Secret police force of the Nazi party.

i.e.: That is.

Mechanized: Made automatic or routine.

Coup: Short for coup d'etat; violent overthrow of existing authority by a small force.

Legation: Diplomatic mission.

For the past two days Budapest has been full of rumors, circulated by the Gestapo, that the great action against the Jews of Budapest is about to begin. I have not yet been able to confirm these rumors.

*On the first of this month I had a conversation with His Excellency **Miklós Horthy**, in the course of which he asked me to provide him with some anonymous written suggestions for actions that might be taken. I submitted one that ended in the demand that individuals with collective passports should be **exempted** from wearing the Star of David, and that the clergy be given greater freedom to speak their mind. On the third of this month, I had a talk with the minister of the interior. He told me that he would welcome an even greater number of Jews leaving for Sweden and confirmed that they might be allowed to stay in special houses under Swedish protection before their departure. The general decision to deport the Jewish population of Budapest was **unresolved**, but they were now in the process of securing reassurances from Germany that no harm would befall them.*

Both meetings were the result of private initiatives.

The Organization of the Rescue Operation

The staff of the B section now consists of forty individuals, organized into reception, registration, treasury, archives, and departments for correspondence, transportation, and housing, each under separate and competent leadership.

Another six-room apartment has been rented in an adjoining building.

*About four thousand applications have been received. No more are being accepted until we have had time to go through and process these. Newly printed protective documents and passport **affidavits** will be sent out as soon as the applications have been approved.*

Miklós Horthy: (Americanized as "Nicholas Horthy"; regent, or acting ruler, of Hungary.

Exempted: Freed from duty or requirement; excused.

Unresolved: Undecided; not yet determined.

Affidavits: A sworn written statement, usually given under oath.

Results Achieved

A number of individuals have avoided detention. Exact numbers will follow in a subsequent report.

Establishment of a Camp

This coming Wednesday or Thursday we will probably be able to empty the rental property Pozsony-utca 3, a Jewish house, of its present occupants and replace them with the same number of Jews under the embassy's protection. It would be most desirable if we could pay the moving costs and a small compensation to those Jews who are now suddenly vacating their homes in this way. The **adjoining** houses in the same street will eventually be transformed into Swedish collection centers. They should be able to hold an average of about a hundred people per house.

Budapest, August 6, 1944
[signed] Raoul Wallenberg
Secretary to the Legation

ROYAL SWEDISH EMBASSY
BUDAPEST
DECEMBER 8, 1944

Dearest Mother,

I really don't know when I'll be able to make it up to you for my silence. Another **diplomatic pouch** leaves today, and once again all you get from me are a few lines written in haste.

The situation is risky and tense, and my workload almost superhuman. **Thugs** are roaming around the city, beating, torturing, and shooting people. Among my staff alone there have been forty cases of kidnapping and beatings. On the whole we are in good spirits, however, and enjoying the fight....

Adjoining: Lying next to.

Diplomatic pouch: Lockable bag for carrying dispatches (important official messages) between offices.

Thugs: Brutal people; killers.

Raoul Wallenberg (1912-c. 1947)

Raoul Wallenberg was born into a distinguished family of bankers and diplomats with close relations to the Swedish Royal family. His father, an officer in the Swedish navy, died of cancer before Raoul was born, but the relationship young Raoul had with his paternal grandfather, Gustof Wallenberg, influenced him profoundly. The elder Wallenberg wished to transform Raoul into a citizen of the world and applauded his plans to study architecture at the University of Michigan. Wallenberg's experiences abroad expanded his imaginativeness and self-reliance, traits that would serve him well in his later role as rescuer during World War II.

As an international banker and trader, Wallenberg traveled throughout Europe and Hungary before the war. In 1944, the American War Refugee Board, the World Jewish Council, and the Swedish Foreign Ministry all agreed Wallenberg possessed the necessary talents to lead a rescue mission of the Jews trapped in Budapest.

Wallenberg arrived in Hungary in July 1944, just as major deportations to the death camps ended—in part as a result of Swedish pressure. In Budapest, Wallenberg first negotiated an agreement to afford protection for anyone, including Jews, who held Swedish protective documents. As a result, he created an entire department dedicated to issuing these "protective passes." Wallenberg remained in Budapest during the Soviet takeover, despite repeated death threats from local fascists who objected to his protection of Jews. (Fascism is a political philosophy that places nation and race above the individual. Fascist governments are run by a single, dictatorial leader and are characterized by extreme social and economic restrictions.) After responding to a request to report to Soviet Army headquarters, Wallenberg disappeared.

Szálasi: Ferenc Szálasi, leader of the Arrow Cross party, took control of Hungary in October 1944.

*We can hear the gunfire of the approaching Russians here day and night. Since **Szálasi** came to power, diplomatic activity has become very lively. I myself am almost the sole representative of our embassy in all government departments. So far, I've been to see the foreign minister about ten times, the deputy premier twice, the minister for the interior twice, the minister of supply once, the minister of finance once, etc.*

The wife of the foreign minister was a pretty close acquaintance of mine. Unfortunately, she has now left for Merano.

Food is very scarce in Budapest. We managed to stockpile a fair amount ahead of time, however. I have a feeling that it will be difficult to leave after the [Russian] occupation, so I doubt I will get to Stockholm until around Easter. But all this is idle speculation. No one knows what the occupation will be like. At any rate, I will try to return home as soon as possible.

It is simply not possible to make plans at the moment. I really thought I would be with you for Christmas. Now I must send you my best wishes for Christmas by this means, along with my wishes for the New Year. I hope the peace so longed for is no longer so far away....

The enormous amount of work makes the time pass quickly, and I am often invited to late-night feasts of roast suckling pig and other Hungarian specialties.

Dearest Mother, I will say good-bye for today. The pouch must be readied. Greetings, tender and heartfelt kisses to you and the whole family....

Affectionately,
R. Wallenberg
(Wallenberg, pp. 168-277)

What happened next...

As the Soviet armies began to occupy Budapest, Wallenberg learned of a joint SS and Arrow Cross plan to blow up both the "international ghetto" and the main ghetto where 70,000 Jews were detained. He brazenly confronted the local German commander, General Schmidthuber, threatening to ensure that the commander would "swing on the gallows" if the liquidation occurred. Wallenberg's bold tactic saved the lives of over 100,000 Hungarian Jews.

When the Soviets were on the verge of capturing Budapest, Wallenberg attempted to negotiate with them for the proper care of the Jews after liberation. Although the Swedish embassy had acted as a diplomatic liaison (connection) between Germany and the Soviet Union during the war, the Soviets distrusted Wallenberg. Responding to their request for a meeting, Wallenberg visited the Soviet army headquarters on January 17, 1945, and was never seen again.

After the war, the Soviets claimed they had no knowledge of any person named Wallenberg. However, German prisoners-of-war returning from Soviet camps testified that they had met Wallenberg at various prisons throughout Russia. The Swedish government and Wallenberg's family demanded that the Soviets provide information about Wallenberg's fate. In 1956, amidst worldwide protest, the Soviet Union claimed to have recovered records indicating Wallenberg died in a prison camp of natural causes in 1947.

Of the estimated 650,000 Jews in pre-war Hungary, about 200,000 survived. Nearly half of the survivors— 100,000 people— were saved by the efforts of Raoul Wallenberg. In recognition of his actions, the U.S. Congress awarded Wallenberg honorary American citizenship and Yad Veshem in Jerusalem awarded him the Righteous Among the Nations medal. Around the world, many schools, streets, and institutions are named in his honor.

Did you know...

- Prior to his mission in Hungary, Raoul Wallenberg did not have experience as a statesman. However, his unique background prepared him for the complex challenges involved in serving as a "volunteer" diplomat. His brief stint in banking helped him organize financial transactions, and even his architecture degree came in handy. During college, Wallenberg completed an assignment to design affordable housing; in Budapest, he found ways to house 35,000 people in buildings designed for fewer than 5,000.

- The U.S. Holocaust Memorial Museum is located at 100 Raoul Wallenberg Plaza in Washington, D.C.

- Wallenberg also personally intervened to save hundreds of individual Jews. He rescued many Jews as the Nazis led them on death marches from Budapest to the Austrian border. Wallenberg drove his car along the line of prisoners and ordered the Nazi guards to release those with protective passports. Since the Germans couldn't read Hungarian, they couldn't check the papers Wallenberg waved in their faces and didn't realize that he was simply saving as many people as he possibly could. He frequently performed similar rescue operations on the trains deporting Jews to extermination camps.

- Raoul Wallenberg came from an influential and well-established family in Sweden. His life accomplishments reflect his family's proud heritage. The motto on the Wallenberg family crest proclaims an honorable, humanitarian aim: "To Be—Not To Be Seen."

For Further Reading

Linneas, Sharon. *Raoul Wallenberg: The Man Who Stopped Death.* Jewish Publication Society, 1993.

Meltzer, Milton. *Rescue: The Story of How Gentiles Saved Jews in the Holocaust.* New York: Harper & Row, 1988.

Wallenberg, Raoul. *Letters and Dispatches, 1924-1944: Raoul Wallenberg.* Originally published in 1987. English translation by Kjersti Board. New York: Arcade Publishing, 1995.

Schindler's List

Excerpt from book by Thomas Keneally

First published in 1982

After invading Poland in September 1939, the German Nazi (National Socialist) party divided the country up according to the goals of the Third Reich, as the government under Nazi leader Adolf Hitler was called. To gain additional *lebensraum,* or living space, they annexed a portion of Poland and called the new territory Warthegau. As part of their plan to reorganize the races of Europe, the Nazis ordered the evacuation of all Poles and Jews from Warthegau to the southeastern portion of Poland. Only Polish people who resembled the ideal Aryan race (tall, blond, blue-eyed, with chiseled features)—and were not Jewish—were allowed to remain in the annexed portion. Hitler and other Nazi chiefs envisioned "the old and new Reich area" to be "cleansed of Jews, Pollacks and company" so that racially pure Germans could establish colonies on vacated land. Those Polish people who resembled the Aryan ideal were allowed to stay in segregated areas and undergo a "re-Germanization" program.

In the southeastern portion of Poland, the Nazis set up a civil administration called the *Generalgouvernement,* or General Government. Under the supervision of Governor-General Hans Frank, this area became the designated holding place for Polish Jews and all others deemed unfit for Reich citizenship. Of the 22 million people in German-occupied Poland, over two million were Jews. About 600,000 Jews lived in the Warthegau area and 1.5 million in the Generalgouvernement. In accordance with a directive issued by Nazi leader Reinhardt Heydrich, local Nazi officials began forcing Polish Jews into certain sections of the larger cities within the *Generalgouvernement.* Heydrich's written orders stipulated that the resettlement efforts take place in those cities "which are either rail-

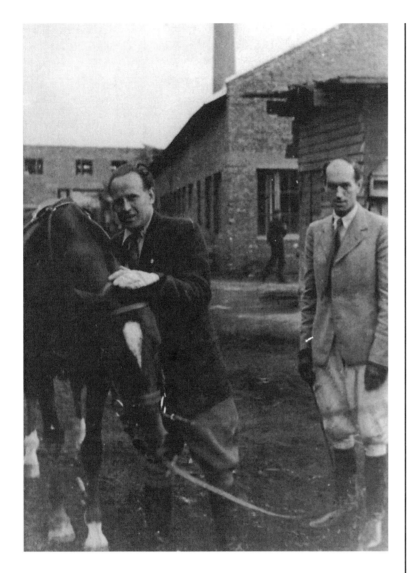

Oskar Schindler and his horse at the "Emalia" enamelware factory in Krakow (Poland).

road junctions or at least along railroad lines" so that "later measures will be easier." After forcing the Jews into ghettos, the Nazis planned to deport them by train to the death camps, which were also located within the Generalgouvernement.

In addition to forced displacement, the German authorities subjected Jewish Poles to violence and discrimination. They humiliated and even assaulted Jews wearing traditional, religious garb, drove them away from food lines, and randomly seized them off the streets for forced labor assignments. Many Jews lost their jobs without receiving compensation or the prospect of securing a new position. In addition, the Nazis issued numerous anti-Jewish decrees, including (1) the requirement that they wear arm bands depicting the Star of David, (2) a ban on owning radios, and (3) a ban on travel by train. But the most damaging orders were the ones that forbid Jews from participating in economic activities and ordered the confiscation of Jewish property.

Chaos ensued as large groups of people, both Poles and Jews, left their homes and possessions behind and traveled across Poland. As a result of this massive upheaval, many businesses closed because they lacked both workers and employers. These abandoned businesses provided entrepreneurs with an ideal opportunity: Aryan businesspeople could take over a deserted factory, start a business in support of the German war effort, and pay practically nothing for the plant or the labor to run it.

Inhabitants of the Jewish ghettos served as virtual slave laborers in such factories. Jews who obtained the designation of a "skilled laborer"—meaning they were employable in factories essential to war production—were assured some level of protection from Nazi *Aktions* (actions; operations) within the ghetto. (Note that among these "actions" were deportation and gassing at the death camps.) When the Nazi government began to prepare for the Soviet invasion, their planning organization—known as the Main Armaments Board—asked businesses in occupied Poland to produce supplies for the German troops. One person who responded to their request was Oskar Schindler.

As a native of the Sudetenland, a region located between Austria and Germany, Schindler was considered an ideal Germanic, or Aryan. In order to avoid military service, he had joined the German intelligence network known as *Abwehr* and traveled to Poland following the invasion in 1939. His involvement with *Abwehr* and his natural sales ability allowed him to establish important connections within both the Polish business community and the German military. Through these influential relationships, Schindler acquired a contract for supplying kitchenware to the military and opened a manufacturing plant in Cracow.

To operate the factory, Schindler began to rely on the Jewish population interned in the local ghetto, and later, from the labor camp. At some point, Schindler ceased being an ordinary employer and began functioning more as a savior to his employees. He fiercely argued with the Nazi police force in charge of the Jews, the SS, to prohibit random acts of terror against "his Jews," claiming they were essential to the German war effort. When the Nazis began the final liquidation of the Polish Jews, Schindler invented a scheme to move his Jewish laborers to a remote and safe location away from the enemy lines. To ensure that the Nazis would grant his request to relocate the Jews, he promised to open a munitions (ammunition) company that would supply much-needed weaponry to the beleaguered German forces.

Schindler was a most unlikely hero. Nothing in his past suggested or predicted that he would one day risk his life to save others. During the course of the war, however, Schindler fulfilled an astonishing promise he made to his Jewish employees—he told them that he would treat them well and that they would survive the war. The heroic actions of this mysterious and complex man saved the lives of more than 1,200 Jews.

Things to Remember While Reading the Excerpt from *Schindler's List*:

- Schindler's ghetto employees in Poland had identified him as a Jewish sympathizer and put him in touch with a secret Jewish relief organization in Hungary. The excerpt below begins with a description of a meeting in the capital city of Budapest between Schindler and two Jewish Hungarian resistance agents, Dr. Rezso Kastner and Samu Springmann. While rumors about Nazi atrocities had reached their country, the two Hungarians hoped to obtain from Schindler an actual firsthand account of the treatment of Jews detained in the Polish ghettos.

- As the Russian forces closed in on eastern Poland in 1944, the Germans began the final liquidation of the Jewish ghetto in Cracow and the local Plaszow labor camp. To save his Jewish workers, Schindler decided to seek permission from the Nazis to move them to Brinnlitz, where he would open a munitions factory. He prepared a list containing the names of all the Jewish prisoners he knew, hence the legendary name "Schindler's List."

- To run a successful business in occupied territories, entrepreneurs had to engage in extensive bribery. Corruption prevailed throughout the various branches of the Nazi organization. Fortunately, Schindler had access to cash and could frequently "buy favors."

Schindler's List

*D*r. Sedlacek [Schindler's initial contact person with the Jewish underground] had promised an uncomfortable journey, and so it was. Oskar traveled in a good overcoat with a suitcase and a bag full of various comforts which he badly needed by the end of the trip. Though he had the appropriate travel documents, he did not want to have to use them. It was considered better if he did not have to present them at the border. He could always then deny that he had been to Hungary that December.

*He rode in a freight van filled with bundles of the Party newspaper, Völkischer Beobachter, for sale in Hungary. Closeted with the **redolence** of printer's ink and among the heavy Gothic print of Germany's official newspaper, he was rocked south over the winter-sharp mountains of Slovakia, across the Hungarian border, and down to the valley of the Danube.*

*A reservation had been made for him at the Pannonia, near the University, and on the afternoon of his arrival, little Samu Springmann and an associate of his, Dr. Rezso Kastner, came to see him. The two men who rose to Schindler's floor in the elevator had heard fragments of news from **refugees**. But refugees could give you little but threads. The fact that they had avoided the threat meant that they knew little of its geography, its intimate functioning, the numbers it ran to. Kastner and Springmann were full of anticipation, since—if Sedlacek could be believed—the **Sudeten** German upstairs could give them the whole cloth, the first full-bodied report on the Polish **havoc**.*

Redolence: Odor or fragrance.

Refugees: People who flee to a foreign country to escape danger or persecution.

Sudeten: Descendant of Sudetenland area of Czechoslovakia, a mountainous region on the Polish-Czech border that was occupied by Germany from 1938 to 1945.

Havoc: Destruction.

A portrait of some of the "Emalia" factory office staff.

In the room the introductions were brief, for Springmann and Kastner had come to listen and they could tell that Schindler was anxious to talk. There was no effort, in this city obsessed with coffee, to formalize the event by calling Room Service for coffee and cakes. Kastner and Springmann, after shaking the enormous German by the hand, sat down. But Schindler paced. It seemed that far from Cracow and the realities of **Aktion** and ghetto, his knowledge disturbed him more than it had when he'd briefly informed Sedlacek. He rampaged across the carpet. They would have heard his steps in the room below—their chandelier would have shaken when he stamped his foot, miming the action of the **SS** man in the execution squad in Krakusa, the one who'd pinned his victim's head down with a boot in full sight of [a] child at the tail of the departing column.

Aktion: Organized roundup of ghetto inmates.

SS: Political police of the Nazi party who operated the concentration camps.

He began with personal images of the cruel **parishes** of Cracow, what he had beheld in the streets or heard from either side of the wall, from Jews and from the SS. In that connection, he said, he was carrying letters from members of the ghetto, from the physician Chaim Hilfstein, from Dr. Leon Salpeter, from Itzhak Stern. Dr. Hilfstein's letter, said Schindler, was a report on hunger. "Once the body fat's gone," said Oskar, "it starts to work on the brain."

The ghettos were being wound down, Oskar told them. It was true equally of Warsaw as of Lodz and of Cracow. The population of the Warsaw ghetto had been reduced by four-fifths, Lodz by two-thirds, Cracow by half. Where were the people who had been transferred? Some were in work camps; the gentlemen here this afternoon had to accept that at least three-fifths of them had disappeared into camps that used the new scientific methods. Such camps were not exceptional. They had an official SS name—"Vernichtungslager": Extermination Camp.

In the past few weeks, said Oskar, some 2,000 Cracow ghetto dwellers had been rounded up and sent not to the chambers of Belzec, but to labor camps near the city. One was at Wieliczka, one at Prokocim, both of these being railway stations on the Ostbahn line which ran toward the Russian front. From Wieliczka and Prokocim, these prisoners were being marched every day to a site at the village of Plaszow, on the edge of the city, where the foundations for a vast labor camp were being laid. Their life in such a labor camp, said Schindler, would be no holiday—the barracks of Wieliczka and Prokocim were under the command of an SS **NCO** named Horst Pilarzik who had earned a reputation last June when he had helped clear from the ghetto some 7,000 people, of whom only one, a chemist, had returned. The proposed camp at Plaszow would be under a man of the same caliber. What was in favor of the labor camps was that they lacked the **technical apparatus** for **methodical slaughter**. There was a different rationale behind them. They had economic reasons for existing....

Parishes: Subdivision of a county.

NCO: Noncommissioned officer.

Technical apparatus: Complex equipment designed for a specific operation.

Methodical slaughter: Planned, deliberate, well-engineered killing.

*The forced-labor camps would be run by men appointed for their severity and efficiency in clearing the ghettos. There would be **sporadic** murders and beatings, and there would certainly be corruption involving food and therefore short rations for the prisoners. But that was preferable to the assured death of the Vernichtungslagers. People in the labor camps could get access to extra comforts, and individuals could be taken out and smuggled to Hungary.*

These SS men are as corruptible as any other police force, then? the gentleman of the Budapest rescue committee asked Oskar. "In my experience," growled Oskar, "there isn't one of them who isn't."...

*At some point in any discussion of Schindler, the surviving friends of the Herr Direktor will blink and shake their heads and begin the almost mathematical business of finding the sum of his motives. For one of the commonest sentiments of Schindler Jews is still "I don't know why he did it." It can be said to begin with that Oskar was a gambler, was a **sentimentalist** who loved the transparency, the simplicity of doing good; that Oskar was by temperament an **anarchist** who loved to ridicule the system; and that beneath the hearty sensuality lay a capacity to be outraged by human savagery, to react to it and not to be overwhelmed. But none of this, jotted down, added up, explains the **doggedness** with which, in the autumn of 1944, he prepared a final haven for the graduates of **Emalia**.*

And not only for them. In early September he drove to Podgorze and visited [Julius] Madritsch, who at that point employed more than 3,000 prisoners in his uniform factory. This plant would now be disbanded. Madritsch would get his sewing machines back, and his workers would vanish. If we made a combined approach, said Oskar, we could get more than four thousand out. Mine and yours as well. We could relocate them in something like safety. Down in Moravia.

Sporadic: Occurring only occasionally or in scattered instances.

Sentimentalist: One who is governed by feelings or emotions.

Anarchist: One who rebels against any authority or ruling power.

Doggedness: Stubborn determination.

Emalia: Another name used to refer to Schindler's kitchenware factory.

*Madritsch would always and justly be **revered** by his surviving prisoners. The bread and chickens smuggled into his factory were paid for from his pocket and at continuous risk. He would have been considered a more stable man than Oskar. Not as **flamboyant**, and not as subject to obsession. He had not suffered arrest. But he had been much more humane than was safe and, without wit and energy, would have ended in Auschwitz.*

Now Oskar presented to him a vision of a Madritsch-Schindler camp somewhere in the High Jeseniks; some smoky, safe little industrial hamlet.

*Madritsch was attracted by the idea but did not rush to say yes. He could tell that though the war was lost, the SS system had become more instead of less **implacable**. He was correct in believing that, unhappily, the prisoners of Plaszow would—in coming months—be consumed in death camps to the west. For if Oskar was stubborn and possessed, so were the SS Main Office and their prize field **operatives**, the commandants of the Concentration Camps.*

*He did not say no, however. He needed time to think about it. Though he couldn't say it to Oskar, it is likely he was afraid of sharing factory **premises** with a rash, **demonic** fellow like Herr Schindler.*

*Without any clear word from Madritsch, Oskar took to the road. He went to Berlin and bought dinner for Colonel Erich Lange. I can go completely over to the manufacture of **shells**, Oskar told Lange. I can transfer the heavy machinery.*

*Lange was **crucial**. He could guarantee contracts; he could write the hearty recommendations Oskar needed for the Evacuation Board and the German officials in Moravia.*

*Later, Oskar would say of this shadowy staff officer that he had given consistent help. Lange was still in that state of **exalted***

Revered: Honored; held in high esteem.

Flamboyant: Characterized by colorful behavior; calling attention to oneself.

Implacable: Not capable of being appeased, soothed, or satisfied.

Operatives: Secret agents.

Premises: A building and its grounds.

Demonic: Possessed or influenced by a demon or evil spirit.

Shells: Projectiles containing an explosive bursting charge.

Crucial: Absolutely necessary.

Exalted: Elevated in status.

desperation and moral disgust characteristic of many who had worked inside the system but not always for it. We can do it, said Lange, but it will take some money. Not for me. For others....

[Oskar] had drawn up what he called a preparatory list and delivered it to the Administration Building. There were more than a thousand names on it—the names of all the prisoners of the backyard prison camp of Emalia, as well as new names. Helen Hirsch's name was freshly on the list, and Amon was not there to argue about it.

And the list would expand if Madritsch agreed to go to Moravia with Oskar. So Oskar kept working on Titsch, his ally at Julius Madritsch's ear. Those Madritsch prisoners who were closest to Titsch knew the list was under compilation, that they could

Oskar Schindler with a group of Jews he rescued. This picture was taken one year after World War II ended.

*have access to it. Titsch told them without any **ambiguity**: You must get on it. In all the reams of Plaszow paperwork, Oskar's dozen pages of names were the only pages with access to the future.*

But Madritsch still could not decide whether he wanted an alliance with Oskar, whether he would add his 3,000 to the total.

There is again a haziness suitable to a legend about the precise chronology of Oskar's list. The haziness doesn't attach to the existence of the list—a copy can be seen today in the archives of the Yad Vashem. There is no uncertainty as we shall see about the names remembered by Oskar and Titsch at the last minute and attached to the end of the official paper. The names on the list are definite. But the circumstances encourage legends. The problem is that the list is remembered with an intensity which, by its very heat, blurs. The list is an absolute good. The list is life. All around its cramped margins lies the gulf.

Some of those whose names appeared on the list say that there was a party at [Amon] Goeth's villa, a reunion of SS men and entrepreneurs to celebrate the times they'd had there. Some even believe that Goeth was there, but since the SS did not release on bail, that is impossible. Others believe that the party was held at Oskar's own apartment above his factory. Oskar had for more than two years given excellent parties there. One Emalia prisoner remembers the early hours of 1944 when he was on night watch duty and Oskar had wandered down from his apartment at one o'clock, escaping the noise upstairs and bringing with him two cakes, two hundred cigarettes, and a bottle for his friend the watchman.

At the Plaszow graduation party, wherever it took place, the guests included Dr. Blancke, Franz Bosch, and, by some reports, Oberführer Julian Scherner, on vacation from his partisan-hunting. Madritsch was there too, and Titsch. Titsch would later say that at it Madritsch informed Oskar for the first time that he would not be going to Moravia with him. "I've done everything I can for the

Ambiguity: Uncertainty.

Jews," Madritsch told him. It was a reasonable claim: he would not be persuaded although he said Titsch had been at him for days.

Madritsch was a just man. Later he would be honored as such. He simply did not believe that Moravia would work. If he had, the indications are that he would have attempted it.

What else is known about the party is that an urgency operated there, because the Schindler list had to be handed in that evening. This is an element in all the versions of the story survivors tell. The survivors could tell and expand upon it only if they had heard it in the first place from Oskar, a man with a taste for **embellishing** a story. But in the early 1960's Titsch himself **attested** to the substantial truth of this one. Perhaps the new and temporary Commandant of Plaszow, a Hauptsturmführer Büscher, had said to Oskar, "Enough fooling around, Oskar! We have to finalize the paperwork and the transportation." Perhaps there was some other form of deadline imposed by the Ostbahn, by the availability of transport.

At the end of Oskar's list, therefore, Titsch now typed in, above the official signatures, the names of Madritsch prisoners. Almost seventy names were added, written in by Titsch from his own and Oskar's memories. Among them were those of the Feigenbaum family—the adolescent daughter who suffered from incurable bone cancer; the teen-age son Lutek with his shaky expertise in repairing sewing machines. Now they were all transformed, as Titsch scribbled, into skilled **munitions** workers. There was singing in the apartment, loud talk and laughter, a fog of cigarette smoke, and, in a corner, Oskar and Titsch quizzing each other over people's names, straining for a clue to the spelling of Polish **patronyms**.

In the end, Oskar had to put his hand on Titsch's wrist. We're over the limit, he said. They'll balk at the number we already have. Titsch continued to strain for names, and tomorrow morning would wake damning himself because one had come to him too

Embellishing: Enhancing; adding ornamental details to.

Attested: Stated as true.

Munitions: War materials, weapons, or ammunition.

Patronyms: Names derived from the father's side of the family (taken from "paternal" ancestry).

Blasphemously:
Irreverently; lacking proper honor or respect.

late. But now he was at the limit, wrung out by this work. It was **blasphemously** *close to creating people anew just by thinking of them. He did not begrudge doing it. It was what it said of the world—that was what made the heavy air of Schindler's apartment so hard for Titsch to breathe.*

(Keneally, pp. 153-291)

What happened next...

With the permission of the German government, Schindler and his Jewish workers left Poland and relocated in the Sudetenland region to open an armaments factory in a town called Brinnlitz. Schindler managed to officially classify his workers as skilled craftsmen who were essential to the war effort—an accomplishment that saved them from the gas chambers at Auschwitz. When the Nazis mistakenly routed a trainload of his Jewish female workers to Auschwitz, Schindler personally intervened and bribed the death camp authorities. He fought to persuade them that returning the Jewish prisoners would be "for the good of the war effort." As the officials considered his plea, they housed his employees in a separate area in Auschwitz. While most prisoners transported to death camps died within hours, his workers managed to survive. When they arrived by boxcar to Brinnlitz, however, many women were starving and in poor health. Schindler made sure that those who died were given a proper Jewish burial—which was an unusual event since Jews under Nazi rule were banned from practicing their religion in public.

The local Brinnlitz labor camp, like the one in Poland, was run by the Nazi SS. Once again the conditions within the armaments factory were considerably better than those in the labor camp. Schindler insisted that the SS not disturb his workers within the factory, arguing that the assembly of secret weapons required intense concentration. With incredible fearlessness, he prohibited guards from entering the factory. At his own expense, he provided his Jewish employees with a life-sustaining diet, unlike the starvation-level rations mandated by the Nazis.

Oskar Schindler (1908-1974)

Oskar Schindler was born in Zwittau, Austria, which is a region known as both the Sudetenland and Moravia. When Schindler was born, the territory was part of the Austrian empire, then under the rule of Emperor Franz Josef. Schindler's family groomed him to inherit the family farm equipment business. This background in machinery combined with his fierce aggressiveness led the young Schindler to competitive motorcycle racing. He served briefly in the Czech army, but did not enjoy life in the service.

During the depression (a period of severe economic slowdown), Schindler found employment by relying on his natural charisma and selling skills. His contact with the German intelligence division allowed him to follow the German advance into Poland in 1939. Schindler took over the operation of a bankrupt kitchenware factory outside Cracow, employing Jewish prisoners from the local ghetto. Later he moved his employees to his home region of the Sudetenland and opened an armament factory. This plant and labor camp was dissolved when the war ended on May 8, 1945. With the support of his prisoners, he and his wife reached the American forces.

After the war, Schindler and his wife immigrated to Argentina, where they tried their hand—unsuccessfully—at farming. Schindler returned to Germany and opened a cement factory in Frankfurt in 1961; this venture also failed. Upon hearing of his plight, some of the Jews he had saved combined their resources to provide financial aid to Schindler. During the last decade of his life, he split his time between Israel and Frankfurt, Germany. Yad Vashem bestowed upon Schindler the Righteous Among Nations honor in recognition of his efforts to save 1,200 Jews in Cracow and Brinnlitz. He died in Frankfurt in 1974.

Production at the Brinnlitz plant can only be described as a farce. Schindler no longer attempted to fulfill his contracts with quality goods—he only wanted to keep the hoax up long enough to survive the war. The Jewish workers deliberately and skillfully rigged the factory equipment so that it passed Nazi inspection and yet continually produced defective ammunition. To save Jews from other labor camps, Schindler demanded that the Nazis direct more laborers to his ammunition plant. When the SS questioned him regarding his use of child labor, Schindler argued that their long, small fingers were necessary to polish the inside of specially constructed anti-tank shells. Since the few shells produced at Brinnlitz failed all inspection criteria, they were not sent to the fighting fields. This greatly relieved Schindler, who did not wish unsuspecting German soldiers to die as a result of his deliberately inferior products.

Schindler's "confidence game," or con game, continued until the end of the war. As a final act of courage, he convinced the SS guard brigade to lay down their weapons and refrain from exterminating their prisoners when the Soviet troops began approaching the Brinnlitz factory and labor camp. The constant need for capital to pay bribes and the lack of successful production at Brinnlitz left Schindler with little hard currency or gems with which to barter at the end of the war. What little he had he used to buy his transport to the American front. The man who started as a profiteer (one who makes an unreasonable profit, often at the expense of others during times of emergency) ended the war penniless, but he is remembered as a savior and hero to many.

Did you know...

- The book *Schindler's List* by Thomas Keneally is regarded as a combination of documentary and dramatization. While it is impossible to recreate his entire story, all people and events cited are accurate, and all conversations were reconstructed based on eyewitness reports and available records.

- Producer-director Steven Spielberg brought the film adaptation of *Schindler's List* to the big screen. The enormously successful motion picture—starring Liam Neeson in the title role—won seven Academy Awards in 1993.

- After World War II, Oskar Schindler could never repeat his wartime business successes. He failed at both farming and manufacturing. The people he helped save, who came to be called "Schindler Jews," provided him with financial support as he grew older. Some Schindler Jews agreed to donate one day's pay each year towards his financial support.

- Even after receiving the Yad Vashem honor, Schindler met with harassment and abuse in Germany. While people around the world praised his courageousness, workmen jeered at him on the streets of Frankfurt. Once, he ended up in a local court for punching a man who had called him a "Jew Kisser." After he died in Frankfurt on October 9, 1974, his body was flown to Jerusalem for burial in accordance with his wishes.

For Further Reading

Adelson, Alan. *Lodz Ghetto.* New York: Viking, 1989.

Keneally, Thomas. *Schindler's List.* Originally published in 1982. New York: Simon & Schuster, 1993.

Kuper, Jack. *Child of the Holocaust.* New York: Berkley Books, 1993.

Stradtler, Bea. *The Holocaust: A History of Courage and Resistance.* West Orange, NJ: Behrman House, 1973.

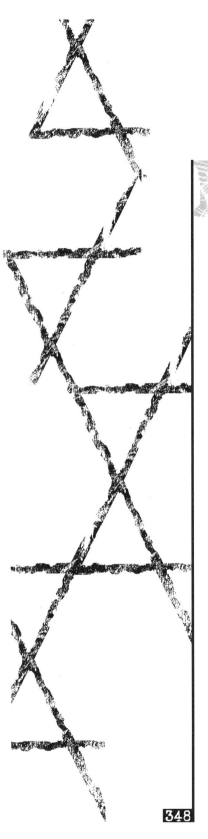

liberation HOLOCAUST

The collapse of Germany in the spring of 1945 allowed the world to witness up close the extent and effects of Nazi hatred. As the German army retreated in the face of advancing Allied forces, they left behind evidence of their brutal actions. Although reports of Nazi atrocities had reached the West throughout World War II, no one was prepared for the conditions discovered in the extermination and concentration camps at the time of liberation. Battle-hardened soldiers wept at the sight of the horrors found behind the camps' barbed wire fences. The few emaciated survivors were living alongside corpses stacked in piles throughout the camp grounds.

During the last days of fighting, radio correspondent **Edward R. Murrow** traveled into Germany behind the American forces. His emotional report of the liberation of the Buchenwald concentration camp became one of the most famous radio broadcasts in history. The text of Murrow's radio report was published in a collection of his works titled *In Search of Light.*

Nine months before the war ended, the Allies had broadcast throughout Europe their intentions and preparations for the end of Nazi rule. In their radio announcement, which aired on September 23, 1944, the Allies promised to repeal Nazi racialist laws that oppressed the Jews living in German-controlled territory. After gaining power in 1933, the Nazis had escalated their campaign of terror and violence against Jewish people. By the end of the war in 1945, over 6 million Jews had died in Nazi-controlled extermination and concentration camps.

Those Jews who survived the Holocaust provided shocking firsthand testimony concerning the brutality of Nazi policies. **Fania Fénelon** was one of the people who managed to stay alive despite the horrendous conditions of the camps. In her book *Playing for Time,* she describes her experiences as a member of the women's orchestra at the Birkenau section of Auschwitz. While her unusual job at Auschwitz spared her

A group of American editors and publishers are shown prisoners' corpses during an inspection of Dachau on May 4, 1945.

Two survivors lie among corpses in the Dora-Mittelbau concentration sub-camp.

from lethal work details, Fénelon almost succumbed to typhus before being liberated by the British in April 1945.

Albert Speer, German minister of armaments and war production, remained involved with the inner workings of the Third Reich up until the close of the war. During the Battle for Berlin, he visited Adolf Hitler in the underground bunker located beneath the Chancellory building. In his bestselling book *Inside the Third Reich,* Speer provides one of the few accounts of Hitler's last days.

Rather than return to his job as an architect after the war, survivor **Simon Wiesenthal** dedicated his life to hunting down those responsible for the Holocaust. In *The Murderers among Us,* Wiesenthal describes the painstaking challenges involved in bringing Nazi war criminals to justice.

The search for justice began even before World War II ended. The International Military Tribunal was established by the Allies to punish senior Nazi staff for instituting the

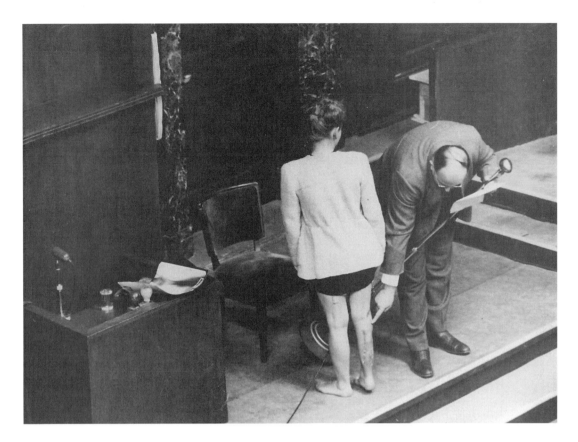

policies that resulted in the extermination of 6 million Jews. Convened in October 1945, these proceedings became known as the Nuremberg Trials. **Justice Robert H. Jackson** gave the opening statement for the United States, which was reprinted in the government document known as *Nazi Conspiracy and Aggression*. A list titled **The Search for Justice Begins** catalogs the sentences handed down by the tribunal to 22 top-level Nazi officials.

Many Nazis fled Germany to avoid prosecution; several committed suicide. **Adolf Eichmann** was responsible for orchestrating the "final solution," or extermination of European Jews. After 15 years of hiding in Argentina, Eichmann was captured and brought to trial in Jerusalem. Scholar **Hannah Arendt** followed the trial and recorded her impressions in *Eichmann in Jerusalem: A Report on the Banality of Evil*. In her controversial analysis, Arendt suggests that Eichmann's behavior demonstrates the existence of evil in ordinary humans.

A Polish survivor shows her scarred leg to the court during Case #1 of the Nuremberg Proceedings.

Edward R. Murrow

Radio Report-- the Liberation of Buchenwald

Excerpt from In Search of Light: The Broadcasts of Edward R. Murrow, 1938-1961
Published in 1967

During its twelve years of rule (1933-1945), the German Nazi (National Socialist) party mastered the tactics of oppression. An essential part of their regime of terror consisted of prisons called *Konzentrationslagers,* or concentration camps. The professed goal of concentration camps was to "reform" political opponents and to transform "anti-social members of society into useful members." Shortly after becoming chancellor of Germany in 1933, Adolf Hitler suspended the constitutional clause guaranteeing personal liberties and ordered the arrest of his political opponents. Thousands of ordinary Germans were taken into "protective custody" because they were members of the Communist party, the Social Democratic party, or powerful trade unions. Eventually the Nazis also detained nonpolitical prisoners who were considered "asocial elements" (those who supposedly lacked the capacity for normal social interactions) such as habitual criminals, tramps, beggars, homosexuals, and Gypsies (a wandering band of people who originated in India and moved to southern Asia, Europe, and parts of North America).

In the early years of the Reich, those imprisoned at concentration camps included German Jews belonging to outlawed political parties and organizations. However, when anti-Jewish measures escalated, so did the proportion of Jewish inmates in the camps. In the wake of the organized violent attack in 1938 known as *Kristallnacht,* or "the night of broken glass," the Nazis imprisoned some 36,000 Jews. At this point, the Nazis hoped to force Jews to emigrate from (or leave) Germany; they released any Jewish prisoner who could produce an emigration visa. Most German Jews who were

imprisoned in concentration camps prior to 1939 managed to secure their own release. But once World War II (1939-1945) broke out, the number of Jewish prisoners in German concentration camps rose again as victims arrived from other German-occupied countries. Then, in 1942, the Nazis ordered the soil of the Reich (Germany) to be *judenfrei,* or "free of Jews," and most Jewish prisoners were sent to the Auschwitz camp in nearby Poland.

In the mid-1930s, there were three main concentration camps in Germany—Dachau, Sachsenhausen, and Buchenwald. Other concentration camps were added as the Nazis continued to arrest anyone who was considered a threat to the Reich. These "enemies of the people" included Catholics, Protestants, Jehovah's Witnesses, pacifists (anti-war supporters), clergymen, monks, even dissident (or rebellious) Nazis. Inmates at concentration camps were tattooed with an identification number and wore a particular colored triangle on their uniform that classified their "crime." Political prisoners

Prisoners from Buchenwald await execution in the forest near the camp.

The End of Nazi Rule

A year before the military struggle ended in Europe, the Allies (forces fighting against Germany) began preparing for the restoration of civilian order in the soon-to-be recaptured lands. Anticipating the fall of Germany, the Allies broadcast a radio statement on September 23, 1944, announcing their intention to repeal (or undo) Nazi racialist laws. The Allied Powers promised to restore full rights of citizenship to Jews when Nazi rule ended. Radio stations across Europe broadcast the announcement, enabling the message to reach millions of people living within Germany and German-occupied countries where normal station operations had been banned.

The Allies expressed their plans to help maintain public order after the defeat of Germany. Nazi administrative officers were instructed to remain at their posts at the end of the war to assure an orderly surrender of funds,

wore a red triangle; criminals wore green; "shiftless elements" (those thought to be inefficient or lazy) wore black; homosexuals wore pink; Jehovah's Witnesses wore purple; Gypsies wore brown; and Jews wore both a yellow triangle and a classification triangle—the yellow triangle pointed up, the other pointed down to form the six-pointed Star of David, which symbolizes Judaism. After the Reich began expanding into other countries, foreign inmates wore signifying letters, such as "P" for Poland or "F" for France.

When Germany began taking over other countries in 1938, the camp system was expanded as well. To accommodate various political and racial goals, the Nazis established an extensive network of camps with differing functions. Most notorious were the extermination camps, which were specially designed for systematic mass murder. The Nazis viewed Jewish people—as well as Poles, Soviets, and Gypsies—as a threat to the "purity" of German blood. By late 1941, the Nazis began to plan for a series of death camps where they could annihilate their genetic enemies. The extensive Nazi camp system also included labor camps, transit camps, and prisoner-of-war (POW) camps. While various camps were built within Germany and throughout occupied territories, death camps existed exclusively in Poland. Two concentration camps—Auschwitz and Majdanek—also functioned as death camps.

Concentration camps provided a ready source of forced labor, which became increasingly important to Germany as the war continued. After 1942, prisoners were systematically drafted for work in the armaments industry. Through a program coordinated by German minister of armaments Albert Speer, state-owned and private companies involved in arms production could tap into the inexpensive labor pool provided by inmates. The demand for prison labor led to some improvement in their living conditions; however, the overall mortality rate remained very high. Due to the intense need for armament factory workers throughout Europe during the later stages of the war, some Jews were diverted to concentration camps instead of being deported directly to death camps.

On April 11, 1945, American troops from the 183rd Engineer Combat Battalion of the United States Third Army were shown a stack of corpses at Buchenwald.

In the spring of 1945, Allied forces (those countries fighting against Germany) descended upon Germany; victory seemed near. After recapturing Poland and Hungary, the Russians marched toward the German capital of Berlin from the east, while the British and American forces advanced deeper into the heart of Germany. By early April, American forces were approaching the Buchenwald concentration camp, which was situated southwest of Berlin. As the Allied forces neared the camp, the SS guards ordered the evacuation of prisoners in a frenzied attempt to cover their treacherous deeds. During the exodus, 25,500 people perished. In these last days, resistance members among the camp population sabotaged, or undermined, the SS plans by slowing down the pace of the evacuation. By April 11, 1945, most of the SS detachment (unit of troops) deserted the camp, and armed prisoners managed to trap the remaining guards. The American army entered Buchenwald that same day, liberating 21,000 prisoners, including 4,000 Jews and 1,000 children.

American reporter Edward R. Murrow had been covering the war since the early days of Hitler's rise to power. He captured a worldwide audience with his radio reports from London, broadcast amidst screeching bombs and gunfire. Now, with victory in sight, Murrow traveled to Germany and arrived in Buchenwald just four days after liberation.

Murrow's broadcast of his impressions reached an audience anxious for news. Just days before, U.S. president Franklin D. Roosevelt had died, and listeners were hungry for news about the new administration of Harry S Truman and about the war in Europe, which finally seemed to be nearing an end. Murrow minced no words in his firsthand account of what he had seen; in a straightforward manner, he described the overwhelming horror he encountered upon entering the concentration camp known as Buchenwald.

Things to Remember While Reading Murrow's Radio Broadcast of His Buchenwald Visit:

- The excerpt below is the text of the famous radio broadcast Murrow gave on April 15, 1945—just four days after the liberation of Buchenwald. Millions of people listened to Murrow's heartfelt and graphic descriptions of the horrors he observed within the camp and the conversations he had with survivors. This radio broadcast aired only three days after the death on April 12 of President Franklin D. Roosevelt.

- Buchenwald was one of the largest concentration camps in Germany, with 130 satellite camps and extension units. Established back in 1937, it was also one of the oldest.

- An inmate's chances of survival were directly related to the color triangle on his or her uniform. German political prisoners typically held top administrative positions, while political prisoners of various nationalities held other key positions at Buchenwald. Notice the principal roles of the German prisoners Murrow met during his visit—one German gave Murrow a tour of Buchenwald, and another was in charge of running the camp's kitchen.

- Murrow's account is consistent with the reaction of other representatives of the Allied countries who entered concentration and extermination camps after liberation. Even members of the military forces who had been hardened by the war were shocked by what they encountered in the camps: namely, the condition of the survivors, the filth, and the indescribable stench. Murrow attempted to give expression to the incomprehensible horrors and cruelties he witnessed.

*During the last week, I have driven more than a few hundred miles through Germany, most of it in the Third Army sector—Wiesbaden, Frankfurt, Weimar, Jena and beyond. It is impossible to keep up with this war. The traffic flows down the superhighways, trucks with German helmets tied to the radiators and belts of machine-gun ammunition draped from fender to fender. The tanks on the concrete roads sound like a huge sausage machine, grinding up sheets of **corrugated** iron. And when there is a gap between **convoys**, when the noise dies away, there is another small noise, that of wooden-soled shoes and of small iron tires grating on the concrete. The power moves forward, while the people, the slaves, walk back, pulling their small belongings on anything that has wheels.*

*There are cities in Germany that make Coventry and Plymouth appear to be merely damage done by a **petulant** child, but bombed houses have a way of looking alike, wherever you see them.*

But this is no time to talk of the surface of Germany. Permit me to tell you what you would have seen, and heard, had you been with me on Thursday. It will not be pleasant listening. If you are at lunch, or if you have no appetite to hear what Germans have

Corrugated: Ridged or grooved.

Convoys: Groups organized for protection during a move.

Petulant: Unreasonably irritable.

done, now is a good time to switch off the radio, for I propose to tell you of Buchenwald. It is on a small hill about four miles outside Weimar, and it was one of the largest concentration camps in Germany, and it was built to last. As we approached it, we saw about a hundred men in **civilian** clothes with rifles advancing in open order across the fields. There were a few shops; we stopped to inquire. We were told that some of the prisoners had a couple of SS men cornered in there. We drove on, reached the main gate. The prisoners crowded up behind the wire. We entered.

And now, let me tell this in the first person, for I was the least important person there, as you shall hear. There surged around me an evil-smelling **horde**. Men and boys reached out to touch me; they were in rags and the remnants of uniforms. Death had already marked many of them, but they were smiling with their

General Dwight D. Eisenhower listens to survivors of Ohrdruf (a sub-camp of Buchenwald) give testimony about atrocities committed in the camp.

Civilian: A person who is not on active duty in the military; in this case, civilian clothes are regular street clothes.

Horde: A large and unorganized crowd.

eyes. I looked out over that mass of men to the green fields beyond where well-fed Germans were ploughing.

*A German, Fritz Kersheimer, came up and said, "May I show you round the camp? I've been here ten years." An Englishman stood to attention, saying, "May I introduce myself, delighted to see you, and can you tell me when some of our **blokes** will be along?" I told him soon and asked to see one of the **barracks**. It happened to be occupied by Czechoslovakians. When I entered, men crowded around, tried to lift me to their shoulders. They were too weak. Many of them could not get out of bed. I was told that this building had once stabled eighty horses. There were twelve hundred men in it, five to a bunk. The stink was beyond all description.*

When I reached the center of the barracks, a man came up and said, "You remember me. I'm Peter Zenkl, one-time mayor of Prague." I remembered him, but did not recognize him. He asked about Benes and Jan Masaryk. I asked how many men had died in that building during the last month. They called the doctor; we inspected his records. There were only names in the little black book, nothing more—nothing of who these men were, what they had done, or hoped. Behind the names of those who had died there was a cross. I counted them. They totaled 242. Two hundred and forty-two out of twelve hundred in one month.

As I walked down to the end of the barracks, there was applause from the men too weak to get out of bed. It sounded like the hand clapping of babies; they were so weak. The doctor's name was Paul Heller. He had been there since 1938.

*As we walked out into the courtyard, a man fell dead. Two others—they must have been over sixty—were crawling toward the **latrine**. I saw it but will not describe it.*

In another part of the camp they showed me the children, hundreds of them. Some were only six. One rolled up his sleeve,

Blokes: British term for "man" or "fellow."

Barracks: Structures that provide temporary housing.

Latrine: Toilet.

liberation

showed me his number. It was tattooed on his arm. D-6030, it was. The others showed me their numbers; they will carry them till they die.

*An elderly man standing beside me said, "The children, enemies of the state." I could see their ribs through their thin shirts. The old man said, "I am Professor Charles Richer of the **Sorbonne**." The children clung to my hands and stared. We crossed to the courtyard. Men kept coming up to speak to me and to touch me, professors from Poland, doctors from Vienna, men from all Europe. Men from the countries that made America.*

*We went to the hospital; it was full. The doctor told me that two hundred had died the day before. I asked the cause of death; he shrugged and said, "**Tuberculosis**, starvation, fatigue, and there are many who have no desire to live. It is very difficult." Dr. Heller pulled back the blankets from a man's feet to show me how swollen they were. The man was dead. Most of the patients could not move.*

As we left the hospital I drew out a leather billfold, hoping that I had some money which would help those who lived to get home. Professor Richer from the Sorbonne said, "I should be careful of my wallet if I were you. You know there are criminals in this camp, too." A small man tottered up, saying. "May I feel the leather, please? You see, I used to make good things of leather in Vienna." Another man said, "My name is Walter Roeder. For many years I lived in Joliet. Came back to Germany for a visit and Hitler grabbed me."

*I asked to see the kitchen; it was clean. The German in charge had been a **Communist**, had been at Buchenwald for nine years, had a picture of his daughter in Hamburg. He hadn't seen her for almost twelve years, and if I got to Hamburg, would I look her up? He showed me the daily ration—one piece of brown bread about as thick as your thumb, on top of it a piece of margarine as big as*

Sorbonne: Major university in Paris, France; also known as University of Paris.

Tuberculosis: A life-threatening disease of the lungs.

Communist: An advocate of a political and economic theory that strives for the formation of a classless society through the communal, or group, ownership of all property.

Edward R. Murrow (1908-1965)

Edward R. Murrow (name originally Egbert Roscoe Murrow) was born in Greensboro, North Carolina. His family moved to Blanchard, Washington, when he was four. While in high school, Murrow shortened his given name to Ed. Later, at Washington State College (now Washington State University) in Pullman, he took the name Edward. Throughout his college years, he participated in debates and attended the country's first course in radio broadcasting. Murrow graduated *Phi Beta Kappa* (with honors) in 1930.

After college, Murrow traveled to Europe and throughout the United States for the National Student Federation and later as the assistant director for the International Institute of Education. He also obtained speakers for the Columbia Broadcasting System (CBS) *University of the Air* radio program.

Murrow's travels allowed him to witness firsthand the brutal repression in Germany when the Nazis seized power in 1933. Through his associations, he helped rescue scholars from

three sticks of chewing gum. That, and a little stew, was what they received every twenty-four hours. He had a chart on the wall; very complicated it was. There were little red tabs scattered through it. He said that was to indicate each ten men who died. He had to account for the rations, and he added, "We're very efficient here."

We went again into the courtyard, and as we walked we talked. The two doctors, the Frenchman and the Czech, agreed that about six thousand had died during March. Kersheimer, the German, added that back in the winter of 1939, when the Poles began to arrive without winter clothing, they died at the rate of approximately nine hundred a day. Five different men asserted that Buchenwald was the best concentration camp in Germany; they had had some experience of the others.

(Continued from previous page)

Germany. In 1935 he was appointed "director of talks" for the 100-station CBS radio network, then became European director two years later. CBS pioneered the radio broadcasting of special events and the establishment of fully-staffed foreign news bureaus. When Germany annexed Austria in 1938, Murrow broadcast to the world Hitler's arrival into Vienna. Murrow's reports of the aerial Battle of Britain and the German blitz (air raid) against London brought the realities of World War II into American homes.

In the years following the end of World War II, television began to replace radio as the most popular news medium. By 1951, Murrow again commanded huge audiences with his *See It Now* telecasts. He continued with the CBS News organization until 1961, when he accepted a position in President John F. Kennedy's administration as director of the U.S. Information Agency. Poor health forced his retirement in 1964, and he died a year later at his home in Pawling, NY.

*Dr. Heller, the Czech, asked if I would care to see the **crematorium**. He said it wouldn't be very interesting because the Germans had run out of coke some days ago and had taken to dumping the bodies into a great hole nearby. Professor Richer said perhaps I would care to see the small courtyard. I said yes. He turned and told the children to stay behind. As we walked across the square I noticed that the professor had a hole in his left shoe and a toe sticking out of the right one. He followed my eyes and said, "I regret that I am so little presentable, but what can one do?" At that point another Frenchman came up to announce that three of his fellow countrymen outside had killed three S.S. men and taken one prisoner. We proceeded to the small courtyard. The wall was about eight feet high; it **adjoined** what had been a stable or garage. We entered. It was floored with concrete. There were two rows of bodies stacked up like **cordwood**. They were thin and very white. Some of*

Crematorium: A furnace for burning dead bodies.

Adjoined: Lay next to.

Cordwood: Neatly stacked wood, often used to refer to wood for cooking or heating.

After liberation, these Jewish children—kept alive at Auschwitz-Birkenau—posed in their concentration camp uniforms.

the bodies were terribly bruised, though there seemed to be little flesh to bruise. Some had been shot through the head, but they bled but little. All except two were naked. I tried to count them as best I could and arrived at the conclusion that all that was mortal of more than five hundred men and boys lay there in two neat piles.

There was a German trailer which must have contained another fifty, but it wasn't possible to count them. The clothing was piled in a heap against the wall. It appeared that most of the men and boys had died of starvation; they had not been executed. But the manner of death seemed unimportant. Murder had been done at Buchenwald. God alone knows how many men and boys have died there during the last twelve years. Thursday I was told that there were more than twenty thousand in the camp. There had been as many as sixty thousand. Where are they now?

As I left that camp, a Frenchman who used to work for **Havas** in Paris came up to me and said, "You will write something about this, perhaps?" And he added. "To write about this you must have been here at least two years, and after that—you don't want to write any more."

I pray you to believe what I have said about Buchenwald. I have reported what I saw and heard, but only part of it. For most of it I have no words. Dead men are plentiful in war, but the living dead, more than twenty thousand of them in one camp. And the country round about was pleasing to the eye, and the Germans were well fed and well dressed. American trucks were rolling toward the rear filled with prisoners. Soon they would be eating American rations, as much for a meal as the men at Buchenwald received in four days.

If I've offended you by this rather mild account of Buchenwald, I'm not in the least sorry. I was there on Thursday, and many men in many tongues blessed the name of [U.S. president Franklin D.] Roosevelt. For long years his name had meant the full measure of their hope. These men who had kept close company with death for many years did not know that Mr. Roosevelt would, within hours, join their comrades who had laid their lives on the scales of freedom.

Back in 1941, [British prime minister] Mr. [Winston] Churchill said to me with tears in his eyes, "One day the world and history will recognize and acknowledge what it owes to your President." I saw and heard the first **installment** of that at Buchenwald on Thursday. It came from men from all over Europe. Their faces, with more flesh on them, might have been found anywhere at home. To them the name "Roosevelt" was a symbol, the code word for a lot of guys named "Joe" who are somewhere out in the blue with the armor heading east. At Buchenwald they spoke of the President just before he died. If there be a better **epitaph**, history does not record it. (Murrow, pp. 90-95)

Havas: French wire or news service.

Installment: One of several parts presented at intervals.

Epitaph: Inscription on a tomb in memory of the person buried there.

What happened next...

The Buchenwald concentration camp operated for eight years, from July 1937 to April 1945. Nearly 239,000 prisoners from 30 countries passed through the main camp and its satellite units, nestled on a mountain outside Weimar, a city in eastern-central Germany. Some 43,000 prisoners perished there, either by execution or due to the harsh conditions.

After liberation, German civilians were forced to visit the Buchenwald camp and view the evidence of the Nazi atrocities. These visitations occurred under escort by the U.S. military. In 1947, 31 members of the camp staff were tried for their crimes before an American military tribunal. Two were sentenced to death; four were given life sentences.

One of those sentenced to life imprisonment was Ilse Koch, an SS officer and guard at the camp who was married to Karl Koch, the commandant of Buchenwald from 1937 to 1941. Ilse Koch, known as the "Witch of Buchenwald," used to ride horseback through the camp and viciously whip prisoners. She also collected lampshades and other household objects fashioned from the tattooed skins of dead inmates. As commandant, her husband had become a millionaire from unscrupulous racketeering (obtaining money illegally, usually through intimidation) and exploitation of camp labor. In 1944, a Nazi court found Karl Koch guilty of corruption. He was hanged a year later.

The decision to reduce Ilse Koch's life sentence to four years aroused international protest because of its "lack of severity." Koch was rearrested in 1949 and brought to trial before a West German court for killing German nationals (citizens). Due to the intense publicity surrounding her case, her name became a byword for horror. In January 1951, she was sentenced to life imprisonment for murder. Sixteen years later, at the age of 61, Koch committed suicide in a Bavarian prison.

Did you know...

- As war spread across Europe, Murrow kept listeners informed with up-to-date news reports. His broadcasts from the rooftops of London, against the noise of sirens, gunfire, and falling bombs, riveted listeners around the world. He opened his narratives with the now-famous line, "This ... is London." Murrow's wartime accounts and his report on the liberation of Buchenwald are among the most famous radio broadcasts in history.

- Before the advent of television, radio was the fastest way to transmit accurate news accounts around the world. Beginning with his coverage of World War II, Murrow revolutionized the broadcast industry with his on-the-scene reports. Today, all major news agencies, both radio and television, use the same innovative reporting style pioneered by Murrow.

- A special division of the SS served as concentration camp guards. These units became known as *SS Totenkopfverbande,* or "Death's Head Units," named after the skeleton-head symbol they wore on the collars of their uniforms.

For Further Reading

Forman, James. *The Survivor.* New York: Farrar, Straus & Giroux, 1976.

Gottschalk, Elin Toona. *In Search of Coffe Mountains.* Nashville, TN: Nelson, 1977.

Karmel-Wolfe, Henia. *Marek and Lisa: A Novel.* New York: Dodd, Mead, 1984.

Murrow, Edward R. *In Search of Light: The Broadcasts of Edward R. Murrow, 1938-1961.* Edited with an introduction by Edward Bliss, Jr. New York: Alfred A. Knopf, 1967.

Fania Fénelon

Excerpt from
Playing for Time

Translated by Judith Landry
Published in 1977

After France fell to the German army in June 1940, the French government offered to sign an armistice, or truce, with Germany to diffuse the chaos that resulted from the early stages of World War II. Under the terms of the agreement, France agreed to disband its military and surrender three-fifths of the country to German control. France became divided into two areas—the occupied zone under German rule and the unoccupied zone under the rule of a new regime established in the town of Vichy in the south of France. The Vichy government quickly established authoritative rule by repealing civil liberties and pledged cooperation with Germany. By collaborating with Nazi Germany, the French hoped to achieve a favorable position within the "New Europe" being created by Adolf Hitler.

About 350,000 Jews lived in France in the summer of 1940, representing less than 1 percent of the population. Only 150,000 were native born; the rest were refugees from Germany, Austria, Czechoslovakia, Belgium, Holland, and Eastern Europe. (Refugees are people who flee to a foreign country to escape danger and persecution.) In the wake of the French defeat, large numbers of Jews fled to the unoccupied zone in the southern portion of the country. Persecution of Jews living in both the German-occupied zone and the Vichy zone began immediately after the armistice was signed. German and French leaders enacted harsh anti-Jewish measures that stripped Jews of their jobs and assets (land, homes, businesses, and anything else of value). Foreign Jews were particularly vulnerable and were the first to be interned (or held) at concentration camps within France or forced into labor brigades (groups of people formed for a specific service, in this case, to support the German war effort).

In the spring of 1942, the Germans and the French police began to organize large-scale deportations (forced exits) of Jews from both zones. In order to assure compliance from the Jewish population, the German and Vichy leaders claimed that the Jews were going to work camps "in the East," when in reality they were being transported to the Nazi-operated death camps in Poland. In July, the French police rounded up over 12,000 Jews in Paris alone. Those individuals without families were sent immediately to Drancy, the major transit camp in France. The remaining 9,000 were crowded into the sports stadium Velodrome d'Hiver, where they spent a week without food, water, or sanitation before being sent to Auschwitz.

A series of massive deportations, which continued into the fall of 1942, helped stir the first serious opposition to the Vichy government. When French Jews became the target of deportation efforts, resistance against the Germans increased. By January 1943, the French police could no longer be trusted to assemble and transport Jews.

Deportations from France continued until the summer of 1944. Allied forces landed in Normandy in June and secured the liberation of France two months later. As Vichy officials fled to Germany, French politician Charles de Gaulle returned from exile in Great Britain and marched triumphantly into Paris as the leader of free France.

But before the Allies liberated France, between 77,000 and 90,000 Jews were killed. The Germans sent the majority of Jews to Auschwitz, the largest Nazi concentration and extermination camp, but they also sent victims to other camps—Majdanek, Sobibor, and Buchenwald. Unlike other countries occupied by Germany during World War II, the Vichy French government had retained considerable autonomy. Historians have determined that without the cooperation provided by French officials, the Germans would not have been capable of deporting such large numbers of Jewish people to their deaths.

One of the French Jews deported to Auschwitz was a young musician and singer named Fania Fénelon. In January

1944, Fénelon arrived at Birkenau, an extension of the main camp at Auschwitz. Nine subunits existed at the Birkenau camp installation, including a women's section as well as gas chambers and crematoriums (furnaces for burning dead bodies). Upon her arrival, Fénelon survived the *Selektion* process that took place at the railway ramp, where Jewish prisoners were directed into two groups—one going immediately to the gas chambers, the other into forced labor. While in the quarantine block awaiting her labor assignment, Fénelon was recognized by another inmate who had seen her musical performances in Paris. Fénelon was selected to become a member of the Birkenau women's orchestra, comprised of over 40 female prisoners.

The Nazis formed orchestras from prisoners in many of the large concentration and extermination camps. These orchestras were forced to play for particular events, including the *Selektion* process, the march to the gas chambers, the procession of prisoners to and from work assignments each day, and the general enjoyment of SS guards (the Nazi political police and operators of the concentration camps). Auschwitz had six orchestras—the largest one consisting of 100 to 120 musicians. Auschwitz camp commandant Rudolph Höss had started the orchestras to provide marching music for the work groups leaving from and returning to the camps each day.

Fénelon and other members of the women's orchestra lived in separate quarters and were spared the life-threatening forced labor details assigned to other prisoners. As one of "the orchestra girls," she received adequate clothing, including an orchestra uniform comprised of a navy blue skirt, black woolen stockings, striped jacket, and a triangle of white cloth worn on top of her head similar to the headdress of German nurses.

Sensing the impending arrival of Allied forces, the Nazis began dismantling the gas chambers and crematoriums at Auschwitz during November and December 1944. Special work groups of male and female prisoners were ordered to clean the crematoriums' pits, cover the human ashes with dirt, and plant grass to hide the murderous evidence. During this time, Fénelon and other orchestra members were transferred to Bergen-Belsen, a concentration camp within northern Germany. Shortly after they arrived, tens of thousands of survivors poured in from death marches; these prisoners had

A prisoners' orchestra performs a Sunday concert for the SS men in Auschwitz.

been evacuated from camps in the East and ordered to walk to installations farther away from encroaching forces. Camp administrators did little to care for this influx of prisoners. Most received no shelter and went without food and water. Total chaos broke out in the camps as conditions reached an all-time low. In early 1945, a typhus epidemic broke out, killing over 18,000 prisoners in the month of March alone. An estimated total of 35,000 perished from typhus between January and April 15, when the British army liberated the camp.

Fania Fénelon was one of those prisoners infected with the deadly disease. In her autobiographical book *Playing for Time,* she describes the day British soldiers entered the Bergen-Belsen camp. As she drifted in and out of consciousness, Fénelon became aware of someone speaking English in her midst. Her orchestra friends forced her to wake up so that she could interpret for them what the soldier was saying. (Fénelon was multilingual.) The British army had liberated Bergen-Belsen.

Things to Remember While Reading
Playing for Time:

- Fénelon was originally deported to Auschwitz in January 1944. After spending 11 months in the women's camp at Birkenau (an extension of Auschwitz), she was transferred to the Bergen-Belsen concentration camp in northern Germany.

- The British army liberated Bergen-Belsen on April 15, 1945. With the British forces approaching, SS commanders ordered the camp guards to destroy all prisoners and burn the entire camp. The guards were prepared to shoot the prisoners at 3 o'clock in the afternoon; fortunately, British soldiers entered the camp four hours earlier.

- Once at Bergen-Belsen, Fénelon remained close to her orchestra friends from Auschwitz. Despite being deathly ill from starvation and typhus, Fénelon—known as the "little singer"—managed to sing for the BBC (British Broadcasting Corporation) after being rescued by a young British soldier.

Playing for Time

"STIRB NICHT!" Don't die.

*The German voice made no sense; it had no power to pull me up out of the black gulf into which I was sinking more deeply every second. For days now, I had no longer possessed the strength to keep my eyes open. I wasn't sure whether it was my urine or the fever which alternately warmed and chilled me. **Typhus** was emptying me of life. I was going to die.*

My head felt terrible. The girls' wailing and sobbing and groanings shattered it into needle-sharp fragments, little scraps of broken mirror which sank razorlike into my brain. I ordered my hand to pull them out, but my hand was a skeleton's claw that didn't obey. The bones must have broken through the skin. Or had

Typhus: Severe disease marked by high fever, dark red rash, intense headache, and delirium; initially transmitted by body lice.

the hand actually come off? Impossible. I must keep my hands to play the piano. Play the piano ... those knucklebones at the end of my arm might just manage **Danse macabre.** *The idea actually made me laugh.*

I was horribly thirsty. The **SS** *had cut off the water. It was days since we'd had anything to eat; but even longer since I'd been hungry. I had become weightless, I was floating on a cloud, I was devoured by quicksand ... no, flying in cotton wool. Odd....*

A trick I'd found to cool myself was to wash in my urine. Keeping myself clean was essential to me, and there is nothing unclean about urine. I could drink it if I was thirsty—and I had done so.

I didn't know the time but I did know the date—the girls kept track of that. It was April 15. What did that matter? It was just a day like any other. But where was I exactly? I wasn't at **Birkenau** *anymore. There, there were forty-seven of us, the "orchestra girls." Here in this windowless shed, there were a thousand of us—* **burgeoning** *corpses. What a stench. Now I remembered: Bergen-Belsen. We had arrived here on November 3, 1944.*

My head was in such chaos that I was no longer sure whether it was day or night. I gave up, it was too painful.... I **foundered.**

Above me, over my face, I felt a breath of air, a vague smell, a delicious scent. A voice cut through the layers of fog, stilled the buzzing in my ears; "Meine kleine Sängerin."

"Little singer," that was what the SS called me.

"Stirb nicht!"

That was an order, and a hard one to obey. Anyhow, I was past caring. I opened my eyes a fraction and saw Aufseherin Irma Grese, the SS warden known as Engel, the Angel, because of her

Danse macabre: "Dance of Death"; refers to image of the dead dancing on their graves to lure the living to the afterworld.

SS: The Nazi political police and operators of the concentration camps.

Birkenau: Extermination camp situated next to the Auschwitz camp in Poland.

Burgeoning: Growing or expanding rapidly.

Foundered: Collapsed.

This column of prisoners, being evacuated by forced march from Dachau, walks along the Noerdlichen Muenchner Strasse in Gruenwald, Germany.

looks. The glorious fair **plaits** which surrounded her head like a halo, her blue eyes and dazzling complexion were floating in a fog. She shook me.

"Stirb nicht! Deine englischen Freunde sind da!…"

"What did she say?" asked Anny and Big Irene.

I repeated the German sentence. Irritated, they insisted: "Tell us in French, translate it."

"I forget…."

"But you just said it in German."

More exhausting people; I retired from the **fray**, defeated.

"Come on." They were pleading. "Don't die."

Plaits: Braids.

Fray: Protracted, or pro-longed, fight.

That triggered it off; I repeated automatically: "Don't die. Your friends the English are here."

They were disappointed.

"Is that all?" muttered Little Irene.

*Florette joined in. "The usual rubbish! We've had that with the Russians, the English, and the Yanks. They fed us that dozens of times in **Auschwitz**."*

I heard Big Irene's calm voice: "What if it's true?"

Anny spoke dreamily: "If only one could believe it and it could all end, now, just like that...."

*I **wafted** off, and most of Florette's colourful **rejoinder** was lost on me. God, how hot I was. My tongue was a hunk of cardboard. I felt myself drifting. Then familiar voices reached me, as if from the end of a funnel: "Look Irene, you can see there's no hope. She's stopped breathing, there is no mist on my bit of glass. This really works, they even do it in hospitals."*

"Try again, you never know."

I wondered who was under discussion. Me? How infuriating they were. Admittedly, I had a pretty bad case of typhus, but I hadn't yet given up the ghost. I had to know the end of the story. I would bear witness.

There were bellowings and whistle blasts around the block; a sudden surge of panic swept through the shed. By way of a full-blooded background to the tramp of boots, the sound of machine guns cut steadily through the silence of the firing range. Their rattle ate into our brains, day and night. Some of these gunners were mere children of fifteen or so.

Auschwitz: Concentration camp in Poland.

Wafted: Drifted.

Rejoinder: A sharp or critical answer to an earlier reply.

"They surely can't be going to have us picked off by those kids?"

"They're not noted for their delicacy of feeling," sneered Florette.

"But they're just children!"

All morning the rumour had been going around that they were going to do away with us. But unlike the rumour about the liberation of the camp, this one rang true. **Lunatic** *laughter burst from all over the shed, from the various tiers of the cojas, the name the Polish girls gave our cagelike bunks. A crazed voice asked, "What time is it? I want to know the time."*

"What the hell does it matter?"

"Because they're going to shoot us at three o'clock," the voice informed us confidentially.

Outside, superficially, all seemed normal; but if one concentrated closely, one could hear new sounds: running and calling. I was completely baffled. My head was swelling until it seemed to fill the whole **barracks**, *to hold all the* **din** *within it like a* **reservoir***. I had no more thoughts, I was sinking into the noise, it absorbed me and digested me. I was an echo chamber, I dreamed of silence.*

No, I wasn't dreaming; the silence was real. The machine guns had stopped. It was like a great calm lake, and I let myself drift upon its waters.

I must have fallen asleep again; suddenly, behind me, I heard the familiar sound of the door opening. From the remotest distance a man was speaking; what was he saying? No one was answering him. That was odd. What was going on? Strange words reached my ears—it was a language I knew. It was English!

Tumult *all around, women* **clambering** *down from the cojas. It couldn't be true, I must be* **delirious***.*

Lunatic: Insane.

Barracks: Structures providing temporary housing.

Din: Loud, continued noise.

Reservoir: A place where something is kept in store.

Tumult: Turbulent uprising; commotion.

Clambering: Climbing awkwardly.

Delirious: Affected with delirium, a mental disturbance characterized by intense confusion, nonsensical speech, and hallucinations.

The girls, those girls of whom I'd grown so fond, threw themselves at me, shaking me.

"Fania, wake up! Do you hear, the English are here. You must speak to them."

An arm was slipped under my shoulders and lifted me up: "Say something."

*I was only too eager, but how could I with that **leather spatula** in my mouth? I opened my eyes and saw dim figures through a fog. Then suddenly one came into focus: he was wearing a funny little flat cap on his head, he was kneeling down and thumping his fist on his chest, rocking to and fro repeating: "My God, my God!" He was like a Jew at the Wailing Wall. He had blue eyes, but it wasn't a German blue. He took off his cap, revealing enchanting red hair. His face was dusted with freckles and big childlike tears rolled down his cheeks. It was both awful and funny. "Can you hear me?"*

I murmured, "Yes."

The girls shrieked, "It's all right! She heard, she answered!"

Madness was unleashed around me. They were dancing, lifting their thin legs as high as they could. Some threw themselves down and kissed the ground, rolling in the filth, laughing and crying. Some were vomiting; the scene was incredible, a mixture of heaven and hell.

There was a flurry of questions: "Where have they come from?" "How did they get this far, to this hellhole?" "Did they know we were here? Ask him."

"We found you quite by luck," he answered. "We didn't know there was a concentration camp here. Coming out of Hanover, we chased the Germans through these woods and we saw some SS coming towards us with a white flag."

"Did you slaughter them?" someone chipped in.

Leather spatula: Fénelon is referring to her tongue.

A group of child survivors from Bergen-Belsen arrive in Tel Aviv after being detained in refugee camps on Cyprus.

He looked uncomprehending. I translated.

"I don't know, I'm just one of the soldiers."

Around us, the girls were **clamouring**. "You must kill them, you must kill them all. All."

I was upset by this outburst of hatred, deeply though I felt it; I too wanted to shout, and tried to sit up, but flopped back, too weak. For the first time now I felt myself slipping. Everything became a haze. Yet I smiled, or at least I think I did. I would have been liberated after all. I let myself drift.

Irene noticed, and shouted: "No, no, not her, it's too unfair."

The "unfair" struck me as wonderfully comical.

"Sing, Fania, sing!" someone shrieked. The order **galvanized** me; I opened my mouth desperately. The soldier thought I was at my last gasp; he lifted me out of my filth, took me in his arms, showing no sign of disgust. How comfortable it was, how light I must feel (I weighed sixty-two pounds). Held firmly, head against his chest, drawing my strength from his, I started on the first verse of the Marseillaise. My voice had not died; I was alive.

The fellow was **staggered**. Carrying me in his arms, he rushed outside towards an officer, shouting, "She's singing, she's singing."

The air hit me like a slap. I choked and was reborn. The girls ran out behind us. Technically no doubt I still had typhus, but the moment I found the strength to sing, I felt I'd recovered. The mists cleared; once more I could look around me and see what was happening. And it was well worth observing: Soldiers were arresting the SS and lining them up against the walls. We had **savoured** the thought of this moment so often and with such passion, and now it was a reality. **Deportees** were emerging from every shed. The men from whom we'd been separated for so long were coming towards us, desperately seeking out relatives and acquaintances.

Then I was in clean surroundings, in the SS block. I was bathing in a marvellous sea of **khaki**, and it smelled so good; their very sweat smelled sweet.

We had been liberated by the **infantry**, and now the motorized units were arriving. Through the window I saw the first jeep enter the camp. An officer jumped out, a Dutchman. He looked

Clamouring: Variation of "clamoring"; noisily shouting and creating a disturbance.

Galvanized: Stimulated or excited interest in something.

Staggered: Reeling, tottering, or moving unsteadily.

Savoured: Variation of "savored"; delighted in or relished.

Deportees: People who have been deported, or forced to leave a country.

Infantry: Soldiers equipped and trained to fight on foot.

Survivors wait for British Army rations at Bergen-Belsen.

Tatters: Ragged, dilapidated clothing.

Wraith: Ghostlike image of a living person.

around dazedly and then began to run like a madman, arms outstretched, calling, "Margrett, Margrett!" A woman staggered towards him, her striped **tatters** floating like rags tied to a pole—his wife, three-quarters dead, in a frightening state of filth and decay; and he hugged her, hugged to him the smiling, living **wraith**.

Someone handed me a microphone.

It was strange. The process of breathing exhausted me, my heart was positively economizing on its beats, life had become a remote possibility, yet I straightened up, galvanized by joy, and I sang the Marseillaise again. This time it emerged with a violence and a strength I had never had before and which I shall probably never have again.

*Clearly moved, a Belgian officer sank his hand into his pocket and handed me the most marvellous present: an old lipstick. I couldn't imagine anything lovelier, three-quarters used as it was and despite its uncertain **pedigree**.*

The microphone holder insisted: "Please, miss, it's for the BBC [British Broadcasting Corporation]."

I sang "God Save the King," and tears filled the British soldiers' eyes.

I sang the Internationale and the Russian deportees joined in.

*I sang, and in front of me, around me, from all corners of the camp, creeping along the sides of the shacks, dying shadows and skeletons stirred, rose up, grew taller. A great "Hurrah" burst forth and swept along like a **breaker**, carrying all before it. They had become men and women once again.*

A few months later I learned that on that day, at that time, in London, my cousin heard me sing on the radio and fainted with shock: simultaneously she learned that I had been deported and that I'd just been liberated. (Fénelon, pp. 3-9)

Pedigree: Origin, background, or history.

Breaker: A wave breaking into foam.

What happened next...

When the British army liberated Bergen-Belsen on April 15, 1945, they found 60,000 prisoners in the camp, the majority of them in critical condition. The sight of thousands of unburied corpses lying around the compound sent many soldiers into a state of shock. Since the British had stumbled upon the camp, they were not prepared for the enormous rescue requirements. During the first five days after liberation, approximately 14,000 prisoners died; another 14,000 perished in the following weeks.

After liberation, Bergen-Belsen served as the site of a displaced person's camp until 1951. The British army medical corps provided help in the physical rehabilitation of the former prisoners. Under the leadership of Josef Rosencraft, the camp developed an active social, cultural, and political life.

In the fall of 1945, a British military court tried 48 members of the staff of Bergen-Belsen, including 16 women. Eleven of the accused were found guilty and sentenced to death—including the commander of Bergen-Belsen, Josef Kramer. Kramer earned the reputation as the "Beast of Belsen" by the international press after the discovery of piles of corpses and mass graves by the British troops who rescued the camp. Transferred to Bergen-Belsen from Birkenau in December 1944, he transformed what had been a camp for the privileged into a camp crowded with prisoners in every stage of emaciation (decline) and disease. Kramer and the other war criminals were executed on December 12, 1945.

At the time of liberation, Fania Fénelon was in her twenties. After surviving the Bergen-Belsen camp, she resumed her life's dream of singing. For 25 years, she traveled throughout East Germany from one town to the next, performing in concert halls. In 1977, more than 30 years after World War II ended, she published *Playing for Time,* a book about her experiences at Auschwitz and Bergen-Belsen.

Did you know...

- While imprisoned at Bergen-Belsen, Fania Fénelon fell ill during the typhus epidemic of early 1945. This was the same epidemic that killed Anne Frank and her sister, Margot, who died in March 1945.

- Despite widespread antisemitism (hatred of the Jews) in France, many French people assisted Jews during World War II. Resistance was found throughout France, but especially among Protestants, who felt themselves to be a vulnerable minority. Perhaps the most remarkable demonstration of French resistance occurred in Le Chambon-sur-Lignon. This small Protestant village served as an underground railway, successfully smuggling several thousand Jews to safety.

- American playwright Arthur Miller adapted Fania Fénelon's story for a 1980 made-for-television movie, starring Vanessa Redgrave as Fénelon and Jane Alexander as the leader of the women's orchestra. *Playing for*

Time won several Emmy Awards, including one for outstanding drama special, one for best teleplay (for Miller), one for best lead actress (for Redgrave), and one for best supporting actress (for Alexander).

• Shortly after their rise to power in 1933, the Nazis gained control of all musical activities in Germany. They appointed composer Richard Strauss as leader of the Reich Music Office, dismissed all Jewish professional musicians from their posts, and banned the performance of works by Jewish composers.

For Further Reading

Fénelon, Fania, with Marcelle Routier. *Playing for Time.* Translated by Judith Landry. New York: Atheneum, 1977.

Rochman, Hazel, and Darlene McCampbell. *Bearing Witness: Stories of the Holocaust.* Orchard Press, 1995.

Rubinstein, E. F. *After the Holocaust.* Hamden, CT: Archon Books, 1995.

Albert Speer

Excerpt from *Inside the Third Reich*

Published in 1970

In the spring of 1945, Allied forces (those fighting against Germany) closed in on Germany from both the eastern and western fronts, signaling the final days of Nazi (National Socialist) rule. As daily air raids from Allied bombers reduced cities to rubble, German citizens desperately hoped the war would end. On April 1, 1945, Adolf Hitler and his closest aides retreated to the shelter of the underground bunker located beneath the Chancellory building in the capital city of Berlin. This refuge was situated 50 feet underground and held ample provisions to sustain its inhabitants during a prolonged siege. Unwilling to concede defeat, Hitler commanded his forces to fight to the last man. To repel oncoming Soviet forces, he issued the following order on April 21: "Any commander who holds his men back, will forfeit with his life within five hours." Traumatized by the impending defeat, Hitler believed his advisors and the German nation had failed him and were therefore unworthy of his genius. The following day he announced to his staff that he would stay in Berlin to the end. In a rage of tears and hysteria, he accused his advisors of treason and lies. Normally alert and sharp, Hitler appeared tired and confused.

In those last days, the bunker in Berlin housed Hitler and nearly 50 people who attempted to coordinate the defense of Berlin and sustain the Nazi government. Included in the group was Hitler's mistress, Eva Braun. To fulfill Braun's dearest wish, Hitler consented to marry her before they committed suicide. They wed in the bunker on April 29, 1945. Following the service, Hitler is said to have retired into his office to dictate his last will and political testament to his sec-

retary. In his personal will, Hitler announced his plan to kill
himself, disposed of his property, and explained the reasons
for his marriage to Braun. In his "political testament" he
named Admiral Karl Doenitz to succeed him as *führer*, or
supreme ruler. Hitler also offered his personal views on the
war, claiming he was compelled to engage in conflict by the
forces of "International Jewry." He also expelled SS chief
Heinrich Himmler and Reich marshal Hermann Goering
from the Nazi party for treason (betrayal of one's country).
(*Reich*, pronounced RIKE, is the German word for "empire";
the "Third Reich" was the name given to the German gov-

ernment that existed under Hitler and the Nazi party from 1933 to 1945.) Hitler ended his testament with the following advice for future leaders of Germany: "Above all I charge the leaders of the nation and those under them to scrupulous observance of the laws of race and to merciless opposition to the universal poisoner of all peoples, International Jewry." On the following day, April 30, 1945, Hitler and Braun are believed to have committed suicide.

Albert Speer, minister of armaments and war production, visited the underground bunker in the Chancellory a few times during April. He observed the destruction of the city and the suffering of the German citizens. He also witnessed the final days of Adolf Hitler—the man to whom he had dedicated the last 12 years of his life. The physical and emotional decline of the führer was visibly evident. In the bunker, Hitler no longer commanded the attention of his staff, but rather wandered about talking incoherently.

Of the many accounts of the Nazi era and the fall of Berlin, Speer's are the most authentic, detailed, and revealing. For over a decade, he had been a close friend of Hitler and a member of the inner power circle of the Nazi leadership. Speer wrote *Inside the Third Reich* while serving a prison sentence after the war. The excerpt below contains what may well be the best view the world will ever have of the last days of Adolf Hitler.

Things to Remember While Reading Speer's Memoirs:

- With defeat approaching, Hitler moved to the *Führerbunker* in Berlin, his underground headquarters built beneath the Chancellory garden. Speer's account of Hitler's final days are the most accurate observations available.

- During his last days, Hitler was in a state of extreme nervous exhaustion. Although he was only 56 years old, he appeared to be prematurely senile. One report claimed that he spent hours before his giant war maps, compulsively planning deployments for battalions (military units) that had long been destroyed.

- Many leaders of the Nazi regime deserted Hitler in the final days of the Reich. Albert Speer fell out of favor with Hitler at the end of the war by disobeying his "scorched earth" policy. Hitler had ordered that all remaining German industry, communications, and transport systems be destroyed rather than fall into the hands of the advancing Allied armies. The führer believed that if *he* did not survive, then all of Germany should be destroyed as well.

Inside the Third Reich

*I*n the last weeks of his life, Hitler seemed to have broken out of the rigidity which had gradually overcome him during the preceding years. He became more accessible again and could even tolerate the expression of **dissent**. As late as the winter of 1944, it would have been **inconceivable** for him to enter into a discussion of the prospects of the war with me. Then, too, his flexibility on the question of the scorched earth policy would have been unthinkable, or the quiet way he went over my radio speech. He was once more open to arguments he would not have listened to a year ago. But this greater softness sprang not from a relaxation of tension. Rather, it was **dissolution**. He gave the impression of a man whose whole purpose had been destroyed, who was continuing along his established **orbit** only because of the **kinetic energy** stored within him. Actually, he had let go of the controls and was **resigned to** what might come.

There was actually something **insubstantial** about him. But this was perhaps a permanent quality he had. In retrospect I sometimes ask myself whether this **intangibility**, this insubstantiality, had not characterized him from early youth up to the moment of his suicide. It sometimes seems to me that his seizures of violence could come upon him all the more strongly because there were no human emotions in him to oppose them. He simply could not let anyone approach his inner being because that core was lifeless, empty.

Dissent: Difference in opinion.

Inconceivable: Not able to be conceived or thought of; impossible to imagine.

Dissolution: Dissolving or breaking up an organization.

Orbit: Sphere of activity.

Kinetic energy: Energy associated with motion.

Resigned to: Accepting something without resistance.

Insubstantial: Lacking substance.

Intangibility: Not real; unable to be touched.

Senile: Exhibiting loss of mental facilities, usually associated with old age.

Obstinacy: Stubbornness; being difficult to help, relieve, or soothe.

Sallow: Greyish, greenish-yellow color.

Scrupulously: Very exacting.

Dignitaries: People holding positions of high rank, dignity, or honor.

Lamentable: Mournful; bringing about strong feelings of sorrow.

Hitler Youth: Youth organization of the Nazi party designed to transmit Nazi goals and values to young Germans.

Entourage: Group of attendants or assistants.

Eva Braun: Mistress and companion to Adolf Hitler from 1933 to 1945. Married Hitler on April 29, 1945, then committed suicide with him the following day.

SS: Political police of the Nazi party and personal bodyguards for Adolf Hitler.

*Now, he was shriveling up like an old man. His limbs trembled; he walked stooped, with dragging footsteps. Even his voice became quavering and lost its old masterfulness. Its force had given way to a faltering, toneless manner of speaking. When he became excited, as he frequently did in a **senile** way, his voice would start breaking. He still had his fits of **obstinacy**, but they no longer reminded one of a child's temper tantrums, but of an old man's. His complexion was **sallow**, his face swollen; his uniform, which in the past he had kept **scrupulously** neat, was often neglected in this last period of life and stained by the food he had eaten with a shaking hand....*

*Hitler's last birthday was not actually celebrated. Formerly on this day lines of cars had driven up, the honor guard had presented arms, **dignitaries** of the Reich and of foreign countries had offered their congratulations. Now all was quiet. For the occasion Hitler had, it is true, moved from the bunker to the upper rooms, which in their state of neglect provided a fitting framework to his own **lamentable** condition. A delegation of **Hitler Youth** who had fought well was presented to him in the garden. Hitler spoke a few words, patted one or another of the boys. His voice was low. He broke off rather abruptly. Probably he sensed that his only convincing role now was as an object of pity. Most of his **entourage** avoided the embarrassment of a celebration by coming to the military situation conference as usual. No one knew quite what to say. Hitler received the expressions of good wishes coolly and almost unwillingly, in keeping with the circumstances....*

*Toward midnight **Eva Braun** sent an **SS** orderly to invite me to the small room in the bunker that was both her bedroom and living room. It was pleasantly furnished; she had had some of the expensive furniture which I had designed for her years ago brought from her two rooms in the upper floors of the Chancellery. Neither the proportions nor the pieces selected fitted into the gloomy surroundings. To complete the irony, one of the inlays on the doors of the chest was a four-leaf clover incorporating her initials.*

We were able to talk honestly, for Hitler had withdrawn. She was the only prominent candidate for death in this bunker who displayed an admirable and superior composure. While all the others were abnormal—**exaltedly** heroic like **Goebbels**, bent on saving his skin like **Bormann**, exhausted like Hitler, or in total collapse like Frau Goebbels—Eva Braun radiated an almost gay **serenity**. "How about a bottle of champagne for our farewell? And some sweets? I'm sure you haven't eaten in a long time."

I was touched by her concern; she was the first person to think that I might be hungry after my many hours in the bunker. The orderly brought a bottle of Moet et Chandon, cake, and sweets. We remained alone. "You know, it was good that you came back once more. The Fuehrer had assumed you would be working against him. But your visit has proved the opposite to him, hasn't it?" I did not answer that question. "Anyhow, he liked what you said to him today. He has made up his mind to stay here, and I am staying with him. And you know the rest, too, of course.... He wanted to send me back to Munich. But I refused; I've come to end it here."

She was also the only person in the bunker capable of humane considerations. "Why do so many more people have to be killed?" she asked. "And it's all for nothing.... Incidentally, you almost came too late. Yesterday the situation was so terrible it seemed the Russians would quickly occupy all of Berlin. The Fuehrer was on the point of giving up. But Goebbels talked to him and persuaded him, and so we're still here."

She went on talking easily and informally with me, occasionally bursting out against Bormann, who was pursuing his **intrigues** up to the last. But again and again she came back to the declaration that she was happy here in the bunker.

By now it was about three o'clock in the morning. Hitler was awake again. I sent word that I wanted to bid him good-by. The day had worn me out, and I was afraid that I would not be able to control myself at our parting. Trembling, the prematurely aged man

Exaltedly: With glorification or praise.

Goebbels, Paul Joseph: Propaganda minister and close advisor to Adolf Hitler.

Bormann, Martin: Hitler's private secretary, chief of staff, and close advisor.

Serenity: Calmness.

Intrigues: Plots.

Albert Speer (1905-1981)

Albert Speer was born in Mannheim, the son of a prosperous architect. While completing his architectural studies at Berlin University, he first heard Adolf Hitler speak in 1930. Impressed with Hitler's charisma, Speer joined the Nazi party one year later. Shortly after the Nazis rose to power in 1933, Speer began to receive commissions from the party, including the job of redesigning the official residence of propaganda leader Dr. Joseph Goebbels. As part of one of his early assignments, Speer perfected the Nazi style of public parades. Using inventive lighting techniques, special flag poles, and other decorative and design effects, he created a majestic sense of pageantry for the annual party rallies held at Nuremberg and for other official celebrations.

Speer's success with these early commissions attracted Hitler's attention, and the two developed close ties of friendship. A frustrated architect himself, Hitler appointed the young Speer to be his chief architect and gave him several important design

stood before me for the last time; the man to whom I had dedicated my life twelve years before. I was both moved and confused. For his part, he showed no emotion when we confronted one another. His words were as cold as his hand: "So, you're leaving? Good. **Auf Wiedersehen**." No regards to my family, no wishes, no thanks, no farewell. For a moment I lost my composure, said something about coming back. But he could easily see that it was a white lie, and turned his attention to something else. I was dismissed.

Ten minutes later, with hardly another word spoken to anyone, I left the Chancellor's residence. I wanted to walk once more through the neighboring Chancellery, which I had built. Since the lights were no longer functioning, I contented myself with a few farewell minutes in the Court of Honor, whose outlines could scarcely be seen

Auf Wiedersehen: German farewell, meaning "till seeing again."

(Continued from previous page)

projects, including the creation of the Reich Chancellory in Berlin and the party palace in Nuremberg. In 1937, Hitler named Speer inspector-general of the Reich, making him responsible for turning "Berlin into a real and true capital of the German Reich."

Throughout the late 1930s, Speer held a succession of posts and received many honorary titles and awards. During Allied bombing, he managed to maintain factory production and is credited with prolonging World War II by two years.

However, toward the end of the war, Speer broke with Hitler by violating his orders to destroy all German areas threatened by advancing Allied armies.

Speer was tried before the International Military Tribunal at Nuremberg and sentenced to 20 years in prison. While serving his sentence at Spandau prison, he began writing his memoirs. After his release in 1966, he published his now-famous autobiography, *Inside the Third Reich*, and a subsequent book, *Spandau: The Secret Diaries*.

against the night sky. I sensed rather than saw the architecture. There was an almost ghostly quiet about everything, like a night in the mountains. The noise of a great city, which in earlier years had penetrated to here even during the night, had totally ceased. At rather long intervals I heard the detonations of Russian shells. Such was my last visit to the Chancellery. Years ago I had built it—full of plans, prospects, and dreams for the future. Now I was leaving the ruins of my building, and of the most significant years of my life....

*That evening I returned to Hamburg. The **Gauleiter** offered to have my speech to the people broadcast by the Hamburg station at once, that is, even before Hitler's death. But as I thought of the drama that must be taking place during these days, these very hours, in the Berlin bunker, I realized that I had lost all urge to con-*

Gauleiter: District manager.

tinue my opposition. Once more Hitler had succeeded in paralyzing me **psychically**. To myself, and perhaps to others, I justified my change of mind on the grounds that it would be wrong and pointles to try to intervene now in the course of the tragedy.

I said good-by to **Kaufmann** and set out for Schleswig-Holstein. We moved into our trailer on Eutin Lake. Occasionally I visited **Doenitz** or members of the General Staff, who like me were at a standstill, awaiting further developments. Thus, I happened to be present on May 1, 1945, when Doenitz was handed the radio message significantly **curtailing** his rights as Hitler's successor. [Hitler had originally appointed Doenitz to succeed him as fuehrer, or supreme leader. The new message appointed Doenitz to the lesser position of Reich president.] Hitler had appointed the cabinet for the new President of the Reich: Goebbels was Chancellor; Seyss-Inquart, Foreign Minister; and Bormann, Party Minister. Along with this message came one from Bormann announcing that he would be coming to see Doenitz shortly.

"This is utterly impossible!" Doenitz exclaimed, for this made a farce of the powers of his office. "Has anyone else seen the radio message yet?"

Except for the radioman and the admiral's **adjutant**, Lüdde-Neurath, who had taken the message directly to his chief, no one had. Doenitz then ordered that the radioman be sworn to silence and the message locked up and kept confidential. "What will we do if Bormann and Goebbels actually arrive here?" Doenitz asked. Then he continued **resolutely**: "I absolutely will not cooperate with them in any case." That evening we both agreed that Bormann and Goebbels must somehow be placed under arrest.

Thus Hitler forced Doenitz, as his first official function, to commit an act of illegality: concealing an official document. This was the last link in a chain of deceptions, betrayals, **hypocrisies**, and intrigues during those days and weeks. **Himmler** had betrayed his Fuehrer by **negotiations**; Bormann had carried off

Psychically: By means of extraordinary telepathic (mind-to-mind) or extrasensory (beyond the senses) mental processes.

Kaufmann, Karl: Gauleiter (district manager) of Hamburg, Germany.

Doenitz, Karl: Admiral and leader of the U-boat fleet and designated successor to Adolf Hitler.

Curtailing: Lessening or shortening.

Adjutant: Assistant.

Resolutely: With firm determination; faithfully.

Hypocrisies: Pretending to be what one is not or to believe what one does not actually believe.

Himmler, Heinrich: Chief of the Gestapo and the SS, making him the highest ranking police official in the Third Reich; by 1945, he was supreme commander of the People's Army.

Negotiations: The process of dealing with, managing, or arranging a business settlement.

Expiated: Extinguished or put to an end.

his last great intrigue against Goering by playing on Hitler's feelings; Goering was hoping to strike a bargain with the Allies; Kaufmann had made a deal with the British and was willing to provide me with radio facilities; Keitel was hiring out to a new master while Hitler was still alive—and I myself, finally, had in the past months deceived the man who had discovered me and furthered my career; I had even at times considered how to kill him. All of us felt forced to these acts by the system which we ourselves represented—and forced also by Hitler, who for his part had betrayed us all, himself and his people.

On this note the Third Reich ended.

On the evening of that May 1, when Hitler's death was announced, I slept in a small room in Doenitz's quarters. When I unpacked my bag I found the red leather case containing Hitler's portrait. My secretary had included it in my luggage. My nerves had reached their limit. When I stood the photograph up, a fit of weeping overcame me. That was the end of my relationship to Hitler. Only now was the spell broken, the magic extinguished. What remained were images of graveyards, of shattered cities, of millions of mourners, of concentration camps. Not all these images came into my mind at this moment, but they were there, somehow present in me. I fell into a deep, exhausted sleep.

Two weeks later, staggered by the revelations of the crimes in the concentration camps, I wrote to the chairman of the ministerial cabinet, Schwerin-Krosigk: "The previous leadership of the German nation bears a collective guilt for the fate that now hangs over the German people. Each member of that leadership must personally assume his responsibility in such a way that the guilt which might otherwise descend upon the German people is **expiated.**

With that, there began a segment of my life which has not ended to this day. (Speer, pp. 471-89)

What happened next...

In 1946, after the war had ended, Speer was brought before the International Military Tribunal at Nuremberg. Unlike other Nazi leaders, Speer acknowledged his responsibility for all crimes committed by the Third Reich, even those which he claimed he had no knowledge of, such as the mass extermination of Jewish people. Speer felt that "there is a common responsibility for such horrible crimes in an authoritarian system." During the trial, he recognized that he was personally responsible for the slave labor used in armament factories under his authority. By collaborating with the SS, Speer had exploited concentration camp prisoners for his war production goals. However, he argued that his work was "technological and economic," not political. During his testimony, he claimed to have rejected violence—not on humanitarian grounds, but because violence against prisoners would hinder his war production output.

The tribunal limited its judgment to Speer's involvement with the slave labor program, finding him guilty of war crimes and crimes against humanity. According to the judges, "in mitigation, it must be recognized that ... in the closing stages of the war he was one of the few men who had the courage to tell Hitler that the war was lost and to take steps to prevent the senseless destruction of production facilities." Speer was sentenced to 20 years' imprisonment, despite the Russian vote to hang him. After serving his complete sentence, he was released in 1966.

While serving his sentence at the Spandau prison, Speer completed the first draft of his memoirs, which became the bestselling book *Inside the Third Reich,* published in 1970. His detailed, dispassionate account gives a firsthand view of the inner workings of the Nazi hierarchy. Scholars continue to debate Speer's repeated claims that he had no knowledge of the murderous actions that took place at the extermination camps. Many contend that he knew far more than he ever admitted publicly.

By ignoring the consequences of his authority and actions, Speer represents the typical Nazi technocrat (a technical expert with managerial authority). Through his absolute loyalty to Hitler and his remarkable talents and efficiencies, Speer—along with others like him—enabled the totalitarian German state to conduct horrendous and lawless activities for 12 years. On September 1, 1981, Speer died during a visit to London.

Did you know...

- Hitler committed suicide on April 30, 1945. Fearing that his body would be desecrated (treated disrespectfully or outrageously) by the Russians when they captured Berlin, he left special instructions for his bodyguards and assistants. According to his wishes, his body and that of Eva Braun were carried into the garden at the Reich Chancellory, covered with fuel, and burned.

- Speer participated in designing the German autobahns, or superhighways, which were used for the rapid transport of troops and armaments during the war. Today, the Autobahn highway system in western Germany is considered to be the finest in Europe. This four-lane superhighway system totals some 34,400 miles and links major German cities, much like the American Interstate Highway system.

- Brought before the International Military Tribunal at Nuremberg in 1946, Speer was one of only two Nazi defendants to admit their guilt in the crimes of the Third Reich.

For Further Reading

Berwick, Michael. *The Third Reich*. New York: Putnam, 1971.

Rubin, Arnold. *The Evil That Men Do: The Story of the Nazis*. New York: J. Messner, 1977.

Speer, Albert. *Inside the Third Reich*. Translated by Richard Winston and Clara Winston. New York: Galahad Books, 1970.

Tunis, John Roberts. *His Enemy, His Friend*. New York: William Morrow, 1967.

Simon Wiesenthal

"The Knife"

Excerpt from *The Murderers among Us: The Simon Wiesenthal Memoirs*

Edited by Joseph Wechsberg
Published in 1967

Shortly after annexing Austria in 1938, German Nazi (National Socialist) leaders established the Mauthausen concentration camp near the town of Linz in Upper Austria. During World War II, the Nazis interned nearly 200,000 people at Mauthausen, where many worked as slave laborers at the nearby granite quarry. Estimates suggest about 120,000 inmates perished there—representing the highest percentage of victims among all the concentration camps in the Nazi system. On April 25, 1945, invading American and Soviet troops converged at Torgau on the Elbe River south of Berlin, effectively cutting off Mauthausen from Germany. American forces liberated the camp on May 5 and found masses of sick and dying people lying among the dead. The International Red Cross transferred thousands of the worst cases to hospitals in Germany, Switzerland, and Sweden. Despite the rescue efforts of the Red Cross and Allied forces, almost 3,000 of Mauthausen's prisoners died after liberation.

One of the prisoners liberated at Mauthausen was Simon Wiesenthal, then a 37-year-old Jewish man from Buczacz, Poland. Nearly six feet tall but weighing less than 100 pounds, Wiesenthal had been assigned to the "death block," which housed prisoners who were not able to work and were therefore expected to die. He arrived at Mauthausen in February 1945, after barely surviving a long, difficult journey from the Buchenwald concentration camp in Germany, which had been evacuated due to the advancing Red (Soviet) Army. Of the 3,000 Buchenwald prisoners placed in open trucks for the journey from Germany to Austria, only 1,200 survived the exposure to the elements and lack of food and

water. Another 180 died during the final four-mile march into the camp compound. Wiesenthal himself had fallen down during that relatively short trek due to exhaustion. One of the SS guards shot at him but missed, leaving his body in the snow to be retrieved by a collection truck sent out before the town's inhabitants awoke. During the night, the workers came upon Wiesenthal's seemingly lifeless body, assumed he was dead, and hoisted him on top of the corpses piled in the back of the truck. At the camp crematorium (furnace for the burning of dead bodies), prisoner workers noticed Wiesenthal was still alive and smuggled him into the

Wiesenthal   **397**

barracks (temporary housing for the prisoners). Fortunately, Wiesenthal survived the three months until American forces took over the Mauthausen camp in May of 1945.

During the four years spent behind the barbed wire of various Nazi institutions, Wiesenthal promised himself that if he survived he would spend the rest of his life as a "deputy for many people who are not alive." Shortly after his release, he began working for the War Crimes section of the U.S. Army, stationed in Austria to track down members of the SS division of the Nazi party. Originally created as a special bodyguard unit for Adolf Hitler and other Nazi leaders, the SS (*Schutzstaffel*), or Security Guard, became a symbol of terror as its members gained increasing power within the party. These black-shirted, black-booted men operated the extensive Nazi camp system. As an organization, the SS was responsible for the deaths of 11 million people, including 6 million Jews and 1 million children. Most perished at extermination camps, but hundreds of thousands died at the concentration camps as well. These innocent victims came from nearly every European country and were killed because the Germans felt they threatened the purity of the Aryan race. Wiesenthal and others focused their efforts on finding fugitive (runaway; escaped) SS members and rarely concerned themselves with the crimes committed by enlisted men in the German armed forces (*Wehrmacht*) or rank and file members (meaning members as distinguished from leaders) of the Nazi party.

As a way to gather evidence against SS men after the war, Wiesenthal organized a network of correspondents at the various displaced-persons (DP) centers set up by the Western Allies to house refugees from the camps. (Refugees are people who flee to a foreign country to escape danger or persecution.) More than 100,000 survivors lived temporarily in about 200 DP centers located in Germany and Austria. According to Wiesenthal's careful directions, correspondents gathered eyewitness reports of killings and torture, disregarding all secondhand accounts of such incidents. Wiesenthal obtained photographs of SS members and circulated copies to the refugee camps, since many inmates were never told their guards' names. He created an extensive cross-index system that allowed connections to be made between the locale of the crimes, the names of the criminals, and the names of witnesses.

In 1947, after leaving the American service, Wiesenthal formed the Jewish Historical Documentation Center in Linz, Austria. His files were first used during preparations for the trials of Nazi war criminals at Nuremberg and later at an American military trial of SS men who had worked as guards at the Dachau concentration camp. In 1959, after 14 years of investigative work, Wiesenthal succeeded in tracking down Adolf Eichmann—the SS lieutenant colonel who organized the transports of Jews from all over Europe to the Nazi death camps located in Poland. After the defeat of Germany, many SS members and high-ranking Nazi officials went underground and relied on the secret organization *Odessa* to arrange for their escape to Buenos Aires, Argentina. Eichmann, whom Wiesenthal traced to Argentina, was brought to Israel for trial, found guilty, and hanged in 1962.

After the Eichmann trial, Wiesenthal accepted an offer to head up a war victims' documentation center in Vienna. A year later, following disputes with the center's board, he started a separate organization called the Federation of Jewish Victims of the Nazi Regime. Since 1947, Wiesenthal has brought 1,100 Nazi war criminals to trial. Having lost 89 family relatives during the Holocaust, he remains committed to seeking justice in the cases of those who escaped punishment after World War II. In the excerpt below from *The Murderers among Us,* Wiesenthal describes the painstaking and difficult challenges involved in the conviction of war criminals. Perhaps one of the most difficult obstacles is time—as the years pass, many Jewish people simply wish to put the horrors of the Nazi regime behind them.

Things to Remember While Reading the Chapter from Wiesenthal's Memoirs:

- Charged with war crimes, Fritz Murer was tried in Graz, Austria, in 1963. As part of an SS detail, Murer had worked at the Vilna ghetto located in what is today Lithuania. ("Vilna" is referred to as "Wilna" in Wiesenthal's account below.)

- Since evidence collected immediately after the war was not allowed to be used in court, testimony against Murer had to be recollected from current sources. This requirement severely limited the prosecution's case, which could only rely on survivors' recollections of events that took place in the Vilna ghetto 20 years earlier.

- When Wiesenthal has evidence against a Nazi war criminal—but does not receive cooperation from the authorities—he reveals his information to the press. Experience has taught him that public outrage is a powerful weapon for bringing criminals to justice.

The Knife

*T*he trial by jury against Murer opened in Graz on June 10, 1963. The **indictment** charged him with having committed "murder by his own hands" in fifteen specific cases; later the public prosecutor added two more cases. Over a dozen witnesses had arrived from Germany, Israel, and the United States. One of the most important witnesses for the prosecution was Jacob Brodi, before whose own eyes Murer had shot his son Daniel at the exit of the Wilna ghetto. Brodi was now sixty-eight. After the war he had emigrated to America, and he now lived alone on a small isolated farm in New Jersey. He was a lonely man. He didn't want to see people, led a simple life, and had refused to accept the German **restitution** money to which he was entitled. Twenty years had gone by since the day he had seen his boy killed by Murer, but the passage of time had not helped Brodi to forget. Every day and almost every night he saw the scene at the entrance to the Wilna ghetto.*

*When I first wrote to ask him to come to Graz to testify, he flatly refused. He explained he couldn't bear the thought of facing the murderer. I wrote him several letters. I said we owed it to our dead to tell the living what had happened. Die Zeit, a respected German weekly, had just protested "against the new wave of distrust" and defended the new generation, "which knows Nazi crimes only from history books." The **apologists** were working*

Indictment: Charging with a crime.

Restitution: Restoration or giving an equivalent for some injury or loss.

Apologists: People who argue on behalf of someone else or a cause.

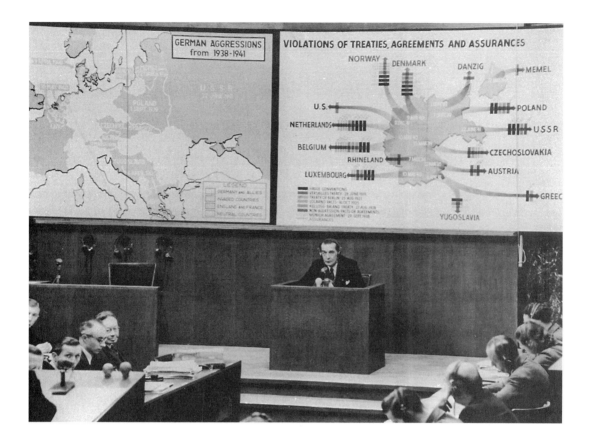

GERMAN AGGRESSIONS
from 1938-1941

VIOLATIONS OF TREATIES, AGREEMENTS AND ASSURANCES

NORWAY

DENMARK

DANZIG

MEMEL

U.S.

POLAND

NETHERLANDS

USSR

BELGIUM

CZECHOSLOVAKIA

RHINELAND

AUSTRIA

LUXEMBOURG

GREEC

YUGOSLAVIA

LEGEND
GERMANY and ALLIES
INVADED COUNTRIES
ENGLAND and FRANCE
NEUTRAL COUNTRIES

overtime. I explained to Brodi that his silence would no longer help his boy, but it might help to save boys of Daniel Brodi's age who knew these crimes only from the history books. A courtroom with a jury, a judge, a prosecutor would make the defendant look real, not like a character out of a history book, certainly not like a hero. There was no answer. I didn't expect to hear from Brodi again. The day before the trial he sent me a cable. He would take a plane and would be there in time.

Four days later I met Jacob Brodi in his room at the Hotel Sonne in Graz, where all witnesses had been put up. He was a tired man with white hair and deep circles around his eyes. With his sunburned, wrinkled face, he looked more like an American farmer from the Middle West than like a refugee from the Wilna ghetto. I told him I was glad he had come. He would be a key witness. His *testimony couldn't fail to **sway** the jury. The trial was not going well, from the prosecution's point of view. After four days, Murer still **cynically** denied everything. One witness after the other had stepped forward and identified him, but Murer said they were making a mistake; they were taking him for somebody else. He had never so much as touched a Jew. He had never seen a dead Jew. He was innocent, victim of a monstrous error.*

*Now Brodi said to me: "I hear that Murer's two sons sit in the front row of the courtroom with his wife and **sneer** at the witnesses."*

*I nodded. The boys thought this was a great show. They laughed and **grimaced**. Two foreign newspapermen who covered the trial were so shocked that they asked the presiding judge why he failed to call the boys to order. He told the correspondents that he hadn't seen the boys.*

Brodi said quietly : "They'll stop sneering when I am called to the stand." He looked at me piercingly and said: "I didn't come here to testify, I came to act." He opened his waistcoat and pulled out a long knife. Brodi spoke without emotion, a man who had made up his mind. "I was able to obtain a plan of the courtroom. I know that the witness stand is close to where Murer sits. Murer killed my child before my eyes. Now I'm going to kill him with this knife before the eyes of his wife and children."

I could see that he was deadly serious. He said he'd thought about it for the past twenty years. He no longer believed in human justice, he said. He had lost faith in God's justice. He would take justice into his own hands. He was not afraid of the consequences. His life was finished anyway. It had been finished that day in the ghetto twenty years ago.

I said: "If you try to kill Murer, you will be treated like a murderer yourself."

Sway: Affect; exerting a guiding or controlling influence on.

Cynically: Shown with distrust.

Sneer: To smile at, laugh at, or mock with facial contortions that express scorn or open disapproval.

Grimaced: Made facial expressions showing disgust or disapproval.

"Yes. But great lawyers will come to my defense."

"That's beside the point. No matter what your motives are, the world will call you a murderer. The Nazis are just waiting for such a thing to happen. They will say: 'Look at these Jews who always talk so much about justice. They accuse Murer of murder, and they are murderers themselves. So Murer killed Jews, and a Jew killed him. What's different about that?' That's the way they will argue."

Brodi gave a shrug, unconvinced.

*"Think of **Eichmann**," I said. "He could have been executed without a trace in Argentina. But the Israelis knew it was necessary to drag him across the ocean and risk **antagonizing** world opinion and being accused of violating international law. Why? Because Eichmann had to be tried. The trial was more important than the defendant. Eichmann was already a dead man when he entered the courtroom. But the trial would convince millions of people—those who knew nothing, or who did not want to know, or those who knew deep in their hearts but wouldn't admit it even to themselves. All of them saw the seedy, bald man in the glass box who had engineered the 'final solution'—the killing of six million people. They heard the evidence, they read the newspapers, they saw the pictures. And at long last they knew not only that it was true but that it was much worse than anyone could imagine."*

Brodi shook his head. "I am not here for the State of Israel. I am not here for the Jewish people. I came here as the father of my murdered child." He stared at me out of hard, pitiless eyes. I wished desperately that he had been able to cry. But perhaps he couldn't cry any more.

I said: "If you try to harm Murer, all our work will have become useless. We cannot achieve our purpose by using their methods.

Eichmann, Adolf: Coordinator of mass deportations of European Jews. He escaped to Argentina after the fall of Germany in 1945; was captured, tried, and executed in 1961.

Antagonizing: To provoke or bring on the hostility of.

You've read the Bible, Jacob Brodi. You know the Commandment: 'Thou shalt not kill.' I want Murer, not you, to leave the courtroom as a convicted murderer."

He shook his head.

"Words, Mr. Wiesenthal, nothing but words. It's so easy for you. Your child was not murdered. My boy was murdered. I told you I did not want to come. You said it was necessary. Well, I am here now. And you know why I came."

I turned away. I couldn't bear the expression in his eyes. I talked for a long time, although I do not remember exactly what I said. I talked about myself: Why I had decided to do what I had done for the past twenty years—because someone had to do it, for our children and for their children—but not out of hatred.

"I still cry sometimes, Mr. Brodi, when I hear what happened to children in the concentration camps," I said. "I did cry when I heard about your boy. Because he could have been my boy. Your child was also my child. Do you really believe I could go on with my work if I didn't feel that way?"

I grasped his shoulders. Suddenly Jacob Brodi put his head on my shoulder. I felt a convulsion go through his body. He cried. We stood there for a while, without saying a word. When I left his room a few minutes later, I carried his knife with me.

Jacob Brodi was called to the stand the following day. He never glanced at Murer. He told his experience in a toneless voice, as though it had happened to someone else. It was very quiet in the courtroom. Even Murer's boys sensed what this lonely man went through during his testimony. They didn't sneer at him. The defense didn't want to question Brodi. He was dismissed. After he left the courtroom, Murer got up and once more said that the witness must have been mistake. Murer had not shot the boy. Maybe it was someone else.

*The trial lasted a week. Foreign journalists sensed that the mood in the courtroom was definitely in favor of the defendant. Some jurors, dressed in the traditional green **loden** costumes, watched Murer with unconcealed sympathy. Some tried to follow the proceedings fairly, but they seemed to be in the minority. The leading paper in Graz supported the arguments of Murer's defense attorneys. He was said to have received many sympathetic letters from political friends.*

The audience was pleased when the defense succeeded in confusing one witness. He became carried away by emotion as he told the court what had happened and mixed up a detail. Another witness was not certain about a date. He described one of Murer's crimes, and then Murer proved conclusively that he had not been in Wilna at that time. Naturally, the testimony of these people was discredited.

Among the witnesses for the defense was Martin Weiss, Murer's former assistant in the ghetto. Weiss had been brought to Graz from Straubing prison in Bavaria, where he was serving a life sentence for mass murder. When Weiss pointed out that "some Lithuanian officers wore uniforms similar to Murer's," there was a satisfied murmur among the audience.

The testimony of the witnesses for the prosecution was received with icy silence. (I was called "manhunter" by Murer's lawyer.) Israel Sebulski, now living in Munich, told the court that his fifteen-year-old son had been mercilessly beaten by Murer, and as a result had lost his mind and the use of his legs and was now in an institution. Mrs. Tova Rajzman of Tel Aviv swore that Murer had shot her sister because she had taken a piece of bread from a Polish woman. In his rage, she said, he had later killed three other women and a man who happened to be standing nearby. As Mrs. Rajzman recalled the scene, she was overcome by the memory and began to scream.

Loden: Thick woolen cloth, usually an overcoat, colored a dull greyish-green.

Simon Wiesenthal (1908—)

Simon Wiesenthal was born in Buczacz, which was part of the Austro-Hungarian empire, then a portion of Poland and now of the Ukraine. After Wiesenthal's father was killed in World War I, his mother took the family to Vienna, Austria, to escape anti-Jewish violence. The family returned to Buczacz when she remarried, enabling Wiesenthal to graduate from the local gymnasium (high school) in 1928. Quota restrictions for Jewish students prevented his admission to the Polytechnic Institute in Lvov, so he attended the Technical University of Prague and received a degree in architectural engineering in 1932. Wiesenthal married Cyla Mueller in 1936 and worked as an architect in Lvov, near Cracow, Poland.

Shortly after taking control of Poland in 1939, the Soviets began harassing native Jews. Wiesenthal lost several family members and was forced to close his business, becoming a mechanic in a bedspring factory. Later he saved himself, his wife, and his mother from deportation (forced exit) by bribing a police commissar (department head). When the Germans displaced the Russians in 1941, Wiesenthal and his

"Don't scream in the courtroom!" said Hofrat Dr. Peyer, the presiding judge.

"Forgive me, Your Honor," said Mrs. Rajzman. "But it was terrible. My sister's blood spilled over my feet."

"Couldn't it have been somebody else who did it?"

"No, Your Honor. It was Murer. I remember him from the time he first came into the ghetto. He beat me in the street. When he walked through the ghetto, everybody had to step down from the pavement, and then had to bow and take off their hats."

Dr. Schumann, the prosecutor, had prepared himself thoroughly for his task. He had studied Murer's files in Frankfurt and

(Continued from previous page)

wife were assigned to a forced labor camp and worked at Ostbahn Works, a railroad repair shop. Due to her "Aryan" appearance and false documentation, his wife managed to escape and go into hiding. In 1943, when all laborers at Ostbahn were ordered to go to the nearby concentration camp, Wiesenthal escaped and hid successfully for nearly six months before being captured.

After being apprehended in June 1944, Wiesenthal was forced to march westward to Plaszow, then on to Gross-Rosen, and on to Buchenwald. This "death march" ended at Mauthausen in upper Austria, with Wiesenthal barely alive. At the time of liberation on May 5, 1945, he weighed less than 100 pounds and could not walk.

At war's end, Wiesenthal dedicated his life to gathering and preparing evidence on Nazi criminals and the atrocities they committed. Since 1947, he and his researchers have brought over 1,100 Nazi criminals to justice. As he approaches his nineties, Wiesenthal continues his relentless search for war criminals. In addition to *The Murderers among Us,* Wiesenthal has published other books, including *I Hunted Eichmann.*

Munich. In his summing up speech, he pointed out that the witnesses had identified Murer beyond any doubt. He appealed to the jury to pass judgment on the defendant as they would on the murderer of their own children.

"In at least six cases there is no reasonable doubt about the defendant's guilt," said the prosecutor. "I want you to know that this trial has already badly hurt the illusion of us Austrians being a Kulturvolk."

After four hours, the jury returned a verdict of "not guilty." In Austria, the exact count of the jury votes is announced in the courtroom. The foreman of the jury said that in two of the seventeen *cases there had been a tie of four to four. He had cast his ballot in favor of Murer.*

I was not in Graz that day. Reporters later told me that the people in the courtroom had cheered and applauded when Murer's acquittal was announced. Some had brought in flowers while the jury was still deliberating. Now they rushed up to Murer with the bouquets.

An American diplomat who visited friends in Graz the following day and wanted to send flowers to his hostess was told in three florist shops that there was nothing left. Everything had been bought up for the trial. Murer left the courtroom a triumphant hero. He was seen being driven off in the Mercedes of Rudolph Hochreiner, a Nazi who had been indicted for the murder of nine Jews and had been acquitted.

*There was a storm of **indignation** throughout Austria. With few exceptions, the Austrian press is anti-Nazi and **democratic**. Newspapers representing nearly all political groups **denounced** the verdict as Justizskandal, a **travesty** of justice. In Vienna, Catholic students pinned yellow stars on their chests and marched in protest through the streets, shouting "Murer is a murderer! Murer must be punished!" Afterward they attended a service of **penitence** in Michaeler Church to express **remorse** for the crimes committed by Christians against Jews.*

The prosecutor appealed the verdict. Austria's Supreme Court has granted an appeal with respect to one charge: a case I had discovered in which Murer had been seen committing a murder by two different witnesses. The witnesses knew nothing of each other, now live in different parts of the world, but described the same scheme independently. Murer will be tried once more. Justice may still prevail.

I met Jacob Brodi in the lobby of a Vienna hotel a few days after Murer's acquittal. He looked through me as if I hadn't been

Indignation: Anger aroused by injustice.

Democratic: Governed by the people.

Denounced: Criticized; proclaimed something to be evil or blameworthy.

Travesty: A distorted imitation; a parody or caricature.

Penitence: Showing sorrow or remorse for sins or faults.

Remorse: Troubles arising from a sense of guilt for past wrongs.

there. I understood. I may have saved Murer's life. It is not a very pleasant thought, but there was nothing else I could have done. (Wiesenthal, pp. 70-77)

What happened next...

As of mid-1997, Simon Wiesenthal continued his quest for justice despite repeated death threats. The neo-Nazi World Union of National Socialists offered $120,000 for his death in 1965. Due to his neighbors' concerns for their safety, he moved the Documentation Center from his apartment in Vienna, Austria, to another building a block away. Nearly two decades later, a bomb planted by neo-Nazis destroyed his home in Vienna. Today, he continues to receive ominous threats and hate mail.

In 1977, the Simon Wiesenthal Center was established in Los Angeles, California. Named in honor of Wiesenthal, the center offers a national outreach program providing education for junior and senior high school students. As part of its commitment to focus on political issues related to the Holocaust, the center campaigned to cancel the statute of limitations on war crimes in West Germany and to force South American governments to surrender Nazi criminals. (A statute of limitations is a law which states that an offense cannot be punished after a certain period of time has elapsed—that is, after a given number of years have passed following the commission of a crime. Although the offenses of the Nazis occurred more than 50 years ago, Wiesenthal wanted to ensure that any surviving Nazis could and would be punished whenever they were caught.) The center's educational services have produced award-winning films, books, publications, and exhibitions, including the 1982 film *Genocide,* which won an Oscar for best documentary. The Simon Wiesenthal Center has offices in Israel, France, and Canada.

Did you know...

- Tracking down Nazi criminals requires painstaking investigative work. For example, some 6,000 SS men worked at Auschwitz, but only 900 are known by name.

Wiesenthal has determined the current names and addresses for one-third of this group, or 300 former SS Auschwitz staff members.

- In 1963, Wiesenthal identified Gestapo officer Karl Silberbauer, who arrested Anne Frank and her family in Amsterdam, Holland. Silberbauer had returned to Austria after the war and resumed his post at the Vienna police department.

- The Berlin Document Center contains the world's largest collection of Nazi documents, totaling over 50 million pages. The repository includes original lists of Nazi party members and SS personnel files.

- Author Ira Levin patterned the character of Jakov Liebermann in *The Boys from Brazil* after Wiesenthal. In the movie version of Levin's novel, Sir Laurence Olivier played the role and received an Oscar nomination for his performance.

- Wiesenthal is also portrayed in Frederick Forsyth's novel *The Odessa File*. In the film version, Israeli actor Shmeul Rodonsky plays Wiesenthal.

- Wiesenthal refers to the Nazis he is looking for as "the heroes." After they are brought to justice and are in custody, he calls them his "clients."

For Further Reading

Friedman, Carl. *Nightfather: A Novel*. New York: Persea Books, 1994.

Noble, Iris. *Nazi Hunter: Simon Wiesenthal*. New York: J. Messner, 1979.

Rochman, Hazel, and Darlene McCampbell. *Bearing Witness: Stories of the Holocaust*. New York: Orchard Books, 1995.

Wiesenthal, Simon. *The Murderers among Us: The Simon Wiesenthal Memoirs*. Edited by Joseph Wechsberg. New York: McGraw Hill, 1967.

Justice Robert H. Jackson

Opening Address for the United States

Delivered at the Nuremberg Trials, November 21, 1945
Text taken from Nazi Conspiracy and Aggression, Volume I

With World War II still raging, the Allied powers (those fighting against Germany) publicly declared their intentions of prosecuting (or bringing legal action against; pursuing punishment of) Nazi war criminals. As early as 1942, American, British, and Soviet representatives began negotiating a series of agreements concerning the standards for punishing those responsible for the Holocaust. Just months after the war ended, the Allies formally agreed to the charter of the International Military Tribunal (IMT), the court formed to prosecute major war criminals of the Axis (Germany and its allies) powers. This agreement, known as the London Agreement of August 8, 1945, was subsequently endorsed by 19 member states of the newly established United Nations.

Opening statements for the public trial of 22 major Nazi war criminals took place on October 18, 1945. The term "major" refers to those military or political leaders whose crimes did not occur in a specific geographical region. After holding the opening session in Berlin, the trial was moved to Nuremberg due to the lack of adequate accommodations in the war-ravaged German capital. One of the reasons the Allied powers chose Nuremberg was for its symbolic significance to the Nazi legacy. The former site of spectacular party rallies, Nuremberg was also the namesake of the Nazi racialist laws that denied German Jews their citizenship status. Due to its location, these proceedings became known as the Nuremberg Trials.

The IMT represented the first time in history that countries aligned themselves to bring to justice those responsible for waging war and mistreating civilians and prisoners of war

The press gallery at the Nuremberg Trials.

(POWs). Never before had legal proceedings been initiated against the leaders of an enemy nation. The establishment of this tribunal created controversy for several reasons: (1) The guidelines for the prosecution and the definitions of the crimes were established on August 8, 1945, three months *after* Germany's surrender; under the widely accepted legal principle of "ex post facto," defendants cannot be prosecuted under laws created after an act is committed. (2) Military justice often shields subordinates who carry out "superior orders," meaning the orders dictated by superior officers. (3) Lastly, individuals who perform actions as representatives of a state or government—a concept referred to as "act of state"—are not held personally accountable. The charter of the IMT expressly prohibited pleas of both "superior orders" and "act of state." After the extent of the crimes committed by the Nazis became apparent through testimony, legal criticism regarding these issues largely subsided.

Reich Marshal Hermann Goering received the death penalty at Nuremberg. Two hours before his scheduled execution, Goering killed himself with a smuggled cyanide (poison) capsule.

The evidence used in the Nuremberg Trials came mostly from Nazis records. Following the defeat of Germany, the Allies found volumes of files and ledgers regarding every aspect of the Nazi government's workings. The invading American armies sent military investigative teams to comb through German records to secure relevant documents. One of their most important acquisitions, found behind a false wall in an old castle in Eastern Bavaria, included the letters of Alfred Rosenberg, one of the party's leading supporters of anti-Jewish ideology.

The Search for Justice Begins

The results of the International Military Tribunal held in Nuremberg, Germany, returned the following verdicts:

Hermann Goering, Reich Marshal, Commander-in-chief of *Luftwaffe*—*Death Penalty.*

Rudolf Hess—*Life in Prison.*

Joachim von Ribbentrop, Reich Foreign Minister—*Death Penalty.*

Ernst Kaltenbrunner, Chief of the Security Police—*Death Penalty.*

Wilhelm Keitel, Chief of the High Command of the Armed Forces—*Death Penalty.*

Alfred Rosenberg, Party philosopher and Reich Minister—*Death Penalty.*

Hans Frank, Governor-General of Polish-occupied territory—*Death Penalty.*

Wilhelm Frick, Former Minister of the Interior—*Death Penalty.*

Julius Streicher, Founder of antisemitic newspaper *Der Sturmer*—*Death Penalty.*

Walther Funk, President of the *Reichsbank,* 1939—*Life in Prison.*

Hjalmar Schacht, Minister of Economics and President of the *Reichsbank,* 1933-1939—*Acquitted.*

The IMT tried the defendants according to several major categories of crimes, including crimes against peace, war crimes, and crimes against humanity. The prosecution of "crimes against peace" upheld the principle that the only legal war was one of self-defense or against aggression (in response to unprovoked attack). The definition of "war crimes" included the ill-treatment of civilians in occupied territory and prisoners of war. And acts of persecution against civilian (nonmilitary) groups on the basis of religion, race, or politics constituted "crimes against humanity." The violence perpetrated against European Jews by the Nazis fell into the categories of war crimes and crimes against humanity.

Excerpted below is an opening statement from the Nuremberg Trials by the American chief counsel, Justice

(Continued from previous page)

Karl Doenitz, Supreme Commander of the Navy, German Chancellor (Successor to Adolf Hitler)—*10 Years.*

Erich Raeder, Supreme Commander of the Navy, 1928-1943—*Life in Prison.*

Balder von Schirach, Führer of Hitler Youth—*20 Years.*

Fritz Sauckel, Plenipotentiary for Labor Allocation—*Death Penalty.*

Alfred Jodl, Chief of Operations Staff of the Armed Forces—*Death Penalty.*

Franz von Papen, Ambassador in Vienna, 1934-1938, Ambassador in Turkey, 1939-1944—*Acquitted.*

Artur Seyss-Inquart, Minister of the Interior, Reich Governor of Austria, Reich Commissioner for the occupied Netherlands—*Death Penalty.*

Albert Speer, Minister of Armaments and War Production—*20 Years.*

Constantin von Neurath, Minister of Foreign Affairs, 1932-1938; Reich Protector of Bohemia and Moravia, 1939-1943—*15 Years.*

Hans Fritzsche, Head of Radio Division of the Propaganda Ministry—*Acquitted.*

Martin Bormann (*in absentia*), Deputy Führer—*Death Penalty.*

Robert H. Jackson. The world watched and listened as prosecutors from each of the major Allied nations—the United States, Great Britain, France, and the Soviet Union—presented the case against the 22 accused Nazi leaders. Twenty of these accused men attempted to persuade the court of their innocence.

Things to Remember While Reading Justice Jackson's Address at the Nuremberg Trials:

- The following address by Justice Robert H. Jackson opened the American case before the International Military Tribunal on November 21, 1945. Jackson had been appointed representative of the United States and chief of council by an executive order signed by President Harry S Truman.

- Justice Jackson refers to the United Nations in his remarks cited below. This international organization was founded on October 24—less than a month before Jackson's speech.

- During the war, the Allies agreed to a series of provisions concerning the future punishment of Nazis who committed war crimes. On November 1, 1943, the Allied nations signed the Moscow Declaration, granting local authorities access to war criminals who were not tried internationally.

OPENING ADDRESS FOR
THE UNITED STATES

May it please Your Honors,

*The privilege of opening the first trial in history for crimes against the peace of the world **imposes** a grave responsibility. The wrongs which we seek to condemn and punish have been so calculated, so **malignant** and so devastating, that civilization cannot tolerate their being ignored because it cannot survive their being repeated. That four great nations, flushed with victory and stung with injury **stay the hand of vengeance** and voluntarily submit their captive enemies to the judgment of the law is one of the most significant tributes that Power ever has paid to Reason.*

*This **tribunal**, while it is novel and experimental, is not the product of **abstract** speculations nor is it created to **vindicate** legalistic theories. This **inquest** represents the practical effort of four of the most mighty of nations, with the support of seventeen more, to utilize International Law to meet the greatest **menace** of our times—aggressive war. The common sense of mankind demands that law shall not stop with the punishment of petty crimes by little people. It must also reach men who possess themselves of great power and make deliberate and concerted use of it*

Imposes: Establishes; brings with it.

Malignant: Evil in nature.

Stay the hand of vengeance: Stop, halt, or suspend the types of punishment that would result from feelings of revenge.

Tribunal: Court of justice.

Abstract: Difficult to understand.

Vindicate: Confirm; justify; defend.

Inquest: Official inquiry or examination before a jury.

Menace: Threat; danger.

to set in motion evils which leave no home in the world untouched. It is a cause of this magnitude that the United Nations will lay before Your Honors.

In the prisoners' **dock** sit twenty-odd broken men. **Reproached** by the humiliation of those they have led almost as bitterly as by the **desolation** of those they have attacked, their personal capacity for evil is forever past. It is hard now to perceive in these miserable men as captives the power by which as Nazi leaders they once dominated much of the world and terrified most of it. Merely as individuals, their fate is of little consequence to the world.

What makes this inquest significant is that those prisoners represent sinister influence that will lurk in the world long after their bodies have returned to dust. They are living symbols of racial hatreds, of terrorism and violence, and of the arrogance and cruelty of power. They are symbols of fierce nationalisms and militarism, of **intrigue** and war-making which have embroiled Europe generation after generation, crushing its manhood, destroying its homes, and impoverishing its life. They have so identified themselves with the philosophies they conceived and with the forces they directed that any tenderness to them is a victory and an encouragement to all the evils which are attached to their names. Civilization can afford no compromise with the social forces which would gain renewed strength if we deal **ambiguously** or indecisively with the men in whom those forces now **precariously** survive.

What these men stand for we will patiently and **temperately** disclose. We will give you undeniable proofs of incredible events. The catalogue of crimes will omit nothing that could be conceived by a **pathological** pride, cruelty, and lust for power. These men created in Germany, under **Fuehrerprinzip**, a National Socialist **despotism** equalled only by the dynasties of the ancient East. They took from the German people all those dignities and freedoms that we hold natural and inalienable rights in every human being. The people were compensated by inflaming and gratifying hatreds

Dock: A place in a criminal court where prisoner sits or stands.

Reproached: Disgraced; expressed disapproval.

Desolation: Sadness; loneliness; ruin.

Intrigue: Plots.

Ambiguously: With doubt or uncertainty.

Precariously: Dependent on chance, circumstances, or uncertain developments.

Temperately: Marked by moderation.

Pathological: Abnormal; diseased.

Fuehrerprinzip: "Leadership principle"; Hitler's concept of a brutal authoritarian state.

Despotism: Government in which a single ruler has complete and absolute power.

Arrogance: Feelings or impressions of superiority.

Serfdom: The state of existing in the lowest class of a hierarchical society; members of such a class are bound to an agricultural life, have no hopes of ever owning their own land, and are subject to the will of a master or king.

Invincible: Incapable of being conquered.

Hapless: Unfortunate.

Bestiality: Status of a lower animal.

Prostrate: Completely exhausted or overcome; reduced to helplessness.

Demoralized: Thrown into disorder.

Litigation: Legal contest using formal judicial processes (judge and jury).

Well thumbed precedents: Frequently used examples that serve as a model for something else.

Commence: Begin.

SS: Secret police of the Nazis who operated the concentration camps.

*toward those who were marked as "scape-goats." Against their opponents, including Jews, Catholics, and free labor the Nazis directed such a campaign of **arrogance**, brutality, and annihilation as the world has not witnessed since the pre-Christian ages. They excited the German ambition to be a "master race," which of course implies **serfdom** for others. They led their people on a mad gamble for domination. They diverted social energies and resources to the creation of what they thought to be an **invincible** war machine. They overran their neighbors. To sustain the "master race" in its war making, they enslaved millions of human beings and brought them into Germany, where these **hapless** creatures now wander as "displaced persons." At length **bestiality** and bad faith reached such excess that they aroused the sleeping strength of imperiled civilization. Its united efforts have ground the German war machine to fragments. But the struggle has left Europe a liberated yet **prostrate** land where a **demoralized** society struggles to survive. These are the fruits of the sinister forces that sit with these defendants in the prisoners' dock.*

*In justice to the nations and the men associated in this prosecution, I must remind you of certain difficulties which may leave their mark on this case. Never before in legal history has an effort been made to bring within the scope of a single **litigation** the developments of a decade, covering a whole Continent, and involving a score of nations, countless individuals, and innumerable events. Despite the magnitude of the task, the world has demanded immediate action. This demand has had to be met, though perhaps at the cost of finished craftsmanship. In my country, established courts, following familiar procedures, applying **well thumbed precedents**, and dealing with the legal consequences of local and limited events, seldom **commence** a trial within a year of the event in litigation. Yet less than eight months ago today the courtroom in which you sit was an enemy fortress in the hands of German **SS** troops. Less than eight months ago nearly all our witnesses and documents were in enemy hands. The*

Wilhelm Keitel, Chief of the High Command of the Armed Forces, also received the death penalty at Nuremberg. Despite his request to be shot as a soldier, Keitel was hanged on October 16, 1946.

law had not been **codified**, no procedure had been established, no Tribunal was in existence, no usable courthouse stood here, none of the hundreds of tons of official German documents had been examined, no prosecuting staff had been assembled, nearly all the present defendants were at large, and the four prosecuting powers had not yet joined in common cause to try them. I should be the last to deny that the case may well suffer from incomplete researches and quite likely will not be the example of professional work which any of the prosecuting nations would normally wish

Codified: Systematized.

Jackson

Render: Deliver; agree upon and report.

Candidly: Honestly; without bias.

Disparity: Having marked distinctions or differences.

Temperate: Moderate; mild.

Victor: The winner in a fight or struggle.

Vanquished: Defeated.

Futility: Uselessness.

Station: Position or level of authority in an organization.

Notoriety: Being widely and unfavorably known.

Retribution: Punishment.

Poisoned chalice: To kill the Nazis without a fair trial.

Detachment: Separation; freedom from prejudice.

Integrity: Soundness; honesty.

Commend: Recommend as worthy of notice.

Posterity: Future generations.

*to sponsor. It is, however, a completely adequate case to the judgment we shall ask you to **render**, and its full development we shall be obliged to leave to historians.*

*Before I discuss particulars of evidence, some general considerations which may affect the credit of this trial in the eyes of the world should be **candidly** faced. There is a dramatic **disparity** between the circumstances of the accusers and of the accused that might discredit our work if we should falter, in even minor matters, in being fair and **temperate**.*

*Unfortunately, the nature of these crimes is such that both prosecution and judgment must be by **victor** nations over **vanquished** foes. The worldwide scope of the aggressions carried out by these men has left but few real neutrals. Either the victors must judge the vanquished or we must leave the defeated to judge themselves. After the First World War, we learned the **futility** of the latter course. The former high **station** of these defendants, the **notoriety** of their acts, and the adaptability of their conduct to provoke retaliation make it hard to distinguish between the demand for a just and measured **retribution**, and the unthinking cry for vengeance which arises from the anguish of war. It is our task, so far as humanly possible, to draw the line between the two. We must never forget that the record on which we judge these defendants today is the record on which history will judge us tomorrow. To pass these defendants a **poisoned chalice** is to put it to our own lips as well. We must summon such **detachment** and intellectual **integrity** to our task that this trial will **commend** itself to **posterity** as fulfilling humanity's aspirations to do justice.*

At the very outset, let us dispose of the contention that to put these men to trial is to do them an injustice entitling them to some special consideration. These defendants may be hard pressed but they are not ill used. Let us see what alternative they would have to being tried.

More than a majority of these prisoners surrendered to or were tracked down by forces of the United States. Could they expect us to make American custody a shelter for our enemies against the **just wrath** of our Allies? Did we spend American lives to capture them only to save them from punishment? Under the principles of the Moscow Declaration, those suspected war criminals who are not to be tried internationally must be turned over to individual governments for trial at the scene of their outrages. Many less responsible and less **culpable** American-held prisoners have been and will be turned over to other United Nations [members] for local trial. If these defendants should succeed, for any reason, in escaping the condemnation of this Tribunal, or if they obstruct or abort this trial, those who are American-held prisoners will be delivered up to our continental Allies. For these defendants, however, we have set up an International Tribunal and have undertaken the burden of participating in a complicated effort to give them fair and **dispassionate** hearings. That is the best known protection to any man with a defense worthy of being heard.

If these men are the first war leaders of a defeated nation to be prosecuted in the name of the law, they are also the first to be given a chance to plead for their lives in the name of the law. Realistically, the Charter of this Tribunal, which gives them a hearing, is also the source of their only hope. It may be that these men of troubled conscience, whose only wish is that the world forget them, do not regard a trial as a favor. But they do have a fair opportunity to defend themselves—a favor which these men, when in power, rarely extended to their fellow countrymen. Despite the fact that public opinion already condemns their acts, we agree that here they must be given a presumption of innocence, and we accept the burden of proving criminal acts and the responsibility of these defendants for their commission....

We would also make clear that we have no purpose to incriminate the whole German people. We know that the Nazi Party was

Just wrath: Rightful anger.

Culpable: Criminally guilty.

Dispassionate: Not affected by personal or emotional involvement.

*not put in power by a majority of the German vote. We know it came to power by an evil **alliance** between the most extreme of the Nazi revolutionists, the most unrestrained of the German **reactionaries**, and the most aggressive of the German militarists. If the German populace had willingly accepted the Nazi program, no Stormtroopers would have been needed in the early days of the Party and there would have been no need for concentration camps or the **Gestapo**, both of which institutions were **inaugurated** as soon as the Nazis gained control of the German state. Only after* these lawless innovations proved successful at home were they taken abroad....

This war did not just happen—it was planned and prepared for over a long period of time and with no small skill and **cunning**. The world has perhaps never seen such a concentration and stimulation of the energies of any people as that which enabled Germany twenty years after it was defeated, disarmed, and dismembered to come so near carrying out its plan to dominate Europe. Whatever else we may say of those who were the authors of this war, they did achieve a stupendous work in organization, and our first task is to examine the means by which these defendants and their fellow conspirators prepared and **incited** Germany to go to war....

It is my purpose to open the case, particularly under Count One of the **Indictment**, and to deal with the common plan or conspiracy to achieve ends possible only by resort to crimes against peace, war crimes, and crimes against humanity. My emphasis will not be on individual **barbarities** and **perversions** which may have occurred independently of any central plan. One of the dangers ever present is that this trial may be **protracted** by details of particular wrongs and that we will become lost in a "wilderness of single instances." Nor will I now dwell on the activity of individual defendants except as it may contribute to **exposition** of the common plan.

The case as presented by the United States will be concerned with the brains and authority [behind] all the crimes. These defendants were men of a station and rank which does not soil its own hands with blood. They were men who knew how to use lesser folk as tools. We want to reach the planners and designers, the **inciters** and leaders without whose evil architecture the world would not have been for so long **scourged** with the violence and lawlessness, and **wracked** with the agonies and convulsions, of this terrible war. (Jackson, pp. 114-20)

Alliance: Bond or connection.

Reactionaries: Those who resist or oppose a force.

Gestapo: Police force of the Nazi party.

Inaugurated: Begun.

Cunning: Craftiness; cleverness.

Incited: Moved to action; spurred on.

Indictment: Being charged with a crime.

Barbarities: Acts of extreme cruelty.

Perversions: Corruptions.

Protracted: Prolonged.

Exposition: An example or explanation to convey something difficult to understand.

Inciters: Ones who move others to action.

Scourged: Afflicted; chastised.

Wracked: Ruined; destroyed.

Robert H. Jackson (1892-1954)

Robert H. Jackson was born in Spring Creek, Pennsylvania, and practiced law in Jamestown, New York. He gained prominence in the New York State Democratic party in the late 1920s, when future U.S. president Franklin D. Roosevelt was New York governor. In 1938, Jackson became U.S. solicitor general; two years later he was appointed by President Roosevelt to the post of attorney general. From 1941 until his death in 1954, Jackson served as associate justice of the U.S. Supreme Court, the highest court in the land. American president Harry S Truman signed an executive order making Jackson chief counsel, or representative of the United States, at the Nuremberg Trials from 1945 to 1946. Throughout his tenure on the Supreme Court, he fought for civil liberties and supported judicial restraint.

What happened next...

The Nuremberg Trials ended on October 1, 1946—which happened to coincide with Yom Kippur, the "Day of Atonement" (making amends for a wrong or injury) in the Jewish faith. Most defendants either claimed that they had followed orders or that they had no knowledge of the atrocities being committed. Of the 22 Nazi leaders tried, twelve were sentenced to death, three received life imprisonment, four received prison terms of 10 to 20 years, and three were found not guilty.

Several notorious Nazi leaders escaped prosecution. Adolf Hitler and his propaganda minister Joseph Goebbels committed suicide on April 30, 1945. Martin Bormann, Hitler's closest aide, is suspected to have died in the fall of Berlin at the close of the war. Chief of the SS (security guard) and Interior Minister Heinrich Himmler committed suicide while in the custody of the British on May 23, 1945. And Adolf Eichmann, the Nazi leader responsible for organizing Jewish deportations to death camps, escaped from an American internment camp in 1946. (Survivor Simon Wiesenthal tracked Eichmann to Argentina in 1958; Eichmann was brought to Israel for trial, found guilty, and hanged in 1962.)

The term "Nuremberg Trials" is also used to refer to proceedings other than those held in 1945-1946. The city hosted trials for 177 additional criminals charged with membership in criminal organizations, including members of the Gestapo, SS, civil servants, and industrialists. A multinational tribunal also convened to examine Japanese war crimes. The vast majority of war crime proceedings involved "minor" war criminals who were prosecuted in the countries where the crimes had taken place.

Did you know...

- The entire transcript of the International Military Tribunal fills 42 thick volumes.

- Spandau Prison, situated in West Berlin, became the exclusive location for the internment, or holding, of the Nazi war criminals convicted at the Nuremberg Trials. France, England, the Soviet Union, and the United States rotated guard responsibilities on a monthly basis.

- The last surviving defendant from the Nuremberg Trials, Rudolf Hess, died in his prison cell at Spandau Prison on August 17, 1987. British authorities claim the 93-year-old inmate hanged himself after 41 years of imprisonment. Hess's family, however, disputes the circumstances of his death.

For Further Reading

Altshuler, David A. *Hitler's War against the Jews: A Young Reader's Version of "The War against the Jews, 1933-1945."* Original version by Lucy S. Dawidowicz. New York: Behrman House, 1978.

Berwick, Michael. *The Third Reich*. New York: Putnam, 1971.

Nazi Conspiracy and Aggression, Volume I. Office of United States Chief of Counsel for Prosecution of Axis Criminality. Washington, DC: U.S. Government Printing Office, 1946.

Hannah Arendt

Excerpt from *Eichmann in Jerusalem*

First published in 1963

Efforts to punish the criminals responsible for the Holo-caust continued long after the end of World War II. Adolf Eichmann, one of the most notorious criminals of the Nazi regime, escaped prosecution by disappearing after the war. Considered a specialist in "Jewish affairs," Eichmann had played a critical role in the Nazi plot by organizing and implementing the party's anti-Jewish measures. Among his dubious accomplishments was the establishment of the ghetto system, where Jews in occupied countries were forced to live during the war years. His office also coordinated the transport of masses of people by rail to the ghettos, transit camps, concentration camps, and extermination centers.

In 1944, Eichmann personally supervised the rapid deportation of hundreds of thousands of Hungarian Jews. Between March and July of that year, over 440,000 victims were rounded up and transported to labor and death camps—a staggering number in just over three months. Toward the end of 1944, when the gas chambers at Auschwitz ceased functioning and the rail system became less reliable, Eich-mann ordered 76,000 Jews to embark on "death marches" from Hungary to Austria.

When the war ended, Eichmann was arrested by Allied forces (those countries fighting against Germany) who were unaware of his key role in the Holocaust. He escaped unrec-ognized from a minimum security internment camp in the American zone and went into hiding. His flight from justice ended 15 years later, when Israeli agents seized him in Argentina, where he had been living with his family. The Israelis brought him to Jerusalem to face trial for war crimes.

Confronting a panel of three judges, Eichmann and his attorney based his defense on five arguments: (1) They contended he could not receive a fair trial in the Jewish state of Israel, before Jewish judges. (2) They claimed Eichmann was the victim of kidnaping, since he had been captured and transported against his will. (3) According to the defense, Eichmann was charged with violating laws put into effect after World War II; under the legal concept of "ex post facto," these laws should not have applied to him. (4) Since the alleged crimes occurred in Nazi Germany, the defense argued that the courts of Israel did not have jurisdiction to prosecute.

(5) The defense contended that Eichmann had merely carried out "acts of state" and should not be held personally accountable for the policies of his government. The judges rejected all of these arguments and ordered the trial to proceed.

Scholar Hannah Arendt followed the trial and wrote her observations in a well-known book titled *Eichmann in Jerusalem*. Born in Germany, Arendt herself experienced the terror of Nazism before fleeing to France. In her controversial analysis, she proposes that Eichmann demonstrated the existence of true evil in ordinary humans.

Things to Remember While Reading *Eichmann in Jerusalem*:

- After 14 years of investigative research, Simon Wiesenthal, a Holocaust survivor, tracked Eichmann to Argentina. Eichmann had been living under an assumed name with his family in suburban Buenos Aires, Argentina.

- Eichmann pleaded "not guilty *in the sense* of the indictment" to each count of the indictment. His unusual qualification was never questioned by the prosecution, nor the defense attorney, nor any of the three judges. It can be assumed that Eichmann meant that he was not guilty of any crimes because he acted as a representative of the German government, obeying laws imposed by Adolf Hitler.

- The trial of Eichmann in Jerusalem was modeled after the Nuremberg Trials of major Nazi war criminals held in 1945-1946.

Eichmann In Jerusalem

Née: Used to identify a woman by her maiden name.

*Otto Adolf, son of Karl Adolf Eichmann and Maria **née** Schefferling, caught in a suburb of Buenos Aires on the evening of May 11, 1960, flown to Israel nine days later, brought to trial in the District Court in Jerusalem on April 11, 1961, stood accused on fifteen counts: "together with the others" he had committed* crimes against the Jewish people, crimes against humanity, and war crimes during the whole period of the Nazi regime and especially during the period of the Second World War. The Nazis and Nazi **Collaborators** (Punishment) Law of 1950, under which he was tried, provides that "a person who has committed one of these … offenses … is liable to the death penalty." To each count Eichmann pleaded : "Not guilty in the sense of the **indictment**."

In what sense then did he think he was guilty? In the long cross-examination of the accused, according to him "the longest ever known," neither the defense nor the prosecution nor, finally, any of the three judges ever bothered to ask him this obvious question. His lawyer, Robert Servatius of Cologne, hired by Eichmann and paid by the Israeli government (following the **precedent** set at the Nuremberg Trials, where all attorneys for the defense were paid by the **Tribunal** of the victorious powers), answered the question in a press interview: "Eichmann feels guilty before God, not before the law," but this answer remained without confirmation from the accused himself. The defense would apparently have preferred him to plead not guilty on the grounds that under the then existing Nazi legal system he had not done anything wrong, that what he was accused of were not crimes but "acts of state," over which no other state has **jurisdiction** ("par in parem imperium non habet"), that it had been his duty to obey and that, in Servatius' words, he had committed acts "for which you are decorated if you win and go to the **gallows** if you lose." (Thus [Nazi propaganda leader Paul Joseph] Goebbels had declared in 1943: "We will go down in history as the greatest statesmen of all times or as their greatest criminals.") Outside Israel (at a meeting of the Catholic Academy in Bavaria, devoted to what the Rheinischer Merkur called the "ticklish problem" of the "possibilities and limits in the coping with historical and political guilt through criminal proceedings"), Servatius went a step farther, and declared that "the only **legitimate** criminal problem of the Eichmann trial lies in pronouncing judgment against his Israeli captors, which so far has not been done"—

Collaborators: Those working jointly with others or together.

Indictment: Formal written explanation of criminal charges.

Precedent: Something done that may serve as a rule to follow in future situations of a similar nature.

Tribunal: A court of justice.

Jurisdiction: Power.

Gallows: Frame used to execute a prisoner by hanging.

Legitimate: In accordance with the law.

Journalists at the Eichmann trial, May 30, 1961.

a statement, incidentally, that is somewhat difficult to **reconcile** with his repeated and widely publicized utterances in Israel, in which he called the conduct of the trial *"a great spiritual achievement,"* comparing it favorably with the Nuremberg Trials.

Eichmann's own attitude was different. First of all, the indictment for murder was wrong: *"With the killing of Jews I had nothing to do. I never killed a Jew, or a non-Jew, for that matter— I never killed any human being. I never gave an order to kill either*

Reconcile: To make consistent.

a Jew or a non-Jew; I just did not do it," or, as he was later to qual-
ify this statement, "It so happened ... that I had not once to do it"—
for he left no doubt that he would have killed his own father if he
had received an order to that effect. Hence he repeated over and over
(what he had already stated in the so-called Sassen documents, the
interview that he had given in 1955 in Argentina to the Dutch jour-
*nalist Sassen, a former **S.S.** man who was also a **fugitive** from jus-*
tice, and that, after Eichmann's capture, had been published in part
by <u>Life</u> *in this country and by* <u>Der Stern</u> *in Germany) that he could*
*be accused only of "aiding and abetting" the **annihilation** of the*
Jews, which he declared in Jerusalem to have been "one of the great-
est crimes in the history of Humanity."...

Would he then have pleaded guilty if he had been indicted as
*an **accessory** to murder? Perhaps, but he would have made impor-*
tant qualifications. What he had done was a crime only in retro-
spect, and he had always been a law-abiding citizen, because
Hitler's orders, which he had certainly executed to the best of his
ability, had possessed "the force of law" in the Third Reich. (The
*defense could have quoted in support of Eichmann's **thesis** the tes-*
timony of one of the best-known experts on constitutional law in
the Third Reich, Theodor Maunz, currently Minister of Education
and Culture in Bavaria, who stated in 1943 ...: "The command of
the Führer ... is the absolute center of the present legal order.")
Those who today told Eichmann that he could have acted differ-
ently simply did not know, or had forgotten, how things had been.
He did not want to be one of those who now pretended that "they
had always been against it," whereas in fact they had been very
eager to do what they were told to do. However, times change, and
he, like Professor Maunz, had "arrived at different insights." What
he had done he had done, he did not want to deny it; rather, he pro-
*posed "to hang myself in public as a warning example for all **anti-***
***Semites** on this earth." By this he did not mean to say that he*
*regretted anything: "**Repentance** is for little children."...*

S.S.: Nazi political police
and operators of concen-
tration camps.

Fugitive: A person who
flees or tries to escape.

Annihilation: Complete
destruction.

Accessory: Contributor
to a crime.

Thesis: A proposition that
needs to be proved.

Anti-Semites: Persons who
discriminate against Jews.

Repentance: Regret
of misdeeds.

*Even under considerable pressure from his lawyer, he did not change this position. In a discussion of [German Nazi leader and chief of police Heinrich] Himmler's offer in 1944 to exchange a million Jews for ten thousand trucks, and his own role in this plan, Eichmann was asked: "Mr. Witness, in the negotiations with your superiors, did you express any pity for the Jews and did you say there was room to help them?" And he replied: "I am here under oath and must speak the truth. Not out of mercy did I launch this transaction"—which would have been fine, except that it was not Eichmann who "launched" it. But he then continued, quite truthful: "My reasons I explained this morning," and they were as follows: Himmler had sent his own man to Budapest to deal with matters of Jewish **emigration**. (Which, incidentally, had become a flourishing business: for enormous amounts of money, Jews could buy their way out. Eichmann, however, did not mention this.) It was the fact that "here matters of emigration were dealt with by a man who did not belong to the Police Force" that made him **indignant**, "because I had to help and to implement **deportation**.... Matters of emigration, on which I considered myself an expert, were assigned to a man who was new to the unit.... I was fed up.... I decided that I had to do something to take matters of emigration into my own hands."*

*Throughout the trial, Eichmann tried to clarify, mostly without success, this second point in his plea of "not guilty in the sense of the indictment." The indictment implied not only that he had acted on purpose, which he did not deny, but out of base motives and in full knowledge of the criminal nature of his deeds. As for the base motives, he was perfectly sure that he was not what he called an "innerer Schweinehund," a dirty bastard in the depths of his heart; and as for his conscience, he remembered perfectly well that he would have had a bad conscience only if he had not done what he had been ordered to do—to ship millions of men, women, and children to their death with great zeal and the most **meticulous** care. This, admittedly, was hard to take. Half a dozen psy-*

Emigration: Moving persons from their home country to another.

Indignant: Filled with anger caused by injustice.

Deportation: Forcibly sent out of the country.

Meticulous: Extremely careful.

Hannah Arendt (1906-1975)

Hannah Arendt was born in Hannover, Germany. She was educated at the universities of Marburg, Freiburg, and Heidelberg, and left Germany for France in 1933, when the Nazis took over Germany. When France fell to Germany, Arendt fled to the United States. She worked for Jewish relief agencies until 1952, then devoted herself primarily to university teaching and writing. Arendt was a teacher, writer, and political philosopher, holding professorial positions at Princeton University, the University of Chicago, and the New School for Social Research. Her writings and teachings expressing bleak views on the human condition have generated much controversy. Arendt's books include: *The Origins of Totalitarianism* (1951), *The Human Condition* (1958), *Eichmann in Jerusalem* (1963), *On Revolution* (1963), *On Violence* (1970), *Crises of the Republic* (1972), and *The Life of the Mind* (1977).

chiatrists had certified him as "normal"— "More normal, at any rate, than I am after having examined him," one of them was said to have exclaimed, while another had found that his whole psychological outlook, his attitude toward his wife and children, mother and father, brothers, sisters, and friends, was "not only normal but most desirable"—and finally the minister who had paid regular visits to him in prison after the Supreme Court had finished hearing his appeal reassured everybody by declaring Eichmann to be "a man with very positive ideas." Behind the comedy of the soul experts lay the hard fact that his was obviously no case of moral let alone legal insanity. (Mr. Hausner's recent revelations in the <u>Saturday Evening Post</u> of things he "could not bring out at the trial" have contradicted the information given informally in Jerusalem. Eichmann, we are now told, had been alleged by the psychiatrists to be "a man obsessed with a dangerous and **insatiable** urge to kill," "a perverted, **sadistic** personality." In which case he would have belonged in an insane **asylum**.) Worse, his

Insatiable: Incapable of being satisfied.

Sadistic: Delighting in cruelty.

Asylum: Institution for the care of the mentally disturbed.

was obviously also no case of insane hatred of Jews, of fanatical anti-Semitism or **indoctrination** *of any kind. He "personally" never had anything whatever against Jews; on the contrary, he had plenty of "private reasons" for not being a Jew hater. To be sure, there were fanatic anti-Semites among his closest friends, for instance László Endre, State Secretary in Charge of Political (Jewish) Affairs in Hungary, who was hanged in Budapest in 1946; but this, according to Eichmann, was more or less in the spirit of "some of my best friends are anti-Semites."*

Alas, nobody believed him. The prosecutor did not believe him, because that was not his job. Counsel for the defense paid no attention because he, unlike Eichmann, was, to all appearances, not interested in questions of conscience. And the judges did not believe him, because they were too good, and perhaps also too conscious of the very foundations of their profession, to admit that an average, "normal" person, neither feeble-minded nor indoctrinated nor **cynical**, *could be perfectly incapable of telling right from wrong. They preferred to conclude from occasional lies that he was a liar—and missed the greatest moral and even legal challenge of the whole case. Their case rested on the assumption that the defendant, like all "normal persons," must have been aware of the criminal nature of his acts, and Eichmann was indeed normal insofar as he was "no exception within the Nazi regime." However, under the conditions of the Third Reich only "exceptions" could be expected to act "normally." This simple truth of the matter created a dilemma for the judges which they could neither resolve nor escape....*

Eichmann, it will be remembered, had steadfastly insisted that he was guilty only of "aiding and abetting" in the commission of the crimes with which he was charged, that he himself had never committed an **overt** *act. The judgment, to one's great relief, in a way recognized that the prosecution had not succeeded in proving him wrong on this point. For it was an important point; it touched*

Indoctrination: Instruction in a particular opinion or point of view.

Cynical: Showing distrust.

Overt: Open to view.

upon the very **essence** of this crime, which was no ordinary crime, and the very nature of this criminal, who was no common criminal; by implication, it also took **cognizance** of the weird fact that in the death camps it was usually the inmates and the victims who had actually wielded "the fatal instrument with [their] own hands." What the judgment had to say on this point was more than correct, it was the truth: "Expressing his activities in terms of Section 23 of our Criminal Code Ordinance, we should say that they were mainly those of a person **soliciting** by giving counsel or advice to others and of one who enabled or aided others in [the criminal] act." But "in such an enormous and complicated crime as the one we are now considering, wherein many people participated, on various levels and in various modes of activity—the planners, the organizers, and those executing the deeds, according to their various ranks—there is not much point in using the ordinary concepts of counseling and soliciting to commit a crime. For these crimes were committed **en masse**, not only in regard to the number of victims, but also in regard to the numbers of those who perpetrated the crime.... The extent to which any one of the many criminals was close to or remote from the actual killer of the victim means nothing, as far as the measure of his responsibility is concerned. On the contrary, in general the degree of responsibility increases as we draw further away from the man who uses the fatal instrument with his own hands...."

What followed the reading of the judgment was routine. Once more, the prosecution rose to make a rather lengthy speech demanding the death penalty, which, in the absence of **mitigating circumstances**, was mandatory, and Dr. Servatius replied even more briefly than before: the accused had carried out "acts of state," what had happened to him might happen in the future to anyone, the whole civilized world faced this problem, Eichmann was "a **scapegoat**," whom the present German government had abandoned to the court in Jerusalem, contrary to international law, in order to clear itself of responsibility. The competence of the

Essence: The real or ultimate nature of a hing or an idea.

Cognizance: Knowledge; awareness.

Soliciting: Requesting.

En masse: A group or collection considered as a whole.

Mitigating circumstances: Conditions that make something less severe.

Scapegoat: One that bears the blame for others.

The main hall at Beit Ha'Am in Jerusalem. It was in this area that most of the Eichmann trial took place.

Statute of limitations: Time limit after which legal action cannot proceed.

court, never recognized by Dr. Servatius, could be construed only as trying the accused "in a representative capacity, as representing the legal powers vested in [a German court]"—as, indeed, one German state prosecutor had formulated the task of Jerusalem. Dr. Servatius had argued earlier that the court must acquit the defendant because, according to the Argentine **statute of limitations**, *he had ceased to be liable to criminal proceedings against him on May 7, 1960, "a very short time before the abduction"; he now argued, in the same vein, that no death penalty could be pronounced* *because capital punishment had been abolished unconditionally in Germany.*

*Then came Eichmann's last statement: His hopes for justice were disappointed; the court had not believed him, though he had always done his best to tell the truth. The court did not understand him: he had never been a Jew-hater, and he had never willed the murder of human beings. His guilt came from his obedience, and obedience is praised as a **virtue**. His virtue had been abused by the Nazi leaders. But he was not one of the ruling **clique**, he was a victim, and only the leaders deserved punishment. (He did not go quite as far as many of the other low-ranking war criminals, who complained bitterly that they had been told never to worry about "responsibilities," and that they were now unable to call those responsible to account because these had "escaped and deserted" them—by committing suicide, or by having been hanged.) "I am not the monster I am made out to be," Eichmann said. "I am the victim of a **fallacy**." He did not use the word "scapegoat," but he confirmed what Servatius had said: it was his "profound conviction that [he] must suffer for the acts of others." After two more days, on Friday, December 15, 1961, at nine o'clock in the morning, the death sentence was pronounced. (Arendt, pp. 21-27; 246-48)*

Virtue: A desirable quality or trait.

Clique: An exclusive group of persons.

Fallacy: Mistaken idea.

What happened next...

Adolf Eichmann's trial took place from April 11 to August 14, 1961. He was found guilty of committing crimes against the Jewish people, crimes against humanity, and war crimes. Following the conviction of Eichmann in the district court of Jerusalem, his case was appealed to the Israeli Supreme Court. After the Supreme Court upheld (agreed with and enforced) the verdict of the lower court, Eichmann was hanged at midnight on May 31, 1962. His body was cremated and the ashes scattered in the Mediterranean Sea, outside the perimeter of Israeli territory.

The Eichmann trial renewed worldwide interest in the atrocities committed at the hands of the Nazis. For many young adults, especially in Israel and Germany, the media coverage surrounding the trial sparked interest in the Holocaust—an event they had only heard about but did not experience firsthand. "Nazi-hunter" Simon Wiesenthal, who helped track down and locate Eichmann in Argentina, received widespread recognition, which in turn allowed him to continue and expand his searches with renewed vigor.

Hannah Arendt, the author who wrote about Eichmann's trial, generated considerable controversy by expressing her personal opinion regarding his guilt. In her book *Eichmann in Jerusalem,* Arendt maintains that Eichmann was an ordinary man, not motivated by any special prejudices or hatreds. By merely following orders, he acted in a manner that was socially accepted at the time. Other scholars have denounced this view, claiming Eichmann to be the personification of the inhumane Nazi ideology—someone who performed his responsibility of exterminating millions of Jewish people with enthusiasm and brutal efficiency. According to his own reports to his superior, Heinrich Himmler, 4 million Jews died in extermination camps and 2 million more were murdered by the mobile killing units known as *Einsatzgruppen.*

Did you know...

- The Eichmann trial generated worldwide publicity and was the first war crimes trial to be shown on television.

- Immediately after World War II, the Nazis used assets they had siphoned from their victims (money and goods stolen from the Jews) to finance an underground organization known as *Odessa.* This secret organization helped Nazis escape to other countries and avoid arrest by the Allies. Travel arrangements were frequently made to Buenos Aires, Argentina. Many former Nazis also fled to Canada and the United States.

- Eichmann was responsible for altering the Theresienstadt ghetto in preparation for the International Red Cross visit in June 1944. Before allowing the Red Cross to tour the ghetto, he arranged for certain temporary improvements, including the installation of dummy

Scholar Hannah Arendt generated considerable controversy by expressing her personal opinion regarding Adolf Eichmann's guilt.

stores, a cafe, a school, and flower gardens. To ease conditions of overcrowding, he also authorized death camp deportations prior to the inspection team's arrival.

- In 1944, when Hungarian Jews were being deported, Eichmann became enraged by the rescue efforts of Swedish diplomat Raoul Wallenberg. Eichmann reportedly threatened to have Wallenberg shot—a warning that did not deter Wallenberg from his dangerous humanitarian work.

For Further Reading

Arendt, Hannah. *Eichmann in Jerusalem.* New York: Penguin, 1994.

Ayer, Eleanor H., with Helen Waterford and Alfons Heck. *Parallel Journeys.* New York: Atheneum, 1995.

Berwick, Michael. *The Third Reich.* New York: Putnam, 1971.

understanding HOLOCAUST

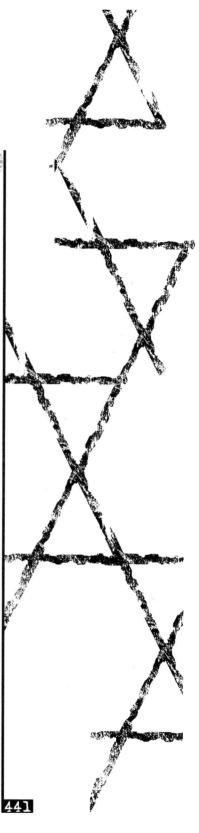

The Holocaust ended over half a century ago, but the world still seeks to understand how such a breakdown in civilization could have occurred in the twentieth century. The murder of European Jews at the hands of the Nazis led to the creation of a new word, *genocide,* which means the use of a deliberate, systematic policy to eliminate an entire racial, political, or cultural group. Those victims who survived the Holocaust provide firsthand testimonies about what happened during this murderous chapter in the history of humankind.

One survivor of the Holocaust, **Elie Wiesel**, has dedicated his life to educating others about the Nazi atrocities so that history never repeats itself. In the essay entitled "Why I Write," Wiesel describes his commitment to honor those who perished during the Holocaust. By writing, he hopes to build bonds between the people who died tragically and those still alive—Jews and non-Jews alike.

Memorials and museums preserve the memory of those who perished in the Holocaust. These centers include the Yad Vashem Heroes and Martyrs Memorial in Jerusalem and the **United States Holocaust Memorial**

Survivors of Bergen-Belsen walk near a large pile of shoes.

Museum (USHMM), which is located in Washington, D.C. The USHMM features comprehensive exhibits for all ages. These exhibits probe the historical, political, social, and religious implications of the Holocaust.

Another Holocaust survivor, **Gerda Weissmann Klein**, spent three years as a slave laborer in German concentration camps. In her memoir *All But My Life,* Weissmann Klein talks about her wartime experiences and the losses she endured. She was liberated in Volary, Czechoslovakia, by Kurt Klein, an American lieutenant whom she later married. Like many survivors of the Holocaust, she learned that "when we bring comfort to others, we reassure ourselves, and when we dispel fear, we assuage [ease] our own fear as well."

The children of Holocaust survivors inherit the emotional scars and broken family heritage of their parents. **Art Spiegelman**, a gifted cartoonist and son of Holocaust survivors, invented a unique form for sharing his family's strug-

gles. In 1986, he published a book about the Holocaust in cartoon format called *Maus: A Survivor's Tale I: My Father Bleeds History.* The sequel, *Maus: A Survivor's Tale II: And Here My Troubles Began*, published in 1991, relates Spiegelman's attempts to understand his father and—through him—to grasp the terrifying realities of the Holocaust. Spiegelman won a special Pulitzer Prize for his *Maus* books in 1992.

Fiction provides authors with the opportunity to illustrate the powerful human emotions that are capable of driving people and countries into war. In *Summer of My German Soldier*, novelist **Bette Greene** explores the universal themes of intolerance and hatred. Drawing from her own childhood experiences growing up in rural Arkansas during World War II, she portrays the many forms of prejudice that exist in American society.

Some people have questioned whether the Holocaust ever really happened. These groups, labeled "**revisionists**,"

Dachau survivors sit on the steps of a barracks after liberation.

Halina Bryks was one of many displaced children whose pictures were published in newspapers in the hope that a family member would see them.

claim the Holocaust can only be considered a theory, not a factual event. Revisionists argue that the survivors and bodies found by Allied forces in the Nazi camps were the victims of typhus epidemics. The essay "Revisionism: Denial of the Holocaust" discusses a pattern frequently seen in antisemitic movements. This pattern requires the belief in a complex "conspiracy" theory. As long as antisemitism exists, there will be people who challenge the reality of the Holocaust and choose to believe that it is nothing more than a myth concocted by scheming historians, survivors, veterans, members of the press, and political leaders.

Elie Wiesel

"Why I Write"

An essay included in *From the Kingdom of Memory: Reminiscences*

The Nazi (National Socialist) party of Germany, which remained in power from 1933 to 1945, attempted to annihilate all Jewish people living in Europe. According to their secret plan, code-named the "Final Solution," they intended to murder 11 million Jews from as nearby as Poland and as far away as England. During World War II, the Nazis occupied 21 countries and controlled the destinies of some 9 million Jews. Nearly 6 million European Jews were exterminated before Nazi Germany surrendered to the Allied forces (the forces fighting against Germany) on May 7, 1945.

So enormous was this catastrophe—the mass murder of millions of people belonging to one particular group—that people worldwide still seek to understand how such a breakdown in civilization could have occurred in the twentieth century. The actions of Nazi rule led to the coining of a new word, *genocide,* which means the use of a deliberate, systematic policy to eliminate an entire racial, political, or cultural group. The Nazi party's attempt to annihilate—or completely wipe out—European Jews and other "enemies" of the German state is also referred to as the Holocaust, taken from the term meaning to sacrifice, destroy, or consume by fire.

Those who witnessed World War II, especially those people who survived the concentration camps, can provide the rest of us with firsthand accounts of what happened during this murderous chapter in the history of humankind. However, no one can fully comprehend why or how such hate-filled policies could consume some people—and why others could not or did not stop them sooner. Perhaps one of the most eloquent and forceful writers exploring the Holo-

Elie Wiesel (second row of bunks, seventh from the left, next to the vertical beam) was an inmate of Buchenwald's "little camp."

caust experience is survivor Elie Wiesel. Wiesel has committed his life to educating others about the Nazi atrocities so that history does not repeat itself. A deeply religious youth when deported to Auschwitz in 1944, he has provided the world with a penetrating view of Nazi death camps.

Wiesel was raised in a religious home in Sighet Marmatiei, a small city located in present-day Romania. Under Hungarian rule from 1940 to 1944, Sighet contained a thriving Jewish community. In 1941, over 10,000 Jews lived in the city, representing nearly 40 percent of the total population. Despite the forced deportation and massacre of "alien" Jews in 1941, the remaining Jews lived in relative stability until 1944. After the Nazis occupied Hungary in March 1944, the party immediately implemented a series of anti-Jewish measures. The situation and safety of all Hungarian Jews deteriorated rapidly in just a few short months. Jews were required to turn over their assets to German authorities, were ordered to wear yellow Star of David arm bands, and were prohibited

The United States Holocaust Memorial Museum

Established by a unanimous act of Congress, the United States Holocaust Memorial Museum (USHMM) serves as a living memorial to the Jewish and non-Jewish victims who perished at the hands of the Nazis. The museum opened in April of 1993 and is located close to the Washington Memorial. Since its opening, it has joined the ranks of the most-visited federally-operated sites in Washington, D.C. The facility includes a permanent exhibition, a learning center, a Hall of Remembrance, a children's wall, and a special exhibit for young children called "Daniel's Story." USHMM also offers educational programs and research opportunities through the Holocaust Research Institute and the Gonda Educational Center.

Special displays, exhibitions, and programs are continually presented and updated. Those who cannot visit the actual museum may visit on-line. The USHMM web site offers excerpts of both the regular and special exhibits as well as access to extensive research tools.

For Further Information:

The United States Holocaust
   Memorial Museum

100 Raoul Wallenberg
   Place SW

Washington, DC
   20024-2150

(202) 488-0400

http:\\www.ushmm.org/
   index.html

---

from dining at restaurants and traveling on trains. By May, the Nazis had forced the Jews from Sighet and nearby rural communities into two ghettos established within city borders. Wiesel and his family were among the nearly 13,000 Jews deported to Auschwitz between May 16 and 22, when the Nazis "liquidated" these ghettos.

Wiesel was not yet 16 years old when he arrived at Birkenau, the depot area and death center of the Auschwitz compound. While still in the train cars, the Jewish captives could see the fires of the camp's furnaces, where the dead bodies of prisoners were being burned. During the *Selektionen,* camp officials directed the deportees into two lines, separating the men from the women. Able-bodied men were "selected" for work assignments, while the elderly, young children, and most of the mothers were led immediately to the gas chambers. The camp guards ordered Wiesel (who had lied about his age) and his father to join the line of prisoners leaving Birkenau and marching to the Auschwitz concentration camp. Wiesel last saw his mother and younger sister as they walked away with thousands of other women and children to their deaths.

During the remainder of 1944, Wiesel and his father managed to physically survive the brutal conditions at Auschwitz; their emotional well-being and spirits, however, were shattered. Despite his religious upbringing, Wiesel began to question how God could allow such horrific events and such twisted, evil men to exist. All day and night, guards attacked and murdered prisoners at will. The inmates grew steadily weaker as they performed exhaustive hard labor in 12-hour shifts, received starvation-quota rations, and slept in filthy, overcrowded barracks. Without adequate sanitation facilities, infectious diseases ravaged the camp population. As individual prisoners fought for their survival, they turned against each other and even their friends and family members. After witnessing a rabbi's son forsake his father, Wiesel vowed that he would never betray his own father in order to save his own life.

In January 1945, as the Soviet army advanced through Poland and toward the compound, the Nazis evacuated Auschwitz. Camp guards ordered the prisoners to march toward Buchenwald, a concentration camp located within Germany. Forced to march for days in the snow without adequate clothing and with little food or water, Wiesel's father arrived at Buchenwald ill and exhausted. When his father was no longer able to get out of bed and no longer eligible to receive food, Wiesel fed him his own meager rations. Wiesel's father died after being violently attacked by a guard who was annoyed by his pleas for water. Wiesel was liberated from Buchenwald by American forces on April 11—less than three months after his father's death. After spending two weeks in the hospital on the verge of death, he was released and eventually settled in Paris, France.

Elie Wiesel first wrote about his experiences as a concentration camp prisoner in his fictional memoir *Un di Velt Hot Geshvigen* (1958). Originally written in Yiddish, this immensely popular work was translated into 18 languages, appearing in English as *Night* in 1960. This book, though considered a novel, serves as Wiesel's personal testimony on the Holocaust.

In "Why I Write," an essay included in the collection *From the Kingdom of Memory: Reminiscences* and excerpted below, Wiesel describes his commitment to honor those who perished during the Holocaust. By writing, the author hopes to build bonds between the people who died tragically at the hands of the Nazis and those still living—Jews and non-Jews alike.

Things to Remember While Reading Wiesel's Essay "Why I Write":

- Wiesel talks about the importance of memory in the Jewish tradition. As a survivor, he views himself as a witness obligated to honor those who died in the camps. By testifying on behalf of the dead, Wiesel hopes to communicate to others the realities of the Holocaust.

- Describing the traumatic events and the sufferings that took place in the Nazi-controlled camps defies language. By finding a way to explain what happened to individuals in the camps, Wiesel exposes the "darkness" so that others may learn. (Wiesel refers to the Holocaust as the "kingdom of night.")

- Wiesel is haunted by all of the people who died in the Holocaust, but perhaps most by the million children who were massacred. On the day he arrived at Auschwitz, he saw hundreds of children lined up with their mothers to be taken to the gas chambers and killed. He will never forget the image of black smoke swirling into the sky as the bodies of victims—adults and children—burned in the crematoria.

- Auschwitz can serve as a symbol of violence, hatred, and death for Jews and non-Jews. Wiesel hopes the Holocaust teaches people about the ever-present dangers of silence, indifference, and inaction and the evils of intolerance and hate that exist even now.

*W*hy do I write? Perhaps in order not to go mad. Or, on the contrary, to touch the bottom of madness.

Like [experimental Irish-born author who wrote primarily in French] Samuel Beckett, the survivor expresses himself "en desespoir de cause," because there is no other way.

Speaking of the **solitude** of the survivor, the great **Yiddish** and **Hebrew** poet and thinker Aaron Zeitlin addresses those who have left him: his dead father, his dead brother, his dead friends. "You have abandoned me," he says to them. "You are together, without me. I am here. Alone. And I make words."

So do I, just like him. I too speak words, write words, reluctantly.

There are easier occupations, far more pleasant ones. For the survivor, however, writing is not a profession, but a calling; "an honor," according to [French philosopher and author Albert] Camus. As he put it: "I entered literature through worship." Other writers have said, "Through anger; through love." As for myself, I would say, "Through silence."

It was by seeking, by probing silence that I began to discover the perils and power of the word.

I never intended to be a novelist. The only role I sought was that of witness. I believed that, having survived by chance, I was duty-bound to give meaning to my survival, to justify each moment of my life. I knew the story had to be told. Not to transmit an experience is to betray it; this is what Jewish tradition teaches us. But how to do this?

"When Israel is in exile, so is the word," says the <u>Book of Splendor.</u> The word has deserted the meaning it was intended to

Solitude: Being alone or remote from society.

Yiddish: A form of German language containing many Hebrew and Slavic words.

Hebrew: The language of the ancient Israelites or Hebrews.

*convey—one can no longer make them coincide. The **displacement**, the shift, is **irrevocable**. This was never more true than right after the upheaval. We all knew that we could never say what had to be said, that we could never express in words—coherent, intelligible words—our experience of madness on an absolute scale. The walk through fiery nights, the silence before and after the **selection**, the toneless praying of the condemned, the **Kaddish** of the dying, the fear and hunger of the sick, the shame and suffering, the haunted eyes, the wild stares—I thought that I would never be able to speak of them. All words seemed inadequate, worn, foolish, lifeless, whereas I wanted them to **sear**.*

*Where was I to discover a fresh vocabulary, a **primeval** language? The language of night was not human; it was primitive, almost animal—hoarse shouting, screaming, muffled moaning, savage howling, the sounds of beating.... A **brute** strikes wildly, a body falls; an officer raises his arm and a whole community walks toward a common grave; a soldier shrugs his shoulders and a thousand families are torn apart, to be reunited only by death. Such was the language of the concentration camp. It **negated** all other language and took its place. Rather than link people, it became a wall between them. Could the wall be scaled? Could the reader be brought to the other side? I knew the answer to be No, and yet I also knew that No had to become Yes. This was the wish, the last will of the dead. One had to shatter the wall encasing the darkest truth, and give it a name. One had to force man to look.*

The fear of forgetting: the main obsession of all those who have passed through the universe of the damned. The enemy relied on people's disbelief and forgetfulness.

Remember, said the father to his son, and the son to his friend: gather the names, the faces, the tears. If, by a miracle, you come out of it alive, try to reveal everything, omitting nothing, forgetting nothing. Such was the oath we had all taken: "If, by some miracle, I survive, I will devote my life to testifying on behalf of all those whose shadows will be bound to mine forever."

Displacement: To expel or force to flee from home.

Irrevocable: Not able to be changed or altered.

Selection: In this case, the selection by the Nazis as to which Jews would live (and be sent into forced labor) and which Jews would die (by being sent straight to the gas chambers).

Kaddish: Jewish prayer of mourning, recited in public at services.

Sear: Burn or scorch.

Primeval: Ancient; primitive.

Brute: Cruel or savage beast.

Negated: Caused to be ineffective or of no value; the cancelling out of each of two things by the other.

This is why I write certain things rather than others: to remain faithful.

Of course, there are times of doubt for the survivor, times when one gives in to weakness, or longs for comfort. I hear a voice within me telling me to stop mourning the past. I too want to sing of love and its magic. I too want to celebrate the sun, and the dawn that heralds the sun. I would like to shout, and shout loudly: "Listen, listen well! I too am capable of victory, do you hear? I too am open to laughter and joy. I want to walk head high, my face unguarded." One feels like shouting, but the shout becomes a murmur. One must make a choice; one must remain faithful. This is what the survivor feels; he owes nothing to the living, but everything to the dead.

*I owe the dead my memory. I am duty-bound to serve as their **emissary**, transmitting the history of their disappearance, even if it disturbs, even if it brings pain. Not to do so would be to betray them, and thus myself. I simply look at them. I see them and I write.*

*While writing, I question them as I question myself. I write to understand as much as to be understood. Will I succeed one day? Wherever one starts from, one reaches darkness. God? He remains the God of darkness. Man? The source of darkness. The killers' **sneers**, their victims' tears, the onlookers' **indifference**, their **complicity** and **complacency**: I do not understand the divine role in all of that. A million children massacred: I will never understand.*

Jewish children: they haunt my writings. I see them again and again. I shall always see them. Hounded, humiliated, bent like the old men who surround them trying to protect them, in vain. They are thirsty, the children, and there is no one to give them water. They are hungry, the children, but there is no one to give them a crust of bread. They are afraid, and there is no one to reassure them.

*They walk in the middle of the road, like **urchins**. They are on the way to the station, and they will never return. In sealed cars,*

Emissary: Designated representative or agent.

Sneers: Smile at with mocking facial contortions, indicating scorn or disgust.

Indifference: Showing a lack of concern.

Complicity: Association or participation in a wrongful act.

Complacency: Self-satisfaction; lack of concern.

we must bear witness

without air or food, they travel toward another world; they guess where they are going, they know it, and they keep silent. They listen to the wind, the call of death in the distance.

All these children, these old people, I see them. I never stop seeing them. I belong to them.

But they, to whom do they belong?

People imagine that a murderer weakens when facing a child. That the child might reawaken the killer's lost humanity. That the killer might be unable to kill the child before him.

Not this time. With us, it happened differently. Our Jewish children had no effect upon the killers. Nor upon the world. Nor upon God.

(From left) Harvey Meyerhoff (chairman of the United States Holocaust Memorial Council), President Bill Clinton, and Elie Wiesel light the eternal flame outside the United States Holocaust Memorial Museum in Washington, DC.

Urchins: Children who aren't cared for and must fend for themselves.

I think of them, I think of their childhood. Their childhood is a small Jewish town, and this town is no more. They frighten me; they reflect an image of myself, one that I pursue and run from at the same time—the image of a Jewish adolescent who knew no fear except the fear of God, whose faith was whole, comforting.

No, I do not understand. And if I write, it is to warn the reader that he will not understand either. "You will not understand, you will never understand," were the words heard everywhere in the kingdom of night. I can only echo them.

An admission of **impotence** *and guilt? I do not know. All I know is that Treblinka and Auschwitz cannot be told. And yet I have tried. God knows I have tried.*

Did I attempt too much, or not enough? Out of some thirty volumes, only three or four try to penetrate the realm of the dead. In my other books, through my other books, I try to follow other roads. For it is dangerous to linger among the dead; they hold on to you, and you run the risk of speaking only to them. And so, I forced myself to turn away from them and study other periods, explore other destinies and teach other tales; the Bible and the **Talmud**, **Hasidism** *and its fervor, the* **shtetl** *and its songs, Jerusalem and its echoes; the Russian Jews and their anguish, their awakening, their courage. At times it seems to me that I am speaking of other things with the sole purpose of keeping the essential—the personal experience—unspoken. At times I wonder: And what if I was wrong? Perhaps I should have stayed in my own world with the dead.*

But then, the dead never leave me. They have their rightful place even in the works about pre-Holocaust Hasidism or ancient Jerusalem. Even in my Biblical and **Midrashic** *tales, I pursue their presence,* **mute** *and motionless.... They appear in Hasidic and Talmudic legends in which victims forever need defending against forces that would crush them. Technically, so to speak, they are of*

Impotence: Lack of power or strength.

Talmud: Authoritative body of Jewish tradition.

Hasidism: Jewish sect practicing strict observance of ritual law.

Shtetl: Small Jewish village formerly found in Eastern Europe.

Midrashic: Explanation of the significance of a given Bible text.

Mute: Unable to speak.

course elsewhere, in time and space, but on a deeper, truer plane, the dead are part of every story, of every scene....

After Auschwitz everything long past brings us back to Auschwitz....

I know Hasidim who never wavered in their faith; I respect their strength. I know others who chose rebellion, protest, rage; I respect their courage. For there comes a time when only those who do believe in God will cry out to him in **wrath** *and* **anguish***. The faith of some matters as much as the strength of others. It is not ours to judge; it is only ours to tell the tale.*

But where is one to begin? Whom is one to include? One meets a Hasid in all my novels. And a child. And an old man. And a beggar. And a madman. They are all part of my inner landscape. Why? They are pursued and persecuted by the killers; I offer them shelter. The enemy wanted to create a society **purged of** *their presence, and I have brought some of them back. The world denied them,* **repudiated** *them: so let them live at least within the feverish dreams of my characters.*

It is for them that I write.

And yet, the survivor may experience **remorse***. He has tried* **to bear witness***; it was all* **in vain***.*

After the liberation, illusions shaped our hopes. We were convinced that a new world would be built upon the ruins of Europe. A new civilization would dawn. No more wars, no more hate, no more intolerance, no fanaticism anywhere. And all this because the witnesses would speak, and speak they did. Was it to no avail?

They will continue, for they cannot do otherwise. When man, in his grief, falls silent, [German poet and dramatist Johann Wolfgang von] Goethe says, then God gives him the strength to sing of his sorrows. From that moment on, he may no longer

Wrath: Anger.

Anguish: Extreme pain, anxiety, or sorrow.

Purged of: Freed from.

Repudiated: Disowned; refused to have anything to do with.

Remorse: Troubled by feelings of guilt for past wrongs.

To bear witness: To give testimony.

In vain: Without success.

Elie Wiesel (1928—)

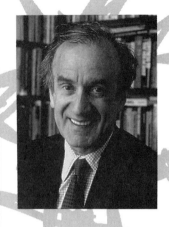

Elie (Eliezer) Wiesel was born in Sighet Marmatiei, a small city in the province of Transylvania that is today part of northern Romania. Wiesel and his three sisters were raised in a religious Jewish home. His parents were shopkeepers, and his father served as an active leader in the Jewish community. In May 1944, Wiesel, his parents, and his younger sister, Tzipora, were deported to Auschwitz. It is presumed that his mother and sister died immediately after their arrival, as they were apparently sent straight to the gas chambers.

Wiesel's father died in January 1945 after being transferred to the Buchenwald concentration camp in Germany. Elie Wiesel was liberated from Buchenwald by American forces on April 11, 1945.

After World War II ended, Wiesel lived in France, where he quickly mastered the French language and studied at the Sorbonne, the University of Paris. During the 1950s, he worked as a foreign journalist and reporter for the Israeli daily newspaper *Yediot Aharonont.* His work as a correspondent

Wrest: Gain with difficulty, as if by force.

Oblivion: The condition of being forgotten or unknown.

Vanquish: Defeat; conquer.

choose not to sing, whether his song is heard or not. What matters is to struggle against silence with words, or through another form of silence. What matters is to gather a smile here and there, a tear here and there, a word here and there, and thus justify the faith placed in man, a long time ago, by so many victims.

*Why do I write? To **wrest** those victims from **oblivion**. To help the dead **vanquish** death. (Wiesel, pp. 13-21)*

What happened next...

Wiesel's passionate commitment to stir the conscience of society earned him the Nobel Peace Prize in 1986. The citation on his award reads: "Wiesel is a messenger to mankind. His message is one of peace and atonement and human dig-

(Continued from previous page)

took him to Israel and finally to United States, where he became an American citizen in 1963. Since 1976, Wiesel has been a professor of humanities at Boston University.

In 1985, Wiesel received the Congressional Gold Medal of Achievement. The same year, former French president François Mitterrand named him commander in the French Legion of Honor. Wiesel was awarded the Nobel Peace Prize in 1986 for his "message" to humanity. The Nobel Committee acknowledged his fight against "blind indifference" and his push to involve people in "truth and justice, in human dignity, freedom, and atonement."

Today, Wiesel continues to give lectures, teach, and write. He lives in New York City with his Austrian-born wife, Marion, who is also a Holocaust survivor. Wiesel prefers to write in French, and Marion translates his work into English. He has written over 40 books, including works of fiction, nonfiction, and plays. In 1995, he published the first volume of his autobiography, *All Rivers Run to the Sea.*

nity. The message is in the form of a testimony, repeated and deepened through the works of a great author." In his Nobel address, Wiesel pledged to "never be silent whenever and wherever human beings endure suffering and humiliation." Silence is not an option, for "neutrality helps the oppressor, never the victim."

Between 1980 and 1986, Wiesel served as the founding chairperson of the U.S. Holocaust Memorial Council. Established by a unanimous vote of Congress in 1980, the Council represents the commitment of the American people and government to remembering the victims of the Holocaust. The council also organized the planning and funding of the United States Holocaust Memorial Museum. During his tenure as chairperson, Wiesel helped institute Days of Remembrance of the Victims of the Holocaust, an annual commemorative program involving local ceremonies as well as a national civic ceremony held in the U.S. Rotunda. His leadership inspired the creation and introduction of Holocaust curricula into junior and senior high schools throughout the United States.

Of Wiesel's 40 published books of fiction and nonfiction, only a small portion deal directly with the Holocaust. His other works explore various aspects of the human experience and Jewish tradition, including reflections on Hasidism, the Talmud, and French existentialism. (Existentialism is a twentieth-century philosophical movement that hinges on the belief in free will, personal responsibility, and the anxiety that accompanies such responsibility. According to existentialist theory, there is no ultimate purpose to the world, and humans will never be able to comprehend their universe.) As Holocaust survivors grow older, Wiesel urges them to write about their experiences. He hopes that "the memory of evil will serve as a shield against evil." As he remarked in a March 5, 1997 *New York Times* interview: "I believe in testimony more than anything else."

Did you know...

- Wiesel is a prolific writer whose works about the concentration camp experience include: *Night* (1960), *Dawn* (1961), *The Accident* (1962), *A Beggar in Jerusalem* (1970), *The Oath* (1973), and *The Fifth Son* (1985).

- When Allied forces liberated Nazi-controlled concentration camps, military adjuncts and press reporters took many dramatic photographs of the prisoners and camp environs. The poor health of the inmates—many of whom resembled living skeletons—and the appalling conditions of the camp shocked the world. Elie Wiesel is featured in one of these famous shots, lying in a crowded bunker in the Buchenwald camp.

- Wiesel's hometown, Sighet Marmatiei, is located in an area once known as the province of Transylvania. When he first arrived in the United States, he introduced himself as someone originally from Transylvania. Only after repeated instances of laughter did he learn of America's fondness for the legend about the Transylvanian vampire Count Dracula. Today, Sighet is part of Romania.

- When the war ended, some 2,300 Jews (out of the original 10,000) remained in Sighet Marmatiei. This small number included a few of the original inhabitants but also a considerable number of Jewish refugees from other parts of Romania.

For Further Reading

Kuper, Jack. *Child of the Holocaust.* New York: Berkley Books, 1993.

Landau, Elaine. *We Survived the Holocaust.* New York: F. Watts, 1991.

New York Times, March 5, 1997.

Wiesel, Elie. *From the Kingdom of Memory: Reminiscences.* New York: Schocken Books, 1990.

Gerda Weissmann Klein

All But My Life

First published in 1957
This version, with epilogue, published in 1995

In the fall of 1939, Nazi Germany invaded Poland, setting off World War II. Of all the countries Germany eventually occupied, Poland had the largest number of Jewish residents—some 3.3 million. By 1945, nearly 3 million had perished, representing one of the greatest losses and tragedies of the war. The slaughter that characterized Nazi rule in Poland wiped out entire families, cutting across generational lines. The majority of those who survived had fled to the Soviet Union and returned after the war. As many as 70,000 Polish Jews managed to stay alive by serving in the Polish Army or as slave laborers in the Nazi concentration camp system. Following the war, the few remaining Polish Jews had neither homes nor families to which they could return. Many small Jewish towns in Poland, called *shtetls,* lost their entire populations, effectively erasing the towns and their entire history.

At the time of the German invasion, approximately 8,000 Jews lived in the town of Bielitz, Poland, near the Czechoslovakian border. Immediately after the war broke out, many Jews fled to either Soviet territory or to the area of Poland incorporated into Greater Germany, hoping to be spared anti-Jewish persecution. By 1940, only 300 Jews remained in Bielitz. The Weissmann family was among the few who stayed. In April 1942, Nazi authorities forced all the Jews into a ghetto near the train depot. The following month, 18-year-old Gerda Weissmann was separated from her parents and transported to a labor camp. For the next three years, she worked as a slave laborer in various work camps attached to factories involved in war production.

At the end of January 1945, Weissmann was among some 4,000 female prisoners who were forced to march through Germany and eventually into Czechoslovakia. Without adequate winter clothing, many prisoners died during these so-called "death marches" from exposure, starvation, and exhaustion. SS guards, members of the Nazi police force, shot prisoners who fell to the ground too tired to continue. It has also been reported that guards would, at times, randomly gather small groups of victims, take them to the woods, and shoot them. Some guards even encouraged prisoners to run away, only to shoot them in the back as they fled. They would later collect a bonus, claiming to have stopped an attempted escape.

Gerda Weissmann was one of 120 women who survived the three-month death march. The ski boots her father had insisted she wear in preparation for the transports and deportations helped save her life. She was liberated in Volary, Czechoslovakia, on May 7, 1945, by Kurt Klein, a lieutenant with the Fifth U.S. Infantry Division. Deathly ill and suffering from severe frostbite, she remained in an American field hospital for several months. She later married Kurt Klein, changing her name to Gerda Weissmann Klein. In 1946, the couple settled in the United States.

Like many survivors of the Holocaust, Weissmann Klein gradually adjusted to life after the war. Grateful to be alive, she enjoyed the many basic pleasures denied her for so long. After facing starvation and living in unsanitary conditions, she was keenly aware of the blessings of abundant food, clean water, and warm clothes. While many treasures of life in America have become commonplace, shadows continue to haunt her. To this day, she still mourns the death of her parents, her brother, and close friends. During the more than 50 years that have passed since liberation, she has often used "the darkness of past despair" to show her "the blessings which I might otherwise take for granted."

In her memoir *All But My Life,* Weissmann Klein talks about her wartime experiences and the losses she endured. The years spent in work camps under Nazi rule have taught her that "when we bring comfort to others, we reassure ourselves, and when we dispel fear, we assuage [ease] our own fear as well." The excerpt below contains her recollections of her early meetings with Kurt and later reflections penned in 1994.

Things to Remember While Reading
All But My Life:

- Since Gerda Weissmann Klein had grown up in a region of Poland that had once been part of the Austro-Hungarian empire, she knew how to speak both German and Polish. Kurt Klein, the American lieutenant who rescued her and became her husband, was originally from Germany. He spoke both German and English.

- Gerda and Kurt shared many similar pains: both lost their parents at the hands of the Nazis, and both knew the suffering involved with never knowing exactly what happened to their loved ones. As the Nazis moved their victims from one place to the next, letters would be returned with the ominous stamped notice: "Moved—left no forwarding address."

- Like many other survivors, Weissmann Klein has said that living through the Holocaust was both a privilege and a burden. As she experienced the bounty of life after her imprisonment during the war, she also recalled those who were less fortunate. From this commitment to both the living and the dead, Weissmann Klein began speaking about her Holocaust experiences and reaching out to children who needed help.

Opposite page:
Concentration camp prisoners on a death march from Dachau to Wolfratshausen.

All But My Life

I don't remember the days that followed too well. The doctors and nurses spent much time over me; I was given injections and pills continuously. My body was rubbed with oil twice a day, for my skin was flaked and dry. I was weighed—sixty-eight pounds. The nurses joked about being able to circle my thigh with their fingers.

My bed seemed very high up, and the distances enormous. I did not feel like talking to anyone; I was strangely silent for the first time in my life. I noticed that many of the girls began to have visitors. I asked for Liesel several times, but was never told where she was.

Revisionism: Denial of the Holocaust

More than 50 years after the end of World War II, some people have questioned whether the Holocaust ever really happened. These groups, labeled "revisionists," claim the Holocaust can only be considered a theory, not a factual event. Revisionists argue that the survivors and bodies found by Allied forces when they liberated the Nazi camps were the victims of typhus epidemics. They also claim that poisonous Zyklon-B gas was used in the camps not as a tool for murder, but as a delousing agent to halt the spread of typhus, which is transmitted by lice. Even though Auschwitz camp commandant Rudolph Höss gave extensive details about the Nazi extermination system in his memoir *Death Dealer*, revisionists discredit his testimony, claiming Höss wrote his confessional memoirs while experiencing the great emotional stress related to his trial and subsequent execution.

Revisionists also question the parameters used to define the Holocaust and the num-

Time and again I thought of the American soldier who had been so kind to me. Just before he had driven off he had said that he would see me again. With a chill, I recalled that the fighting had gone on after I had spoken to him; something might have happened to him!

A week passed. One afternoon an American came in and glanced into each bunk. My eyes met his as he approached.

"It's you I'm looking for!" he said.

I must have frowned as I recognized him. Out of his helmet and battle gear, he looked different.

"Don't you remember me?" he asked.

"Oh yes!" I said quickly, and wanted to add how worried I had been that something might have befallen him, but checked myself.

ber of victims cited. They allege that many Jewish deaths could be attributed to civilian (nonmilitary) losses during the war. The reliability of prewar population estimates are also challenged, especially those concerning Poland and the Baltic States (Estonia, Latvia, and Lithuania). These regions contained the highest number of Jews, but they kept the least accurate records and experienced the greatest mass movement of people. The enormity of the losses makes verification of individual cases impossible.

Antisemitism, or hatred of Jewish people, frequently includes the belief in a "conspiracy" theory. The origins of the Nazi movement that led to the outbreak of World War II can be traced to the belief in an international plot by Jews to take control of the world. The arguments of today's revisionists provide a haunting echo of the Nazi party's belief in the conspiracy of "international Jewry." As long as antisemitism exists, there will be people who challenge the reality of the Holocaust.

He carried a parcel under his arm. "These are for you," he said, unwrapping two magazines.

"Do you know what this means?" he asked, pointing to four bold white letters on a red background.

I gazed at the letters: L-I-F-E.

He repeated his question. "Do you know what it means? It is a fine word for you to learn. I know no better word of introduction to the English language for you."

I pronounced the word and tasted the strange sound of it.

"Say it again," he urged.

I was only too glad to try.

"That's right, that's what I wanted to see."

"To see what?" I asked.

"You smiled," he said. "I wanted to see you smile."

We talked. He told me that he had been busy with large numbers of prisoners, and that was why he had not come sooner. He said that he was stationed in a neighboring village about sixteen miles away. We talked like old friends. There was so much to ask. He seemed amazed at the limited knowledge I had about the development of the war. His German was excellent, though not fluent. At times he substituted an English word for a German one, but I nearly always knew what he meant.

*The nurse came in, bringing my dinner tray, and told him that all visitors had to leave. I would have gladly **foregone** food if he could have stayed.*

He left, and I ate my dinner, realizing that I had again forgotten to ask his name. After eating, until the light grew too poor, I studied the magazines. The pictures of the free world were exciting.

Then, unexpectedly, a voice near me said "Hello" in English. "You're not going to throw me out, are you?"

I was overjoyed to see him. I hadn't occurred to me that he might return in the evening. This time I learned his name.

"Kurt Klein," he said, laughing. "By the way, I wrote the letter to your uncle in Turkey. I hope I can bring you an answer soon."

I told Kurt about the strange sensation I felt every time I saw German soldiers under guard.

"Just hurry up and get well," he said, "and I'll show you how many of them are under guard."

And he told me some of his experiences with the Germans' surprise when they heard about their concentration camps.

Foregone: Done without.

"It seems we fought a war against the Nazis, but I haven't met a Nazi yet," he said wryly.

And I was actually able to laugh. He could make me laugh, but I was ashamed to cry in front of him. I told him about Ilse. He seemed to understand. He didn't tell me to forget, to draw a line through the past, for he knew that I couldn't. He didn't ask questions either. He listened to what I had to tell him. He was silent when he knew that there was no answer. He joked about the present, and again and again I found myself laughing.

His daily visits continued. Although we came from different worlds, we understood each other. I did not want pity. I did not want him to like me because of what I had endured. Without knowing why, I sensed that there was something in his past that made him suffer.

A couple of days after his first visit he brought me some lilies-of-the-valley. The subtle fragrance brought back memories of my garden in May. I clutched the flowers without being able to speak. I remembered the roses in Grünberg which we had not been allowed to touch. But here were flowers that bloomed for me.

I kept my eyes downcast for quite a while, not daring to raise them and have them full of tears.

Finally Kurt asked, "Do you like them?"

My answers must have been written on my face. There was a catch in his voice when he spoke.

"I knew you would. They were my mother's favorite flowers."

"Your mother?" I asked haltingly.

Then for the first time Kurt told me about himself. He had been born in Germany. His older sister had gone to America soon after Hitler came to power, Kurt following her a year later. Finally the older brother had left for America. The parents had stayed behind. With the children safe, they waited, hoping that the Nazi regime would collapse. I remembered when Papa and Mama had talked the same way. Kurt went on to tell me how the children's combined efforts had failed to get their parents out of Germany. The Nazis had deported them to Camp de Gurs, in the south of France, in 1941. For a while letters reached them from America, then in July, 1942 a letter had been returned, stamped "Moved—left no forwarding address." Kurt fell silent. I understood so well. Impulsively I caught his hand.

"There is hope still," I said.

*"Is there?" His voice was slightly **ironical**, but there was some concealed hope in it.*

I had always felt that his understanding of my feelings had been made deeper by tragedy of his own. I was glad now that I had never given him detailed descriptions of cruelty, that I had really never told him what had happened, though he heard it from the others later. Yet the knowledge that I could shield him from pain gave me satisfaction....

From the epilogue to <u>All But My Life</u>, written in 1994

*It is with **trepidation** that I look back at what I wrote nearly a half century ago, in the springtime of my life. A **welter** of emotions **assails** me and must be sorted out. Now that I have reached **autumn**, perhaps I can be more **objective**.*

I have been asked countless times, "How and why did you go on during those unspeakable years?" And then, "How do you cope with the memory of hardships in the work camps and the pain of losing your family?" I admit I no longer remember all the answers I have given, but I am sure that they often varied and depended on my mood.

Ironical: Sarcastic; saying the opposite of what is meant.

Trepidation: Fear.

Welter: State of wild disorder.

Assails: Assaults; attacks.

Autumn: Middle age; now that the author has gotten older.

Objective: Dealing with facts that have not been distorted by personal feelings or prejudices.

Gerda Weissmann Klein (1924–)

Gerda Weissmann Klein was born in Bielitz, Poland. Bielitz, known as "Little Vienna," is a small town at the foot of the Beskide mountain range, near the Polish-Czechoslovakian border. Before the German invasion of Poland in 1939, Weissmann lived a comfortable life with her brother, Arthur, and their parents. In June 1942, she was deported for forced labor, then spent the next three years in various work camps. She was one of the few prisoners to survive a brutal death march from Grünberg to Czechoslovakia, which began at the end of January 1945. On May 7, she was liberated by Kurt Klein, a U.S. Army lieutenant who later became her husband. Gerda was the only member of the Weissmann family to survive the Holocaust.

After the war, Gerda and her husband settled in Buffalo, New York, where they raised three children. In 1957, she published a memoir titled *All But My Life* and later wrote four other books. She has lectured throughout the country for the past 45 years and has received numerous awards and honorary degrees. Today, Gerda and her husband have several grandchildren and live in Arizona.

*The part of my formative years over which fate cast such a large shadow imposes an enormous burden and is not fully sorted out even now. No manual for survival was ever handed to me, nor were any self-help books available. Yet somehow I made my way, grappling with feelings that would let me **reconcile** difficult memories with hope for the future, and balancing pain with joy, death with life, loss with gain, tragedy with happiness.*

*Survival is both an **exalted** privilege and a painful burden. I shall take a few random incidents that have become important in my life and try to make some sense of them. At the same time, I realize that it is impossible to do justice to fifty years of memory.*

Reconcile: To accept something unpleasant.

Exalted: Raised in rank or character.

*The **acuteness** of those recollections often penetrates the calm of my daily life, forcing me to confront painful truths but clarifying much through the very act of **evocation**. I have learned, for the most part, to deal with those truths, knowing well that a painful memory brought into focus by a current incident still hurts, but also that the pain will recede—as it has—and ultimately fade away.*

When, in September 1946, the wheels of the plane bringing Kurt, my husband, and me from Paris and London touched American soil, he tightened his arms around me and said simply, "You have come home." It has been home, better than I ever dreamed it would be. I love this country as only one who has been homeless for so long can understand. I love it with a possessive fierceness that excuses its inadequacies, because I deeply want to belong. And I am still fearful of rejection, feeling I have no right to criticize, only an obligation to help correct. I marvel at my three children's total acceptance of their birthright and rejoice in their good fortune.

*The establishment of the State of Israel in 1948 helped me to become a better American. The pain and loss I experienced in Poland, the country of my birth, **obliterated** the nostalgic thoughts of a childhood home for which I yearn. I have found the answer to that longing in the tradition of my religion and in the land of my ancient ancestors. Israel, by extending the law of return to all Jews, has become the **metaphorical sepulcher** of my parents as well as my spiritual childhood home.*

While my love for Israel represents my love for my parents and our shared past, the United States is my country of choice, my adult home. This country represents the love I harbor for my husband, my children, and my grandchildren. One complements the other; by being mutually supportive, they enrich and heal.

I fell in love with this country from the moment I first stepped upon its soil. It felt so right, so expansive, so free, so hospitable, and I desperately wanted to become part of the American mainstream.

Acuteness: Sharpness; severity.

Evocation: Summoning of a spirit or will.

Obliterated: Totally wiped out.

Metaphorical: Suggesting a likeness between one object and another.

Sepulcher: Receptacle for religious articles.

*I had envisioned Buffalo [New York], which was to become my American home, as a **utopian** city beneath an ever-blue, brilliant sky, and had dismissed Paris, London, and New York, my **way station** to this utopia. During the drive from the grand, imposing New York Central railroad station in Buffalo, I was confronted with my new city's small wooden houses, huddled together like **refugees**, but my disappointment lasted only a few moments. I was ready to love the city and willing to defend it, even to myself. My affection was not misplaced. Buffalo did become a true home. It nurtured me, and later my children played and laughed under rows of elm trees while I immersed myself in a new life.*

*In time we would move from our first apartment to another part of the city, but I would occasionally drive past the familiar location that held so much of our early memories. I would remember how it had seemed to me on my first night in Buffalo, and a picture would flash through my mind. Long after Kurt had fallen asleep, I roamed through the apartment's modest rooms, stopping at the refrigerator in the tiny kitchenette that Kurt's friends had amply stocked. I had always loved fruit, so I took out an apple; but before I could catch the door, it slammed shut with a bang, and terror seized me. How many years had it been since I had lived in a home where I could take whatever I wanted with **impunity**? It was all mine now: the apple and the refrigerator. I opened the door, fully intending to let it slam shut. Instead, I caught it in time, closed it gently, and, grateful, went to bed.*

*Looking up at that third-story window of our first home, I also recalled the day which **catapulted** me into my life's work. I came to Buffalo in September 1946, and the following incident must have happened in late November.*

I loved going to grocery stores and still do. In those days I had the handy explanation that it was a great way to learn English, since I would see pictures on labels of cans that would tell me what was inside—an easy way to learn new words. The truth was dif-

Utopian: Characteristics of an ideally perfect place.

Way station: A station between major stops on a route.

Refugees: People who flee to a foreign country to escape danger or persecution.

Impunity: Freedom from punishment.

Catapulted: Thrown or launched.

Forlorn: Sad; lonely.

Protestations: The act of protesting; declarations or statements made in objection to something.

Articulate: Able to put one's thoughts into groups of clear, concise words.

ferent. I needed to convince myself of the abundance of available food and of its never-ending supply. I wanted the assurance of never being hungry again.

On that particular fall day, I must have dawdled in the market longer than I thought, because when I left the store, a snowstorm was gathering. I made it home, windblown, wet, and cold, and unpacked my bag on the kitchen table. Among my purchases was a loaf of bread. A whole loaf of bread, all mine! I took it into the living room and sat near the window, watching the icy gales swirling outside as I began to eat. Somehow it tasted soggy and a bit salty.

*What was wrong with me? Here I was, sitting in a warm, secure place with a whole loaf of bread. Why, then, did I feel so sad, so **forlorn**? Slowly, the answer began to dawn. During the long years of deprivation, I had dreamed of eating my fill in a warm place, in peace, but I never thought that I would eat my bread alone. Later that evening, I told Kurt that I had been thinking of my friends still in Europe, cold and hungry. I had to do something.*

Out of that need evolved my work with the local Jewish Federation, where I soon found myself putting stamps on envelopes and sealing them. I was immensely proud of having become a volunteer. When Kurt's aunt cautioned me that volunteer work was really for the wealthy, I agreed wholeheartedly. I considered myself rich now.

*It didn't take long before the director of the office suggested that there were other ways to help. Could I tell some of the Buffalo Jewish community what I had seen and lived through? He waved aside **protestations** about my halting, faulty English. It did not matter that I was not **articulate**; he assured me that I would somehow manage to convey my feelings. And so, in the fall of 1946, I tried to tell my story, and I have continued to do so ever since. (Weissmann Klein, pp. 219-22, 247-50)*

What happened next...

Nearly half a century later, Gerda Weissmann Klein returned to Volary, Czechoslovakia, the site of her liberation on May 7, 1945. Gerda, along with her husband and children, visited the abandoned factory where she had spent her last days in Nazi captivity. They also went to the building that had housed the American field hospital, where she recuperated for several months. It was at the field hospital where she and Kurt Klein—her liberator and eventual husband—first talked about their lives and shared hope for a brighter future. Weissmann Klein visited the graves of her friends from the labor camps who did not survive the three-month death march from Grünberg. Standing in the cemetery, she thought about the question she had asked herself many times before: why did she survive when others did not? Through her postwar life's work, she hopes to provide a fragment of the answer to that question.

Did you know...

- Miraculously, Weissmann Klein reacquired the complete collection of her family's photos several years after settling in Buffalo, New York. A distant relative visited her hometown of Bielitz after the war and by chance met a former neighbor of the Weissmann family. In preparing for the forced departure from their home, the Weissmanns had asked the neighbor to store some precious family belongings until their return. Years later, with her entire family gone, Weissmann Klein received a battered box containing some 400 family photos.

- Originally published in 1957, Gerda Weissmann Klein's memoir, *All But My Life,* went through its 38th printing in 1996 and became the subject of a film produced by Home Box Office (HBO) and the United States Holocaust Memorial Museum. The film, *One Survivor Remembers,* won an Emmy Award and the Academy Award for documentary short subject.

- Death marches became especially frequent during the final stage of World War II. About 250,000 prisoners of Nazi concentration camps died on death marches between the summer of 1944 and war's end in the spring of 1945.

For Further Reading

Auerbacher, Linda. *Beyond the Yellow Star to America*. Royal Fireworks Press, 1985.

Fluek, Toby Knobel. *Memories of My Life in a Polish Village, 1930-1949*. New York: Random House, 1990.

Weissmann Klein, Gerda. *All But My Life*. New York: Hill & Wang, 1995.

Art Spiegelman

Maus: A Survivors Tale II: And Here My Troubles Began

Published in 1991

After the Holocaust, survivors were scattered across the globe and faced the prospect of rebuilding their shattered lives. Despite social, economic and cultural differences, they all shared a common bond—they wondered why *they* had survived while so many others had not. Some struggled to tell their stories, confiding in family members and friends. Many began writing and lecturing about their experiences, hoping to honor the deceased and to prevent future atrocities. A few remained silent, vowing never to speak of this terrible chapter in their past. For the survivors who started families after the war, they passed on a unique set of experiences to their children. In addition to the love and nurturing they received from their parents, this second generation inherited the emotional scars and broken family heritage left in the wake of the Holocaust.

During the late 1960s and early 1970s, American social and political activism flourished. Among the numerous campaigns of the era was the "roots" movement, which celebrated family genealogy. At this time, groups of Jewish graduate students in the United States began meeting and exploring their similar experiences as children of survivors. Despite their socioeconomic differences and the varying circumstances of their parents' survival, they shared many of the same struggles. They witnessed and participated in their parents' attempts to cope with the immeasurable loss of community, family, and identity caused by the Holocaust. Early articles discussing these themes appeared in the Jewish publication *Response*. Through grassroots organizations, members of the second generation began to meet with each other,

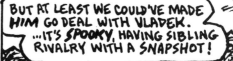

helping to reduce their sense of isolation. The largest group, called the International Network for Children of Survivors, promotes commemoration and education and works toward preventing future genocides (attempted destruction of an entire body of people).

As the children of survivors grew up, they usually learned something of their parents' experiences during the Holocaust. Some survivors, still haunted by fear, never let their children out of their sight and strictly monitored their playtime with friends. Others compulsively counted pieces of food such as slices of bread, crackers, and vegetables due to the chronic hunger they suffered long ago. One of the children of Holocaust survivors, Art Spiegelman, poignantly captured his father's idiosyncratic (odd, eccentric) behavior and painful reminders of the past.

A gifted cartoonist, Spiegelman invented an unusual medium for sharing his family's struggles. In 1986, he published a volume about the Holocaust in comic book format called *Maus: A Survivor's Tale I: My Father Bleeds History.* This first volume of *Maus* ("mouse") introduces readers to characters modeled after Spiegelman and his father, Vladek. As the character Spiegelman tries to understand his father, he learns about the terrifying realities of the Holocaust. In his cartoon strip, Spiegelman uses cats to represent the Nazis and mice to represent the Jews. He also recreates his father's broken English to make the Vladek character more believable. Spiegelman's second volume, *Maus: A Survivor's Tale II: And Here My Troubles Began,* excerpted throughout this entry, further details camp life and work. The author captures the lasting emotions of the Holocaust that haunt survivors and are inevitably passed onto their children.

Things to Remember While Looking at the Pages from Spiegelman's *Maus*:

- Children of survivors become part of their parents' struggle to recover from their concentration camp experiences. Spiegelman faced an unbeatable sibling rivalry with Richieu, his older brother who died as a young child during the Holocaust. Spiegelman refers to Richieu as his "ghost brother" and wonders how he can compete with the ideal and imaginary virtues of a "snapshot."

Opposite page: In panel "A", Spiegelman and his wife are driving to visit his father, Vladek, who survived the Auschwitz concentration camp.

WHAT ARE THEY DOING OVER THERE-DIGGING TRENCHES IN CASE THE RUSSIANS ATTACK?

TRENCHES-HAH! THOSE ARE GIANT **GRAVES** THEY'RE FILLING IN!...

IT STARTED IN MAY AND WENT ON ALL SUMMER. THEY BROUGHT JEWS FROM HUNGARY-TOO MANY FOR THEIR OVENS, SO THEY DUG THOSE BIG CREMATION PITS.

THE HOLES WERE BIG, SO LIKE THE SWIMMING POOL OF THE PINES HOTEL HERE.

AND TRAIN AFTER TRAIN OF HUNGARIANS CAME.

AND THOSE WHAT FINISHED IN THE GAS CHAMBERS BEFORE THEY GOT PUSHED IN THESE GRAVES, IT WAS THE **LUCKY** ONES.

THE OTHERS HAD TO JUMP IN THE GRAVES WHILE STILL THEY WERE ALIVE...

PRISONERS WHAT WORKED THERE POURED GASOLINE OVER THE LIVE ONES AND THE DEAD ONES.

AND THE FAT FROM THE BURNING BODIES THEY SCOOPED AND POURED AGAIN SO EVERYONE COULD BURN BETTER.

- In panel "A," Spiegelman and his wife (represented by two mice) are driving to visit his father in the Catskill Mountains of New York. His father, Vladek, survived the Auschwitz concentration camp.

- Panel "B" opens with Vladek describing how he and another inmate were assigned to help dismantle the crematoriums at Auschwitz in late 1944 as massive numbers of prisoners from Hungary were arriving at the camp.

- During Panel "C," which takes place on the porch at Vladek's bungalow, Spiegelman's wife wonders if Vladek is always upset or if he was particularly tense during their visit because his second wife, Mala, had just run off with his money.

- Notice that in the last frame of Panel "C," Spiegelman gasses the bugs on the porch with an insecticide—an ironic reference to the Nazis' attitude and use of power over their Jewish victims.

About the Author/Illustrator

Art Spiegelman was born in Stockholm, Sweden, to Polish-born survivors of the Auschwitz concentration camp. His older brother died during the Holocaust, three years before Spiegelman was born. Then, when Spiegelman was 20 years old, his mother committed suicide.

During his early career working on underground comics in the 1970s and 1980s, Spiegelman published the *Maus* comic strip in various periodicals, including *Raw*, the magazine founded by Spiegelman and his wife, designer Francoise Mouly. He published his first book-length volume of *Maus* in 1986, achieving widespread accolades. In 1991, he completed a second volume of *Maus*, this one being a semiautobiographical account of the author's relationship with his parents. Spiegelman was awarded a special Pulitzer Prize in 1992 for *Maus*. Additional awards include a Guggenheim fellowship and a nomination for the National Book Critics Circle Award. His work has appeared in the *New York Times*, *Playboy*, and the *Village Voice*. As of 1997, Spiegelman was living in New York City with his family.

Opposite page: Panel "B" opens with Vladek describing how he and another inmate were assigned to help dismantle the crematoriums at Auschwitz in late 1944.

What happened next...

The children of Holocaust survivors have contributed enormously to rebuilding the Jewish history and culture destroyed in World War II. Their unique sense of dedication is helping to restore and recreate lost art, music, literature, and theater. Second-generation interest in the Holocaust propels researchers to investigate the lost Jewish culture of Eastern Europe, to distribute information, and to aid current victims of antisemitism around the world

Spiegelman, like many other children of survivors, has embraced art and literature to express his emotions. His marvelously unique style allows him both to touch and to shock readers. He succeeds in the difficult task of placing the brutalities and the horrors of the Holocaust alongside ordinary human events. Even after his father's death, Spiegelman continues to recover pieces of a rich family heritage.

Did you know...

- The most famous attempt by Jews to resist the Nazis occurred in the Warsaw ghetto in Poland. Starting on April 19, 1943, some 750 resistance fighters managed to fend off Nazi forces for a month before suffering defeat. Members of the Warsaw Ghetto Resistance Organization in the United States persuaded their children to meet and start a second-generation organization.

- Children of survivors began to organize in the late 1960s and early 1970s. These nearly invisible groups received national attention when the article "Heirs to the Holocaust," written by Helen Epstein, was published in the *New York Times Magazine* on June 19, 1977.

- Survivor families in different countries share obvious commonalities, but not all of them face the tragedy of the past in the same way. In Europe, the absence of strong, united Jewish communities—combined with a stunning resurgence of antisemitism (or hatred of Jews)—has obstructed commemorative activities. And in the case of survivors who immigrated to Israel, they represent a minority of the larger Jewish population there, so their children seem less inclined to identify with the terror of the Holocaust.

Opposite page: In the last frames of Panel "C," Spiegelman gasses the bugs on the porch with an insecticide—an ironic reference to the Nazis' attitude and use of power over their Jewish victims.

For Further Reading

Epstein, Helen. "Heirs to the Holocaust." *New York Times Magazine,* June 19, 1977.

Friedman, Carl. *Nightfather: A Novel.* New York: Persea Books, 1994.

Spiegelman, Art. *Maus: A Survivor's Tale I: My Father Bleeds History.* New York: Pantheon, 1986.

Spiegelman, Art. *Maus: A Survivor's Tale II: And Here My Troubles Began.* New York: Pantheon, 1991.

Bette Greene

Excerpt from *Summer of My German Soldier*

Published in 1973

The Holocaust, which refers to the mass murder of 6 million Jewish people by the Nazis during World War II, will stand forever as a reminder of the destructive power of extreme hatred and prejudice. However, the senseless, barbaric acts of the Nazis against Jewish people and other victims did not generate the kind of outrage among other countries that one might expect. Even as countries became aware of the atrocities, few offered any real assistance to the victims. By not relaxing immigration quotas, various nations hindered the attempts of Jews to reach safety. The United States first moved to aid victims of Nazi persecution in January 1944, with the creation of the War Refugee Board. Working with Jewish organizations, neutral diplomats, and resistance groups in Europe, up to 200,000 Jews were saved. Historians wonder how many more lives could have been spared if the efforts had started earlier. Within the United States, widespread racial prejudices, including prejudice within the ranks of the State Department, led to the defeat of efforts to aid even Jewish refugee children.

Intolerance and prejudice know no borders. During the 1940s, strong anti-German sentiments arose throughout America in response to the war in Europe. Japanese-Americans suffered state-sanctioned discrimination throughout the United States. At the time, black Americans lived in a deeply divided and segregated society with separate schools, housing, restaurants, and even water fountains. In her first novel, *Summer of My German Soldier,* author Bette Greene explores the universal themes of bias and hatred against an American

backdrop. Drawing from her own childhood experiences growing up in rural Arkansas during the 1940s, she illustrates the many forms of prejudice that existed at that time in American society.

Things to Remember While Reading *Summer of My German Soldier*:

- Patty Bergen was 12 years old when German prisoners of war (POWs from World War II) were assigned to a location outside Jenkinsville, Arkansas. As a Jewish American preteen in a rural area, she lives with the assumption that everyone she meets can tell she is Jewish.

- Bergen befriends a German prisoner named Anton Reiker, who speaks perfect English. After Reiker escapes from the POW camp, Bergen places herself at great risk by providing him with shelter.

- Patriotism turns to hatred when the townspeople learn of Bergen's actions in aiding Reiker. As she is led away by the sheriff, a riot nearly breaks out as people yell both antisemitic and anti-German jeers.

Summer of My German Soldier

The Germans began trying on the hats, smiling as though they were on a holiday. Reiker had pushed out from the center huddle and was exploring the broader limits of the store.

One very blond prisoner turned to my father. "Der Spiegel?"

My father shook his head. "I don't know what you're talking about."

"Wo ist der Spiegel?" said a second prisoner.

Again my father shook his head. "I don't understand your talk!"

Voices called for Reiker, and at his approach the men parted **like the Red Sea for the Israelites**. Again the word "Spiegel." Reiker turned to my father. "They'd like to see themselves. Have you a mirror?"

Reiker used English cleanly, easily, and with more precision than anyone I know from around these parts. And he didn't sound the least bit like a German. It was as though he had spent his life learning to speak English the way the English do.

Again Reiker left the others to walk with brisk steps across the store.

The corporal was involved in selecting off-duty socks for himself while the other guard leaned heavily against a counter and

Like the Red Sea for the Israelites: The Red Sea is a huge body of water between Arabia and northeastern Africa, which, according to the Old Testament of the Bible, parted for Moses and the Israelites as they marched into Egypt.

rolled himself a cigarette. Neither seemed concerned as Reiker headed unobserved towards the door. He could be gone before they even got their guns out of their holsters. Terrified that the guards' casualness was only a cover for the sharpest-shooting soldiers in anybody's army, I closed my eyes and prayed that he would make it all the way to freedom.

But I heard no door opening, no feet running, and no gun firing. By sheer force of will I opened my eyes to see Reiker calmly examining the pencils at the stationery counter.

Stationery was one of the many departments seen to by Sister Parker. But Sister Parker was busy waiting on a lady customer, and lady customers take half of forever to make up their minds. Who was going to wait on Reiker? I wanted to, but I couldn't. I didn't even have a comb. Why, in God's name, didn't I carry a purse with a fresh handkerchief and a comb like Edna Louise? I ran my fingers through my hair and patted it into place.

I took a few hurried steps and stopped short. Reiker may not wish to be disturbed, anyway not by me. The skin-and-bones girl. But I can wait on him if I want to, it's my father's store. Who does he think he is, some old Nazi?

Pushed on by **adrenalin**, I was at his side. "Could I help you, please?" My voice came out phony. Imitation **Joan Crawford**.

Reiker looked up and smiled. "Yes, please. I don't know the word for it—" Above those eyes with their specks of green were dark masculine eyebrows. "Pocket pencil sharpeners? They're quite small and work on the razor principle."

"Well," I said, reaching towards the opposite end of the counter to pick up a little red sharpener, "we sell a lot of these dime ones to the school children."

"Yes," he said. "Exactly right." He was looking at me like he saw me—like he liked what he saw.

Adrenalin: A hormone, or chemical messenger, that is released by the body during the "fight or flight" response to danger or excitement.

Joan Crawford: 1940s Hollywood star.

"What color would you like?" I asked, not really thinking about pencil sharpeners. "They come in red, yellow, and green."

"I'll take the one you chose," said Reiker. He placed six yellow pencils and three stenographic pads on the counter. "And you did not tell me," he said, "what you call these pocket pencil sharpeners."

He was so nice. How could he have been one of those—those brutal, black-booted Nazis? "Well, I don't think they actually call them much of anything, but if they were to call them by their right name they'd probably call them pocket pencil sharpeners."

Reiker laughed and for a moment, this moment, we were friends. And now I knew something more. He wasn't a bad man....

Later in the text....

"I'm glad you're here." I said. "I want you to stay safe."

"I will. There's no reason why the Americans should bother with one missing prisoner. An ordinary foot soldier." [Anton] adjusted his gold ring, the surface of which had some sort of crest. "Also, I'm lucky. Twice I've been so close to exploding bombs that only a miracle could have saved me. And so I've had a couple of miracles."

He took a quick look out the hide-out's front and back windows. "But suppose I am recaptured. What will the Americans do? Deposit me in the nearest POW camp where I'll have to wait till the end of the war. But in the meantime this day, this month, this year belongs to me...."

"I was wondering how you managed to escape?"

*"The actual mechanics of the escape are not important," he said. "The **pertinent** point is that I was able to create a—a kind of climate that permitted the escape. Specifically, my deception was believed because it was built on a foundation of truth. Hitler taught me that."*

Pertinent: Relevant or important to the matter at hand.

I heard him say it. "Hitler taught you?"

*Anton smiled. "I learned it by analyzing his techniques. Hitler's first layer is an undeniable truth, such as: The German worker is poor. The second layer is divided equally between flattery and truth: The German worker deserves to be prosperous. The third layer is total **fabrication**: The Jews and the Communists have stolen what is rightfully yours."*

"Well, I can see how it helped him, but I don't see how it worked for you."

"Because I had a rock-bottom truth of my own," he said, striking his chest with his index finger. "My excellent English. I let it be known that I had had an English governess. And this gave me the advantage of being considered wealthy. But I didn't have a good workable plan that would capitalize on my believed riches until I saw that pin with the glass diamonds—the one you sold me."

*"Yes! I couldn't for the life of me figure out why you wanted it. So **gaudy** and not at all like something you'd like."*

*"I loved it!" protested Anton. "Because those glass diamonds were going to make me a free man. One of the guards was a simple fellow with financial problems. One day I told him my father would pay five thousand dollars to the person who could get me out of prison. The guard looked too surprised to answer. But eight days later he followed me into the **latrine** and asked, 'What's the deal?' 'Five perfect diamonds, each diamond having been appraised in excess of one thousand dollars, will be given to the person who drives me out beyond those gates,' I told him. So he did, and I paid him with a dollar's worth of glass jewelry."*

"I'm glad you made it," I said, "but that guard—he could get into an awful lot of trouble."

Fabrication: Lie or falsehood.

Gaudy: Flashy, tasteless, or showy.

Latrine: Toilet.

"I don't feel guilty." His hand rubbed across the slight indentation in the chin. "His concern was for reward; mine was for survival. But, on the other hand, I wouldn't wish to **implicate** him."

I nodded. "Now I'm ready to answer your question."

His teeth pressed together, giving new strength to the line of his jaw. "I'm certain you appreciate the seriousness of what you have done, aiding an escaped prisoner of war. I was wondering why you were taking these risks on my behalf. Because of your German ancestry? Perhaps your father is secretly sympathetic to the Nazi cause?"

"That's not true! My father's parents came from Russia and my mother's from Luxembourg."

Anton looked alarmed. "I'm sorry. It's just that Bergen is such a good German name."

"It's also a good Jewish name," I said, pleased by the clean **symmetry** of my response.

His mouth came open. "Jewish?" An index finger pointed toward me. "You're Jewish?"

I thought he knew. I guess I thought everybody knew. Does he think I tricked him? My wonderful Anton was going to change to mean. As I nodded Yes, my breathing came to a halt while my eyes clamped shut.

Suddenly, strong baritone laughter flooded the room. Both eyes popped open and I saw him standing there, shaking his head from side to side.

"It's truly extraordinary," he said. "Who would believe it? 'Jewish girl risks all for German solder.' Tell me, Patty Bergen—" his voice became soft, but with a trace of hoarseness— "why are you doing this for me?"

Implicate: To involve in something; to prove someone's involvement in a crime.

Symmetry: Balance; evenness.

Bette Greene

Bette Greene, a writer of adolescent fiction, was born in a small town in Arkansas. She has also lived in Memphis, Tennessee, and Paris, France. When *Summer of My German Soldier* was published, Greene lived in Brookline, Massachusetts, with her husband and two children.

The award-winning book *Summer of My German Soldier* incorporates many of Greene's own memories of growing up in wartime Arkansas. In 1973, it received the ALA Notable Book Award and the Golden Kite Award. The novel was also a finalist for the prestigious National Book Award and was cited by the *New York Times* as an outstanding book of the year.

Greene has published many other books for young adults, including *Philip Hall Likes Me, I Reckon, Maybe*. A recent work, *The Drowning of Stephan Jones*, received critical acclaim for its portrayal of a young gay man murdered at the hands of his tormentors. A gifted author who generates a strong emotional response among her readers, Greene seeks through her craft to call attention to the potentially devastating effects of intolerance and injustice.

It wasn't complicated. Why didn't he know? There was really only one word for it. A simple little word that in itself is reason enough.

"The reason I'm doing this for you," I started off, "is only that I wouldn't want anything bad to happen to you."

Anton turned his face from me and nodded as though he understood. Outside, a blue-gray cloud cruised like a pirate ship between sun and earth, sending the room from sunshine into shadows....

Pierce walked to the door of my room without entering. "All settled, Mr. Bergen. We're taking the girl into Memphis." Then he gave me a nod. "Better pack a few things."

"How long will she be gone?"

"Don't know, sir. She'd better take a few changes."

I got the smallest of the three suitcases out of the closet and began putting in some clothes like a robot who feels nothing. I wasn't even conscious anymore of wanting anything except maybe to be left alone, and I wasn't even strong on that. Living was too big a deal and dying too much trouble....

*As we came close to my father's store I saw people **milling** in front. Too many people for a weekday unless today is dollar day. Suddenly, the FBI men were walking at my side. "Stay close to me," whispered Pierce. There were ten, more than that, at least fifteen people and all with fixed faces. They know about me. How could they have found out so soon? Then I spotted Jenkinsville's leading gossip merchant, Mary Wren, holding onto the arm of Reverend Benn's wife.*

The agents maneuvered me away from the sidewalk and into the center of Main Street. The crowd followed. A glob of liquid hit me in the back of the neck and when I saw what my hand had wiped away I gagged.

Suddenly a woman's voice called, "Nazi! Nazi!" Other voices joined in. A man's voice, one that I had heard before, shouted, "Jew Nazi—Jew Nazi—Jew Nazi!"

When we reached the car, the mob blocked the doors. "You people are obstructing justice," said Pierce. "Please move back."

"Jew Nazi-lover!" screamed the minister's wife.

Tires screeched to a stop. A car door opened and Sheriff Cauldwell shouted, "Get away from that car. What's the matter with you folks, anyway?"

Milling: To move in a circle; wander.

People slowly moved away from the car, crowding into a huddle on the sidewalk. Sheriff Cauldwell opened the back door of the car for me, and then, whipping out a small black Bible from his shirt pocket, he pressed it into my hand. "Times when I was down this helped lift me up. God bless you."

"Thanks," I said, feeling the tears stinging at my eyes.

McFee drove in second gear all the way down Main Street before taking a right turn onto Highway 64. As we passed McDonald's dairy, I looked down the long dirt road leading to the prison camp. But I knew I wasn't going to find him there or any other place on God's earth. (Greene, pp. 41-43, 93-96, 189-92)

What happened next...

Greene chose an apt setting for a fictional depiction of the pain and suffering caused by intolerance. The 1940s were a time of great upheaval as the world reeled from the effects of war and sacrifice; all around the globe, national loyalties turned into intense patriotism. Hatred against a particular group of people resulted in one of the darkest and most tragic periods of human history. Six million European Jews died as a result of extreme prejudice. In America, racial intolerance and other forms of discrimination were commonplace. Greene's characters illustrate how hatred existed against Germans, Jews, blacks, and women, even in the idyllic setting of a rural American town.

In Green's novel *Summer of My German Soldier*, Anton Reiker successfully flees Arkansas but is killed in New York City while trying to avoid arrest. Patty Bergen is arrested and tried for aiding an escaped prisoner of war. As the story ends, she is in the custody of a juvenile detention center for girls in Arkansas.

Did you know...

- The novel *Summer of My German Soldier* was based loosely on true historical events. Reiker's escape coincided with the actual landing of Nazi saboteurs (the Nazis who attempted to hinder the Allied war effort) on the beaches of the Atlantic coast. The arrival of these spy teams, who were assigned to destroy key installations (military bases) on American soil, set off an intense anti-German reaction within the States.

- Greene wrote a companion volume to *Summer of My German Soldier* titled *Morning Is a Long Time Coming.*

- *Summer of My German Soldier,* Bette Greene's first novel, is regarded as a classic in young adult literature.

- Green's story was the basis of a 1978 television movie of the same name starring Kristy McNichol (as Patty Bergen), Bruce Davison, and Michael Constantine. Esther Rolle won an Emmy Award for her portrayal of Ruth, Bergen's nanny and confidante.

For Further Reading

Greene, Bette. *Summer of My German Soldier.* New York: Dial Press, 1973.

Tunis, John Roberts. *His Enemy, His Friend.* New York: William Morrow, 1967.

Zaiben, Jane Breskin. *The Fortuneteller in 5B.* New York: Henry Holt, 1991.

index

Bold type indicates main documents and speaker profiles
Italic type indicates volume numbers
Illustrations are marked by (ill.)

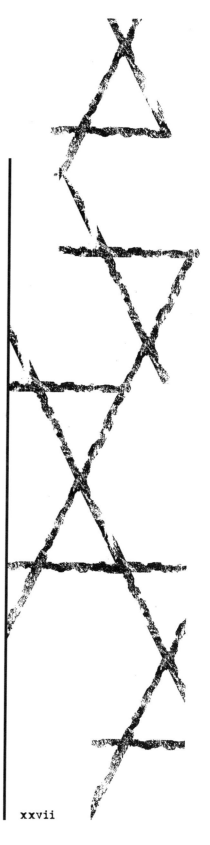

Emmy Award *2:* 383, 473
Enabling Act *1:* 34
Essays on the Inequality of the Human Race 1: 8
Eugenics *1:* 9
Euthanasia *1:* 153-54, 175
Evian, France *1:* 81
Extermination camps *1:* 97, 104, 118-19, 161, 177-78, 192

F

Faith and Beauty" (Glaube and Schonheit) *1:* 72
Fascism *1:* 186, 219; *2:* 328
Federation of Jewish Victims of the Nazi Regime *2:* 399
Fénelon, Fania *2:* 349-50, **368-83**
"Final Solution" *1:* 22, 105, 118, 157, 158, 160, 161, 177-78, 192, 205;
     2: 254-55, 260, 273, 445
Ford, Henry *1:* 16-17
Foundations of the Nineteenth Century 1: 9
Four and a Half Years of Struggle against Lies, Stupidity, and Cowardice 1: 32
Franco-Prussian War *1:* 15
Frank, Anne *1:* 158, **176-91**, 177 (ill.), 183 (ill.), 188 (ill.)
Frank, Edith *1:* 176-77, 179-91
Frank, Hans *1:* 77, 107, 117; *2:* 332, 414
Frank, Margot *1:* 176-77, 177 (ill.), 178, 179-91
Frank, Otto *1:* 176-77, 177 (ill.), 179-91
Frauen, Motherhood Times Ten, and Food to Spare 1: 62-72
Free Corps (Freikorps) *1:* 170
Freisler, Roland *2:* 315, 317
Freud, Sigmund *1:* 34
Frick, Wilhelm *1:* 48-49, 59, 61
Front for Poland's Renewal *2:* 290

G

General government (Generalgouvernement) *1:* 93, 107, 108;
     2: 287, 332-33
Genocide *1:* 16, 155; *2:* 445
Gentile (definition) *1:* 100, 248
German Faith Movement (Deutsche Glaubensbewegung) *1:* 136
Gestapo *1:* 94, 124, 189, 233; *2:* 260, 270-71, 275, 301
Ghetto *1:* 30, 76, 108, 161, 205; *2:* 254-55, 334
Ghetto, Krakow *2:* 254 (ill.)
Ghetto, Kovno (Kaunas) *1:* 122-33
Ghetto, Lodz *1:* 76 (ill.), *2:* 258 (ill.)
Ghetto, Warsaw *1:* 98-106, 99 (ill.), 106, 108-21, 109 (ill.), 112 (ill.)
Gies, Miep *1:* 190
Goebbels, Joseph *1:* 34, 73, 82 (ill.), 90; *2:* 424
Goering, Hermann *2:* 385, 413 (ill.), 414
Greene, Bette *2:* 443, **483-93**
Grunstein, Hirsch *1:* 159, **243-52**
Grynszpan, Hershl *1:* 80-81
Gunther, Rolf *2:* 273
Gypsies *1:* 156, 162, 174; *2:* 352

Voelkisch *1:* 9
Vom Rath, Ernst *1:* 81-82
Von Hindenburg, Paul *1:* 48

W

Wallenberg, Raoul *2:* 257-58, **318-31**, 328 (ill.), 439
Wansee Conference *1:* 158, 161
The Warsaw Diary of Chaim A. Kaplan 1: **93-106**
The Warsaw Ghetto: A Christian's Testimony *2:* 256, **287-300**
Warsaw ghetto uprising *1:* 119-20; *2:* 295 (ill.), 298, 481
Warthegau *1:* 107; *2:* 287, 332
The Watchtower 1: 233
Weimar Republic *1:* 6, 21, 41
Weissmann Klein, Gerda *2:* 442, **460-74**
Westerbork *1:* 193 (ill.), 193-204
White Rose (Weisse Rose) movement *2:* 257, 301-17
"Why I Write" *2:* 441, **445-59**
Wiesel, Elie *2:* 441, **445-59**, 446 (ill.), 453 (ill.), 456 (ill.)
Wiesenthal, Simon *2:* 350, **396-410**, 424, 428
The World Struggle 1: 17
World War I *1:* 1, 2, 6, 8, 19, 21, 48
World War II *1:* 5, 22, 60, 92, 93, 104, 143
WRB (War Refugee Board) *2:* 318, 320, 483

Y

Yad Vashem *1:* 217, 252; *2:* 347
Yom Kippur *2:* 424

Z

Zegota *1:* 120; *2:* 288-90, 298-99
Zionism *1:* 122, 130, 206; *2:* 262
ZOB (Jewish Fighting Organization) *2:* 299
Zyklon-B *1:* 157, 163, 175
ZZB (Jewish Military Union) *2:* 299